2 -

THE BISHOP
JOTS IT DOWN

BISHOP KELLEY
Portrait by Rembski, 1938

MEMORIAL EDITION

The Bishop Jots It Down

An Autobiographical Strain
on Memories

by

Francis Clement Kelley

HARPER & BROTHERS PUBLISHERS

NEW YORK AND LONDON

FOREWORD TO MEMORIAL EDITION

by JOSEPH J. QUINN

B ISHOP Francis Clement Kelley held only three positions in his fifty-four years of the priesthood—pastor of Lapeer, Michigan, President of the Catholic Church Extension Society, and Bishop of Oklahoma City and Tulsa. The first two periods are covered in this volume as an autobiography. The third—his Episcopal career in Oklahoma—remained in his memory, never to be jotted down. Later we shall tell why.

In June, 1924, word quickly spread through Oklahoma that a new Bishop had been named as successor to the late Theophile Meerschaert. His name was Kelley but it seemed too much to hope that it was Monsignor Kelley, head of Extension. After all, he was a world figure, his meteor of fame soaring, bearing his illustrious name among the stars. He had met the distinguished people of his time, popes, presidents, emperors and kings. Everywhere he was looked upon as a giant in the domain of the church. But the incredible news was true; it was the celebrated president of Extension Society, an organization that had proved a fairy godmother to the missions throughout America.

Following his installation in St. Joseph's Cathedral on October 15, 1924, Oklahomans settled down to liking Bishop Kelley. It did not take them long to appreciate their good fortune. No sooner had they lost their initial awe of his greatness than they came to realize how truly kind and simple he was. Let others call him statesman, author, lecturer, soldier, patriot and benefactor. Oklahoma looked upon him as a kindly peacemaker, a man who initiated a reign of good will throughout the new commonwealth, an era of friendliness whose momentum carries through today.

A new spirit was seen in Oklahoma from the moment Bishop Kelley came. He stilled the tongues of venom of former enemies, brought sunlight into dark places, pioneered with smile and logic, and cleared the vision of those who wished to see. Where he made friendships, there the church made friends. His candor and brilliance lifted the non-Catholic people of Oklahoma to a remarkable appreciation of the Faith and its leaders. Loved by Protestants as well as Catholics, Bishop Kelley found willing hands for all his projects. With this co-operation, he went forward on uncharted paths, trail blazing to new heights.

"Catholic Bishops are human," he wrote in this autobiography. But the public liked him because he was human, especially because he wanted to see people happy and had the gifts to bring this about—interest in everyone, kindness, humor, the talent of reaching down into people's souls and having them respond.

Bishop Kelley came to Oklahoma at the twilight of a pioneer period. His predecessor had forded streams, ridden in surries, slept in dugouts, and through patience and adversity had carved the name of Christ upon the cornerstone of a rough empire. But Bishop Kelley was a new bishop and brought a new day. Now there came the dawn of pulsing progress. They began chipping down mountain sides, piling them high and calling them skyscrapers. Boulevards ran along the old cattle trails. The second Bishop of Oklahoma was fifty-three years of age, handsome, with boundless energy, seeking new goals, fanning out the church's influence in every direction.

This new bishop was on the move. Nothing that he took hold of stood still. Organizations sprang up everywhere; missions were started and cornerstones laid; fields white unto the harvest became filled with workers. It was as if a prairie fire of activity had been lighted and swept across the length and breadth of the diocese.

Bishop Kelley's accomplishments during his twenty-three years in Oklahoma would fill volumes. He brought progress everywhere, undertook numerous philanthropic projects, spoke hundreds upon hundreds of times before every type of audience, wrote eight books, built seventy churches, schools, educational halls and hospitals and had the happiness of seeing his clergy increase from 105 to 192. He was exuberant year after year over the fact that Oklahoma made more converts, proportionally, than any other diocese in the country.

Bishop Kelley did more for Oklahoma than any one man in its

history. As the state's greatest booster, he carried its name across the nation and even across the seas. He gave it prestige and standing and was always ready to defend it, surely willing to praise it at all times. In the young commonwealth of Oklahoma, the ancient church blossomed as Bishop Kelley unfolded the beauties of the Faith to thousands who before knew nothing of the glories he pictured.

No priesthood extending over a half century ever radiated greater influence than Bishop Kelley's. Within the fifty-four years of his sacerdotal life were moments that made history, monuments that will endure and marks that are imperishable. Whether in the old world or the new, he met the kind of triumphs that denote genius.

Bishop Kelley's deeds, eloquent with the irresistible eloquence of greatness, wove a golden thread through many countries. His long years of distinction in the realm of the ecclesiastical have many brilliant addenda in other spheres. Each separate achievement would measure greatness in the life of any leader.

He toiled for the oppressed of Mexico, lent a helping hand to the Bishop of Vancouver, negotiated with England in the name of the Vatican. The part he played in the settlement of the Roman Question, a feat that thrilled the Christian nations of the world, will never be forgotten. Knighthood by the King of Italy in recognition of his work on the Roman Question, an award of the Great Golden Cross of Merit with Star by Austria for relieving postwar distress in Vienna, the conferring of the Medal of Isabella the Catholic by Spain for his writings on Mexico are but three of the many citations from foreign countries. Too, there came rewards in the field of education—Doctor of Sacred Theology from Laval, Doctor of Laws from Notre Dame, and Doctor of Philosophy and of Letters from Louvain.

In Bishop Kelley was the enlightened zeal and the tireless vigor of a St. Paul. His steel endurance came not so much from physical strength as from an indomitable will to go forward in everything he visualized. His energy in the progress of the church bespoke his desire for the return of men to their "forgotten God"; his interest in arts and letters reflected his high distinction of mind and elegance. With the nation as his platform, he rose splendidly to every occasion. He used with masterful talent every arm of the church to win new friends to Christ, among them the pen, the pulpit and the radio. In his early years in Oklahoma he laid down lines of Catholic Action that proved a national pattern.

Bishop Kelley was a man of wide reading and culture and his manners matched his mind. His uniform, unfailing kindness was the natural offspring of a tender heart. It was that great heart that made his genius soar like unto a planet's flame but a flame that did not sear. It was that heart that caused him to reach out to aid the helpless of many nations, that inspired him to extend the church into places where the Gospel was never heard. It was that heart that brought a reign of good will to Oklahoma, that built churches, hospitals and schools, that won thousands to his side. And when that great heart stopped, there came to a close the career of a truly faithful apostle, one of America's greatest churchmen, to live forever with an Ireland and a Gibbons.

Most of all Bishop Kelley loved peace. He disliked intensely that adventure of blood and bombs that men call war and in all his rosaries he prayed that peace would come to nations tried in the crucible of horror and despair. Although born on a little island in the upper reaches of the Atlantic, no native American loved this country more. In the order of the love of God he was an internationalist, with charity for all men as brothers and love of country following love of God.

There was a continuous stream of apostolic literature from Bishop Kelley's pen for close to sixty years. He never hesitated to write for any just cause. With pen in hand, he became inspired. His literature was simple yet profound, veined with wit yet always pointing a lesson. Some of his literature will live; in fact, many of his writings are classics. Hundreds of his sentences are. He had the happy facility of dressing his thoughts in an odd simplicity that contained more meaning than first met the eye.

Although one of our greatest authors, yet there was no consensus as to the particular type of writing in which he excelled. Some believed he reached his apex in satire; others in his lucid explanations of doctrine; still others thought that in editorial writing he had the most brilliant pen.

Bishop Kelley's store of experiences was rich and varied. Seemingly he made it a point to remember the bright bits of his seventy-seven years and forget those that carried no interest for the public. Packed in his memory were thousands of incidents that concerned great men and small, facts of history and of the church, all of which he could pull out of memory's hat like a magician and tailor them to fit the crowd.

Greatest compliment to Bishop Kelley was that if you ever heard him speak, you wanted to read one of his books, and if you read one, you looked forward to reading them all. No one who ever heard him will ever forget Bishop Kelley the speaker. He came smilingly to the front of the platform, paid his felicitations to the audience, settled them in a happy mood and kept that mood happy, sometimes for two hours. One often hears of tireless speakers and tired audiences. Bishop Kelley was tireless and his audiences likewise.

A writer appraising Bishop Kelley's sixteen volumes has asserted: "It is the general opinion that *The Bishop Jots It Down* is his greatest work. In this he told a factual story and if there is a better story teller than Bishop Kelley on this hemisphere, no one has come forward and pointed him out."

Practically everyone agrees that *The Bishop Jots It Down* WAS Bishop Kelley. The book is grand writing and better reading. Here he lets you glimpse at his past with its trials and triumphs, its glamour and heartbreaks, its storms and rainbows. It is a big book —not counting all that is said between the lines.

Few know that *The Bishop Jots It Down* was prompted by a suggestion of Henry L. Mencken, the writer. On one of his twenty-six crossings of the Atlantic, Bishop Kelley met the Baltimorean who, upon hearing some of Bishop Kelley's world-wide experiences, urged him to write his autobiography.

And now we will tell you why there was no sequel to the autobiography, why there was nothing jotted down about his memorable years in Oklahoma.

The Bishop was sitting with a small group of friends in his home on October 18, 1942. They had just finished dinner and had retired to a sitting room. Suddenly a strange pallor overspread his face. He felt his side; slumped slightly. It was the first time in his life that he had become really ill. But from the moment of that first heart attack, the pyramid began to crumble. True, he fought to recoup his body to meet the challenge of the spirit. But it was hopeless. It was as if a curtain had been lowered on his dynamic career, never to be lifted. From that moment on he never trod the platform again, never swayed great crowds, and his pen never produced another volume.

At times he would take up his pad and pencil and try to tell of his Oklahoma memories, his travels over the diocese, the brilliant occasions and banquets in his honor, the personalities he had met and the friends he had made. But it was no use. The inspiration was gone; the spark was extinguished. His writing days were over, and "30," the newspaper symbol of the end, could well have been placed on the final chapter of his last volume.

His were five long years of illness! Days, months and years spent resting under the arched elms on his lawn, upon his wide veranda, more often in his room. Friends came to cheer him. There were books, too, but his feeble hands could not hold them. In this circumscribed horizon, narrowing week by week, the radio brought in the news of the outside world.

Even his voice that had charmed a thousand audiences felt the toll of illness. He could no longer spin off the wit that had won him fame. But he never lost the merry dance to his eyes, his appreciation of humor, nor his desire to see all people happy. He stayed young in spirit, even though spell after spell kept wounding his frail body.

Wars and Bishop Kelley's jubilees seemed to coincide. During World War I his Silver Jubilee of the priesthood had to be curtailed. World War II, together with the state of his health, cancelled plans for his sacerdotal Golden Jubilee. There must have been a tinge of regret, a feeling of disappointment, as he stood there alone after fifty golden years of achievement, without the handclasp of friends, hearing only the echo of the music that he had created for the world.

On the occasion of his Golden Jubilee, he was tendered a handsome edition by his diocesan paper, *The Southwest Courier*. This souvenir number contained tributes paid the jubilarian by well-wishers the world over. In its foreword it said:

The records of time will never enroll all the achievements of Bishop Kelley, nor tell of the inspiration he has given to countless thousands, nor reveal the weak made strong through his kind and gentle ministrations. This man of God who has spent his life in having the world know Christ, in lifting faces to see the light, in dispelling darkness with his pen whose passionate cause is Truth, has earned the plaudits of peoples and nations for more than 50 years. But encomiums slip away on the wings of time unless penned in pages. This book is a symposium of tributes that spring from the heart, a bouquet picked here and there from an endless field of flowers. It is our offering to a grand soul, restless, creative, spiritual; our labor of love for one who is a benediction to America, for we know that we shall not meet his like again.

The Holy Father, Pope Pius XII, after having cited His Excellency as the founder of the Catholic Church Extension Society, stated in the souvenir volume:

It was, however, when you were raised to episcopal dignity that your gifts of character and soul most splendidly shone forth to the advantage of the church, for you have industriously discharged its manifold duties, particularly by your eloquence in preaching and by the publication of writings of great utility—brilliant evidences of your learning and piety.

President Franklin D. Roosevelt penned the following:

I know your golden anniversary will bring a flood of memories of your varied activities as priest, missionary, editor and, latterly, for nearly a score of years as Bishop of a great and flourishing diocese. As you reflect on all the events of which you have been a part during the last fifty years, you will say with the Psalmist that the lines have fallen unto you in goodly places.

The forty-page edition was filled with greetings and compliments from cardinals and statesmen, bishops and archbishops, churchmen and laity. Most of the expressions fixed his greatest feat as the founding of the Catholic Church Extension Society. He was lauded as the Bishop of Scouting, the oldest military chaplain, a progressive member of the Administrative Board of the National Catholic Welfare Conference, America's foremost Catholic author, the nation's most versatile prelate and the greatest contributor to the church in the history of the country.

Under the caption *A Disciple Jots It Down*, a churchman destined to be his successor in Oklahoma, revealed how he first met Bishop Kelley. Most Rev. Eugene J. McGuinness, then Bishop of Raleigh, North Carolina, told how he was stationed at the Philadelphia Cathedral in 1917. Archbishop (now Cardinal) Dougherty always heard confessions on Saturday afternoons. But on one particular Saturday afternoon he left his confessional early and the

Cathedral staff of priests wondered why. They discovered he had gone to meet a Monsignor who had come from Chicago. "Who is he?" they all queried. Bishop McGuinness answered the question, "He is the one who saved a certain seminary from the sheriff's sale by cabling over money to the Philippines and the Archbishop never forgot a favor."

Bishop McGuinness continued in the Golden Jubilee number:

A Golden Jubilarian in the priesthood is comparatively rare but to have arrived at it and to find that the church under the American flag has been enriched both spiritually and materially by one's activity is the lot only of Francis Clement Kelley. He, above others, has narrowed the horizon of the Cross, for he has in truth dotted the hillsides and valleys with crosses he made possible by the ordination of countless priests; he adorned and festooned lowly tabernacles throughout the land, and his greatest achievement —he made America mission-conscious.

Bishop William D. O'Brien, who succeeded Bishop Kelley as President of the Catholic Church Extension Society, told this story in the souvenir number:

Here in the office of Extension I will be glad to point out to you a framed Canadian one-dollar bill. It was the first dollar ever contributed to the work of Extension. When Father Kelley was going home from the first meeting of Extension Society, held in the residence of Archbishop Quigley here in Chicago, the newsboy on the train told Father Kelley that he had read in the paper about him being appointed president of a new society. Father Kelley went to work on the newsboy. The result was the gift of the first dollar ever made to the Society. . . . Father Kelley's idea of helping the Home Missions and our dependencies has resulted in $20,000,000 being put into Home Missionary activities in the last generation alone.

During his five years of illness Bishop Kelley never failed to be charmed by beauty. He loved to ride out into the open country and watch the procession of the seasons—spring with its dogwood and red bud opening pink and white umbrellas through the hollows; summer with its wheat fields pressed down to the red earth by the strong south winds; autumn when prairie fires ate their way along the horizon and the crimson sumac shook out its bannerets along the hillsides; winter, too, when the wild grape vines became brown ropes in the thickets and wild geese chanted lonesomely down the airways of the sky.

On summer evenings he would sit on his lawn and go over his memory whirlpool of the years, all the while watching the stars

Foreword

move as if in a drift of the winds. In the sunset of life, with his active career over, he would think back over the years with their trials and triumphs. He must have been dreaming of his native Prince Edward Island washed by blue Atlantic waters, or of Rome where his mind shaped events of history, or of Oklahoma where he built a structure of granite from hard-won quarries. But, above all, he must have reflected on the Cross and the inspiration it gave him to place it on thousands of churches in forgotten places and bring the light of hope and the Faith of our Fathers to forgotten peoples.

During the last solemn days, he remained in his room, with the photograph of Mother Cabrini by his side. He liked to be reminded that he preached the sermon at her funeral in Chicago and had predicted that she would be a saint, for he had said, "She sees the Vision! She is on the mount of her own transfiguration. The light about her is the light of the Blessed for Whom she lived."

Low, gray clouds swept around and over Bishop Kelley's home on February 1, 1948. It was gloomy almost from dawn to death-time. The Bishop had been in a coma for five days. The weakening pulse grew weaker still and the household waited. The medal of St. Frances Xavier Cabrini, pinned on his breast, moved with every labored breath. Then there came a gentle flutter of the eyelids; his head fell gently to the side. At eventide the soul of the great leader went swinging out above the tide that runs around the world.

Friends from as far as three thousand miles, distant Prince Edward Island, came to Oklahoma City in a gesture of final friendship. They gathered at the cemetery, almost in the shadow of the Cathedral, as freezing rain glazed the trees and created a fairyland of ice, something the poet in the soul of Bishop Kelley would have loved. Mourners stood by the gray tomb while fingers of ice grew on the fringes of the canopy under which Bishop McGuinness stood and pronounced the church's last farewell. The close-by elms were crackling under the north wind, as if grieving for the lost leader. But bending low under their burden of ice were clumps of mistletoe, green, standing as symbols of eternal life, of heralds of coming spring and resurrection.

Bishop Kelley's fruitful life needs no future to complete. Still, the ocean at each tide casts sparkling treasures on the beach. So will it be in days to come. Each year will bring to light the hidden deeds, the ungathered bits of gold, of one who was marked by Providence for his era, his church and country, yes, even for the world.

Contents

Contents

THE BISHOP
JOTS IT DOWN

⚜ 1 ⚜

THE ISLAND

E VEN a birth date, being a statistic, sounds like a threat of
dullness. But every life is a series of adventures, so why not
open up with the one, if one there be, that stands out most
vividly amongst the memories of boyhood; an event which might
be called a poor brother of the one to which Dante thus referred:
"In quella parte del libro de la mia memoria dinanzi a la quale
poco si potrebbe leggere"—"In that part of the book of my memory
before which little could be read." I had such an adventure; one
of the kind that every grown person would like to have had early
enough in life to color all of it; wild enough for wonder, dangerous enough for thrills, and unusual enough to treasure. How many
bishops, for example, could jot down the glorious fact that they
began life as sailormen? But I sailed once before the mast. Better
still, I was a sort of officer on shipboard, and that before my first
twelve years had been passed. A fisherman on the Newfoundland
Banks, too, I was. It all came about this way:

My father was a trader in the sense given the word in the
Merchant of Venice. He chartered and loaded ships and sent his
partner off on them to sell their cargoes. All his ships went out
into the Atlantic; some to Newfoundland, some as far as the West
Indies, and some to the French islands called St. Pierre and Mi-
quelon. One never-to-be-forgotten summer he sent me with his
partner on a two-masted schooner to St. Pierre. Because the ship
took no passengers I had to be given a job so I was registered as
assistant supercargo. My only duty, however, was to keep from being seasick, a duty I performed very badly. When we passed the
strait between Nova Scotia and Cape Breton, with the inelegant
name of the Gut of Canso, I gave up my duty and went to bed

in the tiny cabin where there were bunks for the captain, the real supercargo and myself. As soon as we came in sight of St. Pierre I returned to duty. While the cargo was being disposed of I fished for squid in the harbor from the side of the schooner. Then we took on ballast and started for Glace Bay in Cape Breton Island, at which port the charter was to expire.

On the way back the schooner was becalmed on what were then the French Banks. The half-barrel of squid I had caught in St. Pierre became a serious temptation to Captain Boudreau. A sailor sent aloft reported that there was nothing in sight but water so the captain resolved to take a chance and do some illegal fishing. Cod lines were brought out and I was taught how to use them. All the afternoon we fished from the deck until it was slimy with cod. The French cutter we feared did not appear, but the wind did and the schooner headed for port.

With a rough sea I went off duty again. The light schooner pitched and tossed as the darkness came on. I dragged my misery down to the cabin and into my bunk.

About midnight I heard the supercargo get up, draw on his oilskins, and ascend the companionway ladder. When he pushed aside the hatch I could hear the captain shouting orders to his son at the wheel. There was much tramping and calling over my head. The supercargo came down again and I asked him what was wrong, with no great interest because I was under the influence of the deep indifference of the seasick to fate. He answered in two words, "Cape Scatari."

I had heard about the Scatari Island's cape as a maker of storms. Now I knew. The cabin was shaking, the old timbers of the schooner creaking ominously. I seemed to be sometimes on my head with my feet in the air and sometimes standing upright or bracing my small body against the sides of the bunk. I had bumps that hurt all over, caused by my being thrown violently against the wall or the board at the edge of the bunk that protected me from falling out onto the cabin floor. I had to go with the schooner as she had to go with the billows. I never knew how it came about that I fell asleep, but when I opened my eyes daylight was streaming down the hatch. The captain was taking off his oilskins and

4

getting ready for needed sleep. The supercargo was sitting on a locker.

"Well," he was saying to the captain, "you brought her through all right, thank God, but it was a tough job."

"Weeth dat feesh I had to make heem," replied the captain.

He was probably thinking of the money for his haul, all clear gain for himself, and the fact that they were French fish.

"Where are we, Mr. MacDonald?" I asked of the supercargo.

"We have passed around Scatari all right, Sonny, and that's as definite as needs be this fine morning. I'm glad we ain't there yet, washed up under the cliffs. A few bits of prayers wouldn't have come amiss from you. We all have something to be thankful for."

The captain was snoring in his bunk by this time and the cook was coming down the ladder with food. I heard the rattle of a spoon against the tin can that held the welcome tea, but with all the force of my soul I hoped that there might not also be bacon.

It was not until we landed in Glace Bay that I learned what a narrow escape we had had. Over the uneasy and salty road from St. Pierre to Scatari my memory ever keeps going, the lighthouse on the cape showing the way.

Twice later in life the memory of that close call came back with extraordinary vividness: once in a fog over the Gulf of St. Lawrence when the old "Empress of Britain" rammed the steel collier "Helvetia" and sent her to the bottom before my eyes; and once when, in the worst storm in fifty years on the Atlantic, I awaited a call to go with a rescue boat from the "Paris" to the aid of a British freighter that had shipped its rudder. Eighty-five men on the freighter were in danger and, as I was the only priest on the "Paris," the captain had suggested that by going with them I might encourage the rescuers. Outside, the sea behaved as it had off Scatari, only worse. I remembered the sailors' superstition about the third time. But it did not turn out to be the third time. Another British freighter, with decks lower down than those of the "Paris," got to its sister ship before us and took the rescue job off our hands. It was a close call, for in that sea the boats would be in danger of being dashed to pieces against the high sides of our liner. As I waited for the knock on my cabin door that awful night I remembered that my first job had made me a sailorman. It seemed not inappropriate that so the last also should be.

With the memory of the first adventure at sea, how could I begin this story by stating in a trite old way that I was born in Prince Edward Island on November 24, 1870? That would be nothing but the soulless record of a simple fact. Scatari was much more than a simple fact. What's a statistic to such an opening on life?

Some thirty-five years ago I heard an orator say, and prove, that it was nothing short of a special gift of Providence to have been born and reared on an island. I say prove because he called to witness the liberty-loving and philosophic dwellers of the isles of Greece, the defenders of Rhodes, of Cyprus, and of Malta, the soldiers and sailors of Albion, and, above all, his own ancestors, the royal O'Briens of the Island of Saints and Doctors. Then and there I recalled to mind with some pride that I had been born and reared on a seabound island.

It was and is a beautiful island. The blue waters of the gulf wrap it round in the comfort of the mildest of northern climates. Gentle rains and sea mists prepare for it a short, cool summer, when its bright green hills and meadows rival those of Ireland. By historic right it is part of Old Acadia, since on it were settled, and from it were driven, some of those whose sad story Longfellow tells. As strong even as in the Land of Evangeline itself, here

"Loud from its rocky caverns, the deep voiced neighboring ocean
Speaks, and in accents disconsolate answers the wail of the forest."

The forest is no more; the ocean speaks alone; there is no longer need for wailing. Sweet smelling spruce and white blossomed hawthorn line roads to peaceful hamlets, fertile farms, and cheerful homes. Blue rivers and streams flow quietly under rustic bridges. In spring the Mayflowers shoot up right bravely at the edge of the melting snows to hint that the time has come for them to vanish. Quickly follows then the Island's almost solitary wealth, pledge of its quiet and its peace, the green and gold product of well-tilled fields. Paradise of the little churches is my island, the little white churches which fit into dark settings of spruce brightened by the tombstones in the churchyards.

My island is called Prince Edward. It was discovered by Jacques

The Island

Cartier of St. Malo on June 30, 1534, when its only inhabitants were Micmac Indians. The historian records that they called it Abegwet, or Abegwit, or Epagwit; the spelling is disputed as is the meaning to be attached to the names. "Afloat at rest on the waves close by," is one translation. "Moored in the shelter of the encircling shore," "Moored in shelter," "Cradled alongside," or "Lying on the water," are others. A poet must have come along and settled the question. The old name is now spelled Abegweit, and translated "Cradled on the Waves." I am grateful to the poet, if there was one, since it must be admitted that the Micmacs most frequently used the less romantic name "Minagoo," which means simply "The Island." I should not enjoy saying that I had been born in Minagoo, but I do not at all mind admitting that I was cradled on the waves. After the Indians came the French, who changed the name to Ile St. Jean, but I am quite sure that they kept the Minagoo tradition and called it "L'Ile" in ordinary conversation. English rule followed the defeat of the French in the Maritimes and again the name was changed, this time as a compliment for a royal visitor, to Prince Edward Island. Royalty was more to the English than sanctity, as sanctity had been more to the French than poetry. But the people did not forget Minagoo and to this day in the Maritimes, and beyond, my birthplace is simply "The Island."

The parish record of Vernon River, in King's County, gives the date of my birth as October 23rd, 1870. It is not in agreement with the family Bible, which puts the day one month and twenty-four hours later. The parish record, however, is official, and, like so many other things that are official, incorrect. I was the second child and the eldest living son in a family of eight. Two children died in infancy. The place of my birth was a rural school district called Summerville. Sometimes people referred to it as the Town Road, but letters were addressed to "Edmund's Post Office." My father kept a store, owned a farm, and was a rural magistrate. Likewise he had men employed as tanners and shoemakers. In his youth young men were "bound out" to trades and my father had learned these two. He must have been at least a little bit prominent, for he served on a commission concerned with the laying out of the Prince Edward Island Railway. If he was responsible for its windings and turnings he was no success as a railroad builder. That may have been the reason why I had never heard him say anything about the railroad part of his experience in life. An island versemaker who had moved to Boston wrote of the twistings for which Father must have been at least partially responsible and called it "An Ode to the Island Railway":

> "Thy graceful curves the line of beauty shows;
> Present enchanting views on every hand:
> The meek potatoes in their crooked rows,
> The bugs which drop from them into the sand.
>
> "Yes, drop bewildered at thy swift approach,
> And lie and kick the whilst you're going by.
> So swift thy pace that, from the coach,
> Increased in size I see each leg on high."

Mother was the daughter of Andrew Murphy, a neighbor of the Kelleys, who, by the way, spelled the name with only one "e." Father spelled it both ways. Mother alone proved Father's good sense. It is not often that young men marry the obviously right kind of wife, but John Kelley had sense and he did just that.

My memory of old Andrew Murphy cries to be jotted down. He was what the neighbors called "a well-read man." "No one could be quite as wise as he looked." He wore at certain times a dignified stock of the Henry Clay type with collar points sticking out under a determined chin, dressed in broadcloth, and never went off his farm without an ivory-topped walking stick clutched in his hand. He knew all about everything and was the oracle of the countryside. When I looked at his picture in the family album I always felt that it was a real distinction to be the grandson of "Andrew Murphy, Esq." He left Ireland and Fighting Wexford because ill-health forced him to give up studying for the priesthood. His daughter selected the son of a Kilkenny man for a husband. I cannot remember the Kilkenny grandfather but I do remember his funeral. I was on my mother's lap as it passed our house, which was close to the road. Not knowing exactly what a funeral was, I asked her which of the men in the procession was my grandfather. She explained that he was riding ahead, and why.

Folks who had the misfortune to be born elsewhere than on the island, but not too far away to be neighborly, such as the people of Nova Scotia and New Brunswick, used to joke about our habit of

calling our little province simply The Island. They did not re.
member Minagoo.

"What island?" asked a puzzled tourist.

"Why, Prince Edward Island, of course; what other island is
there?"

"How big is Borneo?" was asked one day in school.

"Just a little bigger than The Island," was the answer.

At one tip of our island crescent is a little fishing paradise called
Souris. After a visit to New York a man from Souris met the late
Bishop Shahan, then rector of the Catholic University at Washing-
ton, who had a summer cottage in Nova Scotia.

"What did you think of our great city?" asked the rector.

The islander replied, "Oh, it's bigger than Souris."

There are a few less than 90,000 people at present on the island.
Its capital, Charlottetown, has some 12,000 of them. The industries
in my boyhood days were farming, fishing, and shipbuilding. Today
the shipbuilding is over and done with, and the people devote themselves chiefly to the raising of "the best seed potatoes in the world,
sir!"; with the silver-black fox as an extra industrial asset. It would
be a long story to tell how the fox stole in, too long for this book,
but it would have interested the Abbot Mendel. I can at least record
that the "King of the Black Foxes" was one Charles Dalton, who,
unlike the Abbot Mendel, was no scientist. Later folks called him
Sir Charles, though to his neighbors in Tignish he was always plain
Charlie. He died governor of the island. What is Tignish? It is a
town near the other tip of the island crescent, the west one, not as
large as New York; perhaps even a bit smaller than Souris.

The face of the island used to be referred to in the geographies as
"gently undulating." It runs to little hills and valleys. There is practically no prairie, so one can catch a glimpse of the blue gulf from
almost any hill. There are speckled trout and salmon in the streams,
and the deep sea is inviting for those who love to go after the "big
ones." I never realized what good things the island offered to eat
until long years after I had left. Imagine buying a whole baby lobster for two cents and a mackerel fresh out of the deep for five.
But human nature is perverse and we island boys considered tinned
lobster a great delicacy, probably because it cost so much more than
a fresh one.

9

There was scarcely room at home for all the new arrivals by the cradle route—the families were large—so a constant stream of young people kept leaving the island for Boston. Boston was a general island name for the whole United States. "Distinguished Islander Abroad" became a regular setup in the daily and weekly papers. The island was and is still prolific in successful sons and daughters; especially so in those who started out in life as schoolteachers. I think that was because of the honored place given to mathematics and the classics in the schools. There was nothing "newfangled" about the education you got from the island schoolmaster, who honored tradition and never bothered to study the latest pedagogical theories. Education was like the island table d'hôte of corned beef, potatoes, cakes, and tea—with, of course, a variation for Catholics on Friday. It cost either nothing or a quarter. In school the menu was reading, spelling, writing, grammar, arithmetic, geography, and later on geometry, algebra, Latin, and Greek. Plain old fare but it gave men and women what they needed as a foundation for something higher. Like the table d'hôte, it cost either nothing or the educational equivalent of a quarter. But we'll see more about that later on.

In religion the islanders were Catholics and Protestants, with the numerical proportion roughly set down as half and half and, in my day, the Protestants leading by a nose. There was some religious controversy but much good will. The islanders, being then for the most part of Scotch and Irish descent, were stubborn in their convictions but rather kindly disposed to one another in action. Even in politics the islander is inclined to be judicial and weigh the case. He changes his party affiliation with great ease. His policy is to "live and let live," provided it helps the island. Outsiders are welcome. "Poor fellows! Was it their fault that they were not born on the island? . . . Everybody can't expect to have everything. . . . Yes, of course they may be quite rich but . . . That's a fine field of potatoes over there on the side of the hill. . . . Won't you step into the house for a sup of tea? Mother'll have the cloth on the table in a jiffy. . . . Of course, as I was saying, we can't have everything. . . . It's too bad the good man was raised off the island. . . . The hay looks good for the season."

What has elsewhere to offer such a people? Nothing half as good to eat, nothing approximating the island neighborliness, nothing quite as fine as its content. The islander has a tiny government of his own. If he dislikes it he throws it out of the little House of Parliament in Charlottetown. The king—in practice the Dominion Cabinet—appoints the governor, after trying to find out whom the people really would like to have. There is prohibition, with the usual ships that "stop" in the night. The islander goes to church on Sunday and makes a better than ordinary job of keeping the Commandments. There are no divorces, so homes are not broken up except by death. Of course there are some grass widowers and widows, but they are visitors and do not walk on the grass while on the island. There are two advanced schools for those of the children who have scholastic aspirations. The islander can afford to send his children to them since the cost is small. During the long winter there are social gatherings and in the summer picnics and tea parties. The daily papers will publish letters, essays, and verses, and thank you for sending them. The islander is literary as well as literate and there is even a poetry society. There are balls and receptions at the Government House for the officers of visiting warships, to which anyone who likes to "dress up" may go if he or she really so desires; swimming on the south shore and surf bathing on the north in summer; tobogganing, snowshoeing, hockey and sleigh parties when the ice and snow come to stay awhile, which is usually three or four months. During the long winter there are night gatherings in the country around the queer-looking stoves—I never saw these stoves anywhere but on the island—and stories. Such stories! Mostly about ghosts. The island used to be full of ghosts. I hope none of them have since left for Boston. Every family had its special stories and some had special ghosts. My own family acknowledged an ancestor who fought a ghost all night. We admit with some reluctance that he was coming home rather late from a party; nevertheless he affirmed that he had fought the ghost successfully. To this day there is a saying around one neighborhood, "In the name of God as Kelley fought the spirit." The ghosts are, some of them, like the Irish banshees, while others are "big black dogs." You know! Perhaps you have a family ghost yourself. Then there were the songs, ballads as a rule which began "Come all ye." Strange as it may seem, the people also sang many songs of our South, mostly Stephen Foster's. I shall never forget how my mother sang them. I knew "Nellie Gray" and "Uncle Ned." Through the Scotch we had "Bonnie Dundee" and "The Campbells are Coming." Through the Irish we had the melodies and all the old ballads about Napoleon who was called "Boney."

The islander is a mortal enemy of "putting on," which means affectation. The way he speaks the English tongue shows it, for his slight brogue is only a protest against softness. He does not pronounce *psalm*, for example, as if the "a" were an "ah." The word is "sam." "Calm" and "palm" are "cam" and "pam," since in them the "a" is single and not double. To pronounce otherwise was, in my day, "Bostonian," a form of "putting on." The islander of today has had to reconcile himself to Boston English on account of his many American relatives. Never, never, will he reconcile himself to English English.

"I was going out of London one day on a train that passed Gladstone's house," remarked a traveled islander to me. "I asked the man in the compartment with me to tell me when I could catch a glimpse of Haywarden Castle, the home of the Grand Old Man. What d'ye think he answered, the scut?"

I shook my head despairingly as if I knew it must be something outrageously unlike what he ought to have said.

"Nothing but this: 'We pawss it in a few minutes, sir, but pawdon me if I say that over yar we call the 'ouse 'Arden Cawsle, and Gladstun is not the Grand Ol' Man, sir, but the Grand Ol' 'Umbug, sir.' That's what he said."

In approved form I answered, "D'ye tell me so?"

My friend kept on relating that story for the rest of his life to illustrate how the Queen's English—Victoria was then reigning—was being ruined by the subjects nearest her throne.

I referred to the low cost of living on the island. Food was not only cheap but its distribution in the normal way was positively encouraged. Did I not mention baby lobsters at two cents each? I bought them at that price many times as I passed through the town market on my way home from school. The finest of sea food could be had for almost nothing, and the finest of berries likewise, when they were in season. Small wild strawberries of the field had not then given place to the large garden variety. Time and time again I bought this delicious little berry for five cents the quart. On the matter of sea foods, however, the islander had certain prejudices. It was admitted that mussels, the kind you pay high for in France and Belgium, were fit to eat, but few ate them. They were altogether too plentiful. Clams likewise. While these latter might sometimes be eaten cooked, no islander of my day at least would believe you if you told him that some people actually ate them raw. Never did I meet an islander at home who would touch a dish of frogs' legs. To him frogs' legs were a sign of French decadence; yet there were thousands of French on the island who, though speaking the language, would not go so far in Gallicanism as to eat frogs' legs. There were heresies other than the religious. Even to this day the eaters of uncooked clams, and frogs' legs in any form, are as a rule held in well-merited suspicion. They are for the most part, however, people from "off the island—poor fellows!"

The hospitality of the islander does, however, take in all the things he believes fit for human consumption. It was, and I hope still is, in his blood, this hospitality. When a visitor entered an island home in the rural districts he simply had to eat. The cloth was spread on the table without a word beyond a welcome. Then came tea, bannocks and wild strawberry jam. It was a faux pas to say "preserves." That was "putting on." Jam it was and nothing else, jam made on the farm in the good wife's way. I never saw preserves in jars till long after I had left the island, nor had I used coffee. Tea was the rule for all meals, black, not green tea. The green variety ranked as low as frogs' legs.

The islander had his habits in the matter of eating oysters. His oysters have a salty tang that makes them the most delicious in the whole world. He had them right out of a barrel which many families bought in season. Or he had them by the quart, fresh out of the shell, and all the liquid served with them on a plate. No lemons and no "on the half-shell," for him. When he wanted oysters he wanted oysters undisguised, and not samples—plain oysters and plenty of them.

Charlottetown, capital of the island, is still a quaint city with many marks of the old days remaining, though it now boasts paved streets and honking horns. Along the streets are houses and stores a century old. Fifty years ago Charlottetown had a busy water front, shown by forests of the masts of sailing ships at its many wharves, and warehouses everywhere, even in residential districts. The wharves today are nearly shipless and empty; the warehouses for the most part abandoned. These, however, are signs of change, not of decay. Fifty years ago the island was almost entirely cut off from the mainland in winter. Communication for the mails and a few passengers was maintained by boats equipped with sleigh runners so that they could be rowed by oars in open water or dragged by crew and passengers over floating ice fields. In consequence what goods were needed for the winter had to be imported during the summer and autumn, and stored until sold. For long years the number and size of the warehouses were the signs of mercantile prosperity. Sailing ships did most of the transport business. All was changed when the government of Canada put two huge ice-breaking car ferries into daily service to and from New Brunswick over the narrowest part of Northumberland Strait, and thus linked up its National Railways on the mainland with the island system, changing the narrow gauge to standard. In summer, sleeping cars now connect Charlottetown and Montreal. The sailing ships no longer come as of old, and the wharves and warehouses are therefore not so much needed. The people, too, have become more sophisticated. There are movies and the latest fashions. But all has not gone down under the swell of modernism. The people still hold on to their traditions. Family life is still unsoiled by divorce courts, and for other as well as religious reasons. An editor, replying to the inquiry of a visitor about the islanders' refusal to countenance divorce, said in substance that the islanders looked at the divorce question with a sportsmanlike and businesslike eye, believing that men or women who failed in such fundamental relations to civilized society as those of matrimony could scarcely be considered good risks in the minor relationships of business and society. Note the use of the word "minor." It is important in studying the islander's psychology.

In my boyhood, Charlottetown could easily have provided Dickens with many characters. In that respect it was a diminutive Old London. It even had its slums—one street was named after the infernal regions—and was decidedly Victorian in its aristocracy. But the slums failed to produce a much lower type of crime than could be handled by a stipendiary magistrate specializing in "drunk and disorderly" cases. Theft was on a small scale, robbery almost unknown. Murder produced a community shock that awed and stilled everything and everybody. There have been only two executions in a century, about fifty years apart. The island has never had a penitentiary, but was and still is forced to buy hotel privileges in another province for its major criminals. The island characters of old could have furnished Dickens with no Fagins.

Old Hatch might, however, have suggested a story. I remember well that last of the town criers, but knew him only when he was near the end of his crying. Memory sees him still, with his queer old head cocked to one side and a bad eye closed, ringing his bell on Walker's Corner and shouting, "Oyez! Oyez! Oyez! To be sold at auction, at Lord's Wharf Number Two," etc., etc., as he announced the arrival of a shipload of imported merchandise. He began an itinerant advertising agency of one, before there were many newspapers to take up the white man's burden. Old Hatch was the daily delight of small boys, but he earned his living on the corners till death took the bell out of his hand and called, "Oyez! Oyez! Oyez! at Temperance Hall where he lived in the rear of the stage, Old Hatch lies dead. God save the Queen."

There was an Island poet, John Lepage. He could write popular doggerel and successfully dispose of his wares like newspapers. They were read by the whole town. One still jingles in my memory:

> "Fire! Fire! said the Crier,
> Where? Where? said the Mayor.
> In Pownal Street, said Major Beete,
> Those ancient piles of wood."

But he could also write like this:

> "Dark rising clouds—no feature distorted—
> Mark in the distance the hurricane's home.
> Hark! in the West rolls the deep-toned thunder,
> Pealing along through the wind-fretted dome.
> See! the proud Storm King to fury awakening,
> Flapping his wings as he rides through the rain,
> Bending the trees of the Forest, or breaking,
> Lashing to fury the waves of the main."

There was a queer character who published a scurrilous sheet called after himself, *Rochford's Daily*, full of personalities and jibes, the venom cleverly concealed against possible libel suits. He sold the paper himself while on his regular walk about town, and every-

body bought it to read what he called his "Yanks." No one was safe
from Rochford. Everybody had for him the respect of fear. No one
selected that editor for an enemy. He had none but those of his
own making, and how he enjoyed seeing the list of them lengthen-
ing day by day. I thought him a mild sort of man because he was
friendly to us boys. But I came close to a woodshed interview with
Father for having just once sold papers for him.

From slavery some Negroes had reached the island and inhabited
a street in Charlottetown soon called The Bog. Reading the island
"Memories" of Benjamin Bremner I was reminded of how one of
them actually gave his name—or rather nickname—to a bridge. He
literally lived, though no Diogenes, in a barrel—Mr. Bremner calls
it a puncheon, and puncheon size it must have been—right on one
end of what was called Black Sam's Bridge. The Negro blood has
thinned out. No black faces are seen now save when the Montreal
sleeper stays overnight in the railway yards. Perhaps it was the run-
away slave who brought the songs of the South to the island. The
little Negro colony in The Bog had two real characters in residence:
Black Sam and Nat De Coursey. The latter might well have served
as a prototype of Uncle Tom except possibly for the piety.

I keep wondering why only one novelist discovered the island.
Maud Montgomery could not help herself, for she had genius and
was born there. But at that she used only a section of a section for
her homey sketches of island life. She did not touch the life of the
French fishermen. She perhaps did not know the descendants of
the Catholic Highlanders. The solid but unvarnished product of
Scotch and Irish unions are still to be introduced to the outside
world. But let no novelist try a pen on island life without having
lived it, especially during a long winter when he may meet his
human inspirations around the kitchen stoves blazing red for comfort as well as for tea and bannocks. The life of the visitor to the
island is a summer life; the life of the islander a winter one. And
it is to be studied only on an equality basis, for the islander is not
to be patronized. He takes little or no interest in the tourist except
as a specimen of curious beings who spend money unnecessarily.
Tourists do not, he knows, stay over the winter. But, 'ware the
islander! He may look the innocent but, like Will Cain of New
Perth, be an ex-schoolmaster or school inspector turned back to

16

farming. He may put a "cargo" in Chicago but he knows his geography. He may exhibit curiosity about the Rockies, but he has a brother who made a fortune in Colorado. If he be a Presbyterian, watch him, for it may be his near relative who had a fashionable church on Fifth Avenue, or was both President of Cornell and American Ambassador to Germany. A Catholic may have an archbishop or a professor of philosophy in his family. There are three living archbishops and three living bishops from The Island. Above all, 'ware the seeming guilelessness of the islander! He is not a guileless man. His humor is deep and he loves to enjoy it at the expense of the unperceiving stranger. If you go to the island be humble, with the humility that is not carried as an ornament but as a safety belt.

An atheistic visitor sat expounding his favorite thesis one winter night to a group around the fire in an island farmhouse. Looking straight at Ronnie Donald McPherson he challenged, "Who ever saw God?" Ronnie took up his cap and put on his fur coat before he said anything.

It was as he fastened his overshoes that he remarked quietly, "Richt, mon! Who ever did? But I saw the thracks of Him on the snow this nicht as I kem over here under the light of the staars."

❧ 2 ❧

SCHOOL DAYS

WHEN the family moved to Charlottetown I had to make a new start at absorbing knowledge and was handed over to the care of Miss Fennessy who conducted a primary private school about two blocks from my new home. Charlottetown's children at that time depended on private schools. Miss Fennessy limped. She had, however, the best of reasons for so doing since half of her walked on flesh and bone and half on a wooden stick which she managed quite dexterously through an opening on the side of her black dress, through which she thrust her hand to hold and guide it as she stumped along. I was only a few months over four years of age when I was sent to Miss Fennessy's Select Academy for Advanced Studies in Alphabetics.

I have a distinct recollection of hearing some of my fellow students express regret that, whatever the accident had been which removed one of Miss Fennessy's props, fate had in it shown no sense of the proprieties. A schoolmistress, if she had to lose any limbs, should, they opined, be allowed to keep both legs in exchange for the loss of both arms. I was too young to feel as keenly as others about that, but on certain painful occasions my ears testified to the soundness of the view. While parents believed in corporal punishment, it was not parents but pupils who had to sit on some of Miss Fennessy's stinging judgments. Her lameness, her strict adherence to both rule and ruler, and the opinions of my companions on the latter, sum up the personal recollections of my second school. Of the first I shall speak later.

There was a most interesting place for a small boy to stop on my way to and from school. It was the shop of "M. HENNESSY, CABINET MAKER AND UNDERTAKER." Mr. Hennessy had the distinction of being my uncle by marriage. He had the greater distinction in my eyes of being a man who could plane boards, saw them, and put them together with nails and glue, thus turning them into coffins. I became deeply interested in the art of coffin-making and greatly admired my cousins who seemed destined by inheritance to become masters of the art. In these days on the island one was measured for his coffin as for his clothes. Everybody could enjoy the distinction of having a tailor-made coffin at a reasonable price. Coffin sweatshops had not come in any more than tailor sweatshops. A shoemaker made our boots, a shirtmaker made our shirts, a tailor made our clothes, and an undertaker made our coffins. Everybody therefore had a job, could live and let live; except, of course, those measured for coffins.

"M. Hennessy, Cabinet Maker and Undertaker" was a man who looked at life over glasses. When called upon for conversation he pulled his "specs" down close to the tip of his nose, frowned, and by lifting up a partially concealed chin brought the pressure of the lower lip to bear on the upper in such wise as to indicate deep thought and great erudition. The reason all the chin did not show was that a crop of black whiskers began under the right ear and extended around the neck in crescent shape, terminating exactly under the left ear. This scheme of facial decoration has, alas, gone out with the coming of the machine age, its safety razors and soap-research laboratories. I venture no opinion as to the merits of the change. Many races, as a witty bishop once said, have been won by a close shave. All I wish to insist upon is that my Uncle Mick might not have won a place in my memory without his whiskers. Still, the coffins may have had something to do with it.

I have since speculated as to what that respected uncle by marriage might have said had anyone suggested his opening a funeral parlor or an undertaker's chapel. His sympathies were expressed to the bereaved over his workbench, and made practical with advice not to be too extravagant in the matter of "putting your good money into the ground." That he never became rich will be no surprise to present-day undertakers. He knew nothing about embalming, nor did any of the other undertakers on the island, though in his old age he sadly witnessed his sons going modern and even importing factory-made coffins; but to the day of his death no man, no woman even, dared call him a mortician. He moved his business just once and his sign with it. The old sign remained for years after his passing over the gate which opened into the back yard containing the shop. Once only did good old Uncle Mick take second place at a funeral. It was his own.

My third try at education was under the Brothers of the Christian Schools at St. Patrick's, near the cathedral. It did not last long, for the bishop had come to a "gentleman's agreement" with the City School Board, and as a result St. Patrick's was taken into the new Public School System and its name changed to Queen Square. To all intents and purposes, however, it remained Catholic, as the Wesleyan Academy, changed also in name, remained Protestant. The gentlemen's agreement worked. It did away with a lot of bickering over schools, and stands today, nearly sixty years after, as one of the reasons why the island prays, raises good citizens and plenty of them, and keeps the Commandments with a fair measure of success. All island school children have religious training. I stayed in Queen Square School till I was ready to study Latin. Then I went to St. Dunstan's College. It is around St. Dunstan's that most of my school-day memories circulate.

St. Dunstan's was a combination high school and college, staffed by three priests and six lay teachers; most of these latter intending to become priests themselves. There was, of course, no standardizing. The college conferred no degrees. Tradition made English and mathematics the secular studies held in highest esteem, but one's class was determined by Latin. When you "saw Horace" you were about ready for philosophy, and one had to have seen Horace and the Church Fathers to hold on there. In my day there was a family style about St. Dunstan's. You could go ahead as fast as you liked. If you didn't want to go at all you waited patiently till you were booted out. I owe a great debt to one of the family style instructors at St. Dunstan's, Mr. Alexander McAuley, now an erudite old pastor, but then an enthusiastic youth. He had a taste for letters and history which, without knowing, he communicated to me by the simple method of reading essays at me as I sat on a trunk in his room, and going off on a talking tangent in class. Mr. McAuley was a born trainer of the imagination. He had the desire to be a scholar. He still has it and still thinks the goal far off, which shows that probably he has attained it. What little I have of letters he gave me in seed form. I can still see his enthusiastic face before me as he read, with no little eloquence, his favorite selections and the latest products of his own pen.

Some teachers use books merely to awaken powers in their pupils as well as enthusiasms to go exploring for themselves. Pupils with a natural love of letters are fortunate if they sit at the feet of at least one such burning enthusiast as was McAuley. He is like a guide at the Grand Canyon of the Colorado who neglects to mention the scientific names of the different visible rock strata but who does not neglect to call attention to their magic display of colors. He never fails to call attention to a white cloud trapped halfway down the gorge any more than he will let one miss glimpses of the tumbling and foaming river below, or allow the play of light and shadow on the deep walls of clay and stone, and the green shrubs that ornament them, to go unnoticed. But he knows also when to be silent and allow one to be his own instructor. Such a guide in school is often set down as impractical. His students may fail in examinations. But is it not often the examinations that fail? There are places on every river worth seeing, say where it widens out or runs, as it were, into bays for rest and repose; or where the stream half pauses to receive the homage and gift of a waterfall; or where a few exposed rocks give it an excuse to lash itself playfully into a threat that deceives no one who loves beauty. The pilot who steers by such marks sees only their utility to navigation. But the teacher-enthusiast? Well! I never saw my thought about him put into language to suit me until I ran across Ernest Raymond's description of the eccentric schoolmaster of St. Paul's about whom he said, "He caught us at the right hour—at an age of blossoming and rapid development." That schoolmaster was, he admitted, half mad. His very madness drove him into his outbursts. How fortunate for the many that Elam himself was so unfortunate.

The teacher who taught me best was not a bit mad, not a bit eccentric. He was a sane enthusiast who perhaps did not even dream that he was setting at least one other mind on fire. Any student could trap him into talking and most of them did. He had not the wide range of knowledge that Raymond credits to Elam, but he was then very young. Here, however, is one thing Raymond's mad teacher said that my sane teacher might well have said: "I don't care twopence about giving you *facts*—anybody can give you *facts* . . . I'm going to give you *ideas* . . . I don't want to teach you to *know*, but to *interpret*. Your brain shouldn't be a cold-storage chamber, but a power-house." No, my teacher never said anything like that, leastwise not in words. But just the same I heard it from him. And how I wish I had heeded it more at the time!

Mr. McAuley was not, however, the only one of my old tutors whose work survives. There was Father John, the late Rev. John A. MacDonald, who was called "Black Jack" by the students—though strictly, of course, in private converse. If Mr. McAuley instilled in me the love of letters Father John infused the fear of God, as well as the mechanics of the English speech. Later he introduced me to Shakespeare.

The rector of St. Dunstan's was "Father Charles," another MacDonald. There were MacDonalds in plenty on the island. Father Charles became Bishop of Charlottetown after the death of Bishop McIntyre, and thereby hang two or three tales, but to one only shall I give any notice. Father Charles had a deep appreciation of the fact that he belonged to the MacDonald clan. Though he never openly mentioned it, he could hint at the fact without trying. Every time I visited the island after my ordination I preached in the cathedral, but never once did Father Charles as bishop offer me the compliment of a hearty "well done." I firmly resolved that I would apply pressure to break that Scotch silence. On the occasion of a visit after my service in the war with Spain I delivered a lecture which had in it everything I could put there. After the lecture I walked back to his house with the Bishop. Not a word about the lecture! We went up to the common room. Still not a word. We smoked. The Bishop remained silent. Then out of a clear sky came this Gaelic compliment: "Frank, did you ever hear that one of your great-grandfathers was a MacDonald and that you have the right to wear the tartan of the clan?" I had not heard that, but I knew that I had forced the Bishop into the open. It was one of the real triumphs of my life and one of the hardest to win.

It was in St. Dunstan's that I began journalism, though we had no such course. I founded a little college paper, and Mr. McAuley became its editor. It was called "The Collegium" and consisted of four folio pages. The subscription price was thirty cents a year. It not only got me into journalism but also into hot water.

It must have occurred to Father John—I forgot to say that he was in charge of discipline—that it was not at all good for a boy who had no taste for algebra—he was also in charge of a class in that disgraceful form of annoyance—to be running downtown interviewing printers to the neglect of the plus and minus signs as well as patient grubbing around Greek roots—he taught also a class of Greek. At any rate Father John decided to put an end to my journalistic career. He took my job of business editor away from me and suggested more attention to study, not knowing the depth of the wound he was inflicting. Like many another later on, he failed to note one miserable weakness in me: if pushed too hard I get stubborn. Ordinarily there is no outward sign of that weakness. Nearly always I am quite willing to stop, look, listen, and give ground. But there is a point, you know! The paper was my baby. I had planned it and made it. I was willing to give almost my heart's blood to discipline but not my heart's infant. I countered on Father John and hid the subscription book. The paper came out on time but could not be mailed to its anxiously waiting patrons. A day passed, three days, a week. Search was made but the book was not found. I was commanded to give it up and answered that it was my own property and not even for sale. If "Black Jack" had gone to see my Father he would have won over me by a knockout but he never thought of that. So, I licked him. I was restored to office and journalism.

Father John won the next fight. He got word to my Father that I was not doing all I should in my studies. The effect was everything he could have wished for. Father was a man of few words. I was glad of that for the next day he used all of them on me. What came out of the talk will appear later. In the end, however, it was anything but distressing. Father had no modern ideas about "being a pal" to his sons. Few old-time Irish fathers had. They ruled and never coddled their offspring. One direct-to-the-point lecture always produced a multitude of good results. One of that kind was all I had and all I needed. Yes, Father John won the next fight and found out how to win any that might follow. All he had to do was to see Father. He became very confident in his dealings with me as well as with a few others of his students who had no love for Greek roots, who abominated algebra, and considered calculus a calculated method of mental torture.

St. Dunstan's is now affiliated with Laval University. It has a new building, Dalton Hall, and championship hockey as well as Rugby teams, but it still gets on without frills. One can secure an education there, sans parties, sans dances, sans style, sans everything but work. The old place has traditions but no money. It opened its door to a student in my day for about one hundred and twelve dollars a year, which covered board and tuition, a cot in an open dormitory, and the doctor's care in sickness. The charge is now about one hundred and fifty dollars a year more. The student body does not grow in numbers, but there is a constantly growing list of those who bless its worn floors, dingy classrooms, and memories of devotion. Its present-day graduates get degrees from Laval to take with them out into the world. In the old days we went out when we thought we knew enough for the next move, and all we took was a trunk full of well-worn clothes and a head full of determination to make every ounce of learning count for a ton. It's not how much one has but how far it will stretch that really seems to matter.

The students of St. Dunstan's came as a rule from the little country schools which still flourish on the island and merit attention. By all the present accepted laws of the science of pedagogy the little one-room country school should be put down as a relic of pioneer educational inefficiency and backwardness. Judging from the product, however, that would not be even half-true of the little one-room country school that occupied a half-acre on the corner of an islander's farm. If the building was small and poor the system was neither. It still works and works well. The educational record of these little schools is simply amazing. With time out for potato digging and berry picking they usually opened in the summer. The number of pupils might average thirty. One teacher carried them from the A B C's well into what we might call second year high. The teacher was paid for that extraordinary service the sum of two hundred and twenty-five dollars a year; if he or she possessed a "second-class license." A "first-class license" added about fifty dollars to the yearly salary and a "third-class license" chipped that much off. Sometimes there was a "supplement" of from twenty to thirty dollars a year, paid by the patrons, outside the usual tax. The "supplement" was, of course, a bait for attracting the best talent. The "masters" or "mistresses" did not board at hotels. There were none. Only a mean "master" would shirk duty in potato time, and there were few "mistresses" who would not gladly lend a hand at the churn.

Some might question the ability of a single teacher to carry thirty pupils from the alphabet into the tenth grade with any degree of success. Naturally there were pupils in these little island schools who could not be carried beyond the most elemental knowledge with any degree of success whatever. Examinations, however, showed remarkable results. The little school with a "second-class" teacher brought its graduates through the lower grades, one hundred and twenty pages of algebra, finished the first book of Euclid, covered two hundred pages of elementary Latin, offered the elements of French, and completed the texts of the histories of both Canada and England.

When the aspiring graduate of the little one-room country school wanted to go higher he or she usually went up for the entrance examination at Prince of Wales, the Normal College in Charlottetown. If admitted, one year in this school was required before taking the examination for a teacher's license of the third or second class. Two years were required before the examination for a first-class license. Many of the professional men and women who started on the island went through this Normal and actually taught in the country schools after graduation. Some put in one year of teaching; most put in two. Then, with almost the difference between the sixty dollars a year paid for board and the full amount of the saved salary in pocket, they bravely started out for college. "For college? With less than five hundred dollars to see them through? Are you joking?" No, I am not joking. They started out for college and about half of them did not have to go far. Some went to Dalhousie or Mt. Allison across the Strait of Northumberland. Catholics could stay home, for they had the only full senior college on the island, situated right in its center and only about one mile from Charlottetown.

St. Dunstan's was founded by immigrant Scotch Highlanders.

The Bishop Jots It Down

Who were these people? The most loyal hearts that beat in Scotland, hearts true to the hopeless cause of the Stuarts, the hearts of the heroes of Colloden; honest, plain people who asked no favor but the right to live their lives and worship God in the manner of their fathers.

Wherever Celts settle, love of learning settles with them. It was not strange therefore that the Highlanders built the first college on the island. Today people would laugh at it, for it had no equipment and the building was nothing but a rough old house made over. One may easily imagine the homespun-clad students on the unpainted benches writing on tables that still had the marks of the saw and plane upon them. The whole staff consisted of two teachers and the whole student body of not more than ten. That was well over a hundred years ago. No one had any money. Fees were paid in farm produce and were not high at that. Books had to be passed from hand to hand. The food was of the plainest kind; more porridge and bannocks than meat and cake, not forgetting the potatoes. But out of that college in the woods came real men who handed down traditions that live. St. Andrew's College was its first name; then St. Dunstan's. Today it has a faculty and a good one. Its student body will compare favorably in quality, if not in numbers, with that of any educational institution in the north country. Side by side in the classrooms sit the big-boned descendants of the Highlanders and of the Irish and the French, who came later; all with the same old red soil of the island clinging to their boots. There is not much money amongst them. As of old the table is supplied by the products of the farm. The boys can discuss potatoes in almost the same breath with Greek roots. They are proud of the things that the students of larger colleges scorn, but they think that these are things worth while. St. Dunstan's, like the old fence that used to surround it when I was a boy, is rough-hewn, but it turns out its generous share of scholars.

St. Dunstan's held from the beginning that education is a philosophy of life which should be a definite one, that man needs the stability of faith. And right there is the first and greatest reason why the island education was a good preparation for life. The island boy or girl was forearmed for the reason that he or she was given the answer to the question, "What is man? What his destiny?

What his end?" The islander believes in God, not only as the Creator but as the Providence, not only as the Father but as the Judge. The Catholic parent on the island sees to it that this foundation of a philosophy of life is taught in the schools his children attend. The Protestant islander, both in the districts religiously mixed and those fully Protestant in population, does what Horace Mann thought all parents would do under his system of state-supported non-sectarian schools: actually instructs his own children at home. The American people put only one part of Mann's idea in practice, the islander all. The Catholic child on the island has his Catechism daily; the Protestant his family Bible readings nightly.

I am not blind to advantages which tradition and a lack of money gave the young island student. He aimed at taking a Normal course before entering college. After the Normal he had that opportunity I mentioned to teach. Fortified not only with an education which, if he won a first-class license, entitled him to sophomore standing, he had also his teaching experience to consolidate and make effective his educational gains. That experience was an integral part of his training. Even when the possession of money freed him from the necessity of teaching, the Normal training was well worth while.

A word must be jotted down regarding the islander's reverence for mathematics as an educational advantage, even though for me it was a source of many worries. He believes that mathematics is the great mental test. "A boy who cannot do sums," my father put it to me, "will never amount to anything." One of the most respected men on the island was the father of James Jeffrey Roche, an American poet who was also for years an editor and the grandfather of the late Arthur Somers Roche, the novelist. Mr. Roche was not an imposing figure, but that did not count for he knew mathematics. There were occasions when he was accepted as a greater man than the governor. Even the Bishop deferred to him. When Mr. Roche came to test the classes in mathematics at the college he shone alone. "Mr. Roche," said my father, with great impressiveness, "Mr. Roche knows more mathematics than anyone on the island." It was as if Mr. Roche were another Napoleon. Never did I win the full approval of my father, for Mr. Roche told him that I was a dunce at "doing sums." I retorted that I had no interest in "sums." It was like propounding a heresy to Mr. Roche, and of course Father backed him. Was it retribution that both the son and the grandson of the old mathematician shone in literature rather than in arithmetic? Perhaps that is as it should be, for even in the study of English there was strict adherence to mathematical order and logic on the island. None but a mathematical mind could follow closely its analyzing, parsing, and table-making; nevertheless it worked. Perhaps the difficulty of procuring light reading had something to do with that, for light reading in my day was the British Essayists. There were no novels in the college library or at home. If mathematics taught the island student how to reason, the reading furnished him with models which taught him how to write.

Alas! Father was not too well off financially when I was ready for the Normal and I took advantage of the fact. I never "passed the Board" or taught in one of the little one-room country schools. I could not "do sums" with any solid hope of getting a correct answer. I hated Euclid and all his triangles. I am therefore far from being a perfect islander. But when I heard a tourist who had wandered into my old homeland one summer say that he had never met such "a solid and learned body of clergy anywhere as those on the island," I straightened up as if I had a right to feel complimented. I think I even managed a modest blush, feeling that, if not really one of them, I certainly was at least distantly related.

Of course there were always those who stand out like village Hampdens and leave their mark on our memories of boyhood. For me, one was a governor, one a bishop, one a parish priest and one a schoolteacher. Let me jot down something about each of them, beginning with the schoolteacher.

Jim Doyle worked for my father after school hours making boots. He was an uncle of mine by marriage and used to carry me to school on his back. He also made my first pair of boots. They were good strong boots, though as to the comfort of them no honeyed words are justified. Jim said they would wear well. They did, for I never put them on without deciding to go barefoot. Jim taught me a few letters of the alphabet while he imparted a knowledge of other branches of learning to the bigger boys and girls, who admitted sadly enough that it was no unmixed blessing to have a schoolmaster so accustomed to working with leather. My memory of Jim Doyle's school is, nevertheless, a vivid and a pleasant one. It had but one room, strictly without ornamentation. The seats were old-fashioned benches without backs. Long tables on each side answered for desks. There was a dunce's corner. Some years ago I went to see where the building stood. It was still there but sadly shrunken. Everything we thought big in childhood does that. I once thought that school one of the greatest edifices in the world. Now I know that it could shelter not more than thirty boys and girls at most.

Governor Hodgson was the first of his kind for me. I saw him after we moved to the city, but of course never spoke to him. He was a tall old man with fine white hair, and in his eyes a look of dignified detachment from ordinary things. He had a noble bearing and was always "dressed up" like my Murphy grandfather. He lived in a great house overlooking Charlottetown harbor and near Fort Edward, which boasted of five old muzzle-loading cannon that could not be trusted to defend a bird's nest in these days, but at that time were as impressive as the governor. I saw him opening the tiny Parliament. The soldiers of his guard were farm boys dressed in red uniforms and remarkably well drilled; the kind of boys whose sons gave a fine account of themselves in the Great War. The aides wore cocked hats with plumes. There was a red-coated band with a fat leader. The guns at Fort Edward fired a salute. The governor made a speech from the throne just as did the queen in London. There were loyal replies from Her Majesty's Government and Her Majesty's Opposition. The governor came out and the red-uniformed farm boys presented arms. The plumes on the hats of the aides caught the wind as the carriage drove back to Government House. It was a grand sight, democracy in gold lace and feathers, but real democracy nevertheless. I just cannot get used to the governors I see in these days, governors in business suits and Stetsons who treat me as a civic equal. I am spoiled in the matter of governors. I like them old, white-haired, dignified, with plumed aides beside them and cannon firing salutes in the distance. Not that I did not get along with Governor "Alfalfa Bill" in Oklahoma. I did, and found him well worth while. Bill would be the last man to blame me for not fitting him into the picture of salutes, fuss and feathers that delighted my boyish eyes in 1879 and after.

The Bishop's name was Peter McIntyre. He was a descendant of the Scotch Highlanders. As with governors, so with bishops. I have seen many bishops, even archbishops and cardinals, but none of them ever measured up to Bishop McIntyre. Even when I am shaving, and thus beholding my own countenance in a glass, I find it hard to think that actually I am shaving a bishop. I miss the long, silvery hair, the dignified carriage of the head, the firm mouth, as well as the overhanging eyebrows that looked like turrets guarding two fortresses of stern eyes. I think the bishop who looks least like the bishop of my memories is myself. Perhaps that is why I find it so hard to think of myself as a bishop. When I have to act as one I sense that there is something wrong, that a mistake has been made; and all because I cannot look like Bishop McIntyre. No man was more respected on the island than he. No man was more set in doing things his way; no man could be. As there was "but one Lord, one Faith, and one Baptism," according to Butler's Cathechism, so on the island there was but one bishop, the one Father of all under God, and his name was Peter. Peter means a rock. This Peter was a rock, but the kind of rock that, while able to carry any weight and seemingly impregnable to the force of the elements which dared to throw themselves against it, nevertheless had gathered into its many crevices a considerable amount of alluvial soil from which grew such pretty things as flowers. For Peter the rock was Peter the charitable. With the children Peter the ruler was Peter the gentle. I am afraid that it is not the memory of great shaggy eyebrows and long white hair that makes me appear a very unsatisfactory bishop to myself, but the lack of distinguishing qualities which the first bishop I knew possessed in plenty.

Father James was the Parish Priest. His family name was Phelan but rarely was he known by it. Everywhere and always he was plain Father James. I do not remember having seen him in church before being presented to him when he was making a visit to my father's house, though the story I am jotting down about the visit means that, if I had not seen him in church, I had at least heard him. He was in the "front room"—the islander's modest way of referring to his parlor—when I was called in and my accomplishments explained. Father James was interested. I was lifted on to a chair and, using it as an improvised pulpit, I preached a sermon to Father James in a language that only Heaven understood, and in his own best style. Every time he came to visit our house I had to preach that sermon. Father James always rewarded it by taking up a collection. Being the whole congregation, he himself gave the silver quarter of a dollar which was quite enough for the great preacher's needs at that period of his life. A kindly man was Father James. When my parents moved out of his parish to Charlottetown he still visited us. I liked the visits because of the very agreeable custom of the collection. Though in time I ceased to preach to him, and even forgot the special language I had invented for the purpose, nevertheless at each visit Father James honored tradition and contributed his silver offering.

Father James was building a new church; the finest church then on the island. When my family was moving to the city we drove past his house which was situated on a hill overlooking a little river. We stopped to see the pastor. I was then about four years old. Father James solemnly promised on that occasion that he would give me the old church when the new one was finished. I remember stipulating that a large oil painting behind the altar was to be included in the gift. I am sorry to say that Father James did not keep his promise. He tore down the old church and I do not know what became of the picture. But even at that time I had a suspicion that, if I could not have the old church at Vernon River, some day I would have one of my own anyhow. Was that the aurora of a rising vocation?

Father James grew old in service. He drank plenty of buttermilk and held firm to the faith that it was the water of life. He was old indeed when I met him in Naples more than twenty years ago. He stopped me on the street.

"Don't you know me?" he asked.

"It's not—it can't be—Father James?"

" 'Tis Father James."

"And what are you doing in Italy at this time of your life?"

"I came to see the Pope before I die. Tomorrow I'll be on my way to Rome."

"And what do you intend doing today?"

"I'm going to see the old city that was buried two thousand years ago."

"Pompeii? I'm going there myself with some friends. Come along with us."

"No. I won't be going with your grand friends in my old clothes." Let it be known parenthetically that Father James wore his old clothes for comfort and not because of poverty.

"They are just plain people, Father James, and some of them are priests."

"Does any one of them speak Irish?"

"Come over to the hotel and we'll soon find out."

He came and we found one who could speak Irish. All that Sunday afternoon we tramped over the ancient cobblestones of Pompeii, Father James and his new friend in the rear of the party. They looked neither to the right nor to the left. With eyes on the cobblestones, heads bent, and hands tight clasped behind their backs they conversed in Irish. It may well have been the first time that the spiritual and stubborn accents of the Gaelic were heard on the streets of that old Latin town—but they were heard too late to save poor Pompeii.

⋖§ 3 §⋗

ISLAND TO INLAND

AS I look back to my days at St. Dunstan's I know that two events of the time were major forces in directing the current of my life. One was a series of losses in my father's business; the other an examination, or rather the proximate preparation for an examination.

My father's principal trading market was Boston, though he sent vessels also to the West Indies, Newfoundland, England and, as already mentioned, to the little French islands of the Atlantic. Boston was, however, the port easiest to reach as well as the surest for quick sales. I have already hinted that Boston was the real metropolis of the world for the people of the island. Many families had relatives there and these kept returning home for summer visits, each of which made Boston a greater wonder than ever to the home folks. Through this coming and going, as well as through trade, the islanders of that time were quite American in sentiment. Although the island in 1864 had been host to the very first of the general conferences that ended in the making of the present Dominion of Canada, yet it preserved its independent colonial status for some years and entered the confederation as a province only in 1873. Its insular situation, as well as its comparative isolation, kept it rather aloof from the rest of Canada. The influence of its expatriated sons and daughters, as well as its business relations with the United States, emphasized that aloofness. It was common to refer to Quebec and Ontario as "Canada" long after the island itself had become part of the Dominion.

Something happened to change all that. Trading diminished when the McKinley Bill put a prohibitive tariff on agricultural products imported into the United States. Other markets had to be

33

found for the island and, in the meantime, the business of its traders was paralyzed. Prices fell and sentiment changed. My father struggled to overcome the effects of the blow, all the time realizing that it would take years to develop new trade lines; and his health was none too good.

When all this happened I knew that I should soon have to rely upon myself alone. I was not worried. An unmathematical youth takes dark clouds for mere scenery, and the spirit of adventure is often a boy's temporal salvation; it makes a desert look like an earthly paradise, and a mirage gives courage for the spurt. Without fear I realized that I could not rely on financial support from my father if I were to continue my studies. I left school toward the end of the last semester in St. Dunstan's, to work in a dry-goods store at a salary of two dollars and fifty cents a week. I worked through part of the summer. My father had little to say about it. He never had much to say about anything, but a talk he gave me at that time I have never forgotten. One evening he came into a room where I sat reading.

"Son," he said, "I have something to say to you. I want you to listen and take it to heart. You are working for Mr. MacDonald for an agreed salary. You sold him your time and your loyalty. He pays for both weekly. They are his and not yours. If you don't deliver what you sold you are a thief. Your family would be ashamed to think that we had produced a thief."

That was all and it was enough. I did not stay long in the dry-goods store for I fell sick with typhoid fever and almost died. When I recovered St. Dunstan's was open again. Mother took the sickness as a sign from Heaven. Father scraped together enough to send me back to my books. I myself knew that it was my last year on the island. It was also my best year. Something big had come into my life. True, I did not improve in mathematics, but I did in about everything else I touched that year. Though I had only a general idea where I was going I knew that my feet were on the road. My father's losses, my humble though unfortunate adventure in business, and my sickness had done something to me and for me.

Evidently Father sensed the change, for he took the first opportunity to help again, not with counsel this time but with complaint. "Son," he said, "I have always thought you lazy. You never win any prizes. The prize speaks for its winner. None ever spoke for you. I have wondered whether it was because of a lack of brains or just plain laziness."

He left the matter there. I went back to school and thought it out along the way. I resolved to show him that it was neither stupidity nor sloth that was the matter with me. Deep down in my heart I knew that it had been a combination of both, with the latter predominating. It was stupidity about the mystery of algebra, and indifference about a lot of the rest. I was becoming altogether too fond of Addison, Steele et al. to devote time to studies which made no appeal to me. The essayists I read diligently because I loved them.

I really did get down to work. On Commencement Day Father would know. He told Mother that he did not care to attend the exercises as he had no confidence in the possibility of my getting even an honorable mention. Mother came, however, and nearly died of pride to see the governor pin the English Medal on me and hear me deliver the valedictory. Addison, Steele et al. had been doing their bit for an admirer. I beat her home and went right in to see Father, wearing the medal of course. He looked up from his desk as I entered.

"What's that you have on your coat?" he asked.

"It's the English Medal, the biggest thing of the year." I was talking quickly, almost breathlessly, "And I got four firsts and two seconds. I even got an honorable mention in Greek." I stopped to let that sink in.

Father did not change a line of his face. He looked at me earnestly for a moment with only the suspicion of a smile in his eyes. The triumph might have a bad as well as a good effect, and he was not for spoiling a boy he knew would delight in the process. Before starting to work again he remarked carelessly, "Very good. Now go out and brag to everyone about it."

I did nothing of the kind, though I would have done that very thing if he had not struck the tender spot of my vanity. I went to my room and put the medal away—somewhat soberly.

About the other great event. We had in St. Dunstan's one class with all the advanced students in it. It was so large that it was conducted in the study hall and by the rector himself. The faculty

called it "Higher Catechism." To the students, however, it was
"Theology." As a matter of fact the work did cover quite a lot of
elementary dogmatic theology. I had taken a fair amount of interest
in it, since I still remembered my childish sermon and the early
appeal of the priesthood. As the end of my last year in St. Dunstan's
approached I became more interested in that class; and its prize
was a distinction worth securing. I wanted that medal too as part
of the spoils with which I intended "showing up" Father. The examination was set for a Sunday afternoon at five. I resolved to make
a try for first place. Taking the textbook with me after dinner I
sought a quiet corner on the campus, stretched out on the grass,
and began to review the year's matter. For the very first time I became seriously interested in a textbook for its own sake. I cannot
describe the feeling I had as I read on and on. The contents of that
once uninteresting book became absorbing. Up to this time it had
been for me only bits of history, texts of Scripture, arguments and
doctrines, all semidetached from one another. Now it was a logical
whole, a synthesis of the reasons for faith in the Church Catholic;
her photograph as she was foreseen, foreshadowed, founded, and
sustained. Prophecy fitted into fulfillment, fulfillment into life. I
saw the Church as a whole. The picture charmed me with its beauty
and satisfied me by its logical completeness. I felt as though I had
had a revelation, and wondered how I had missed this "many splen-
dored thing" before. What really happened was that I glimpsed
the philosophy of life that was to guide me to the end.

When the bell rang for the examination, with my first real
understanding of what the mission of Christ meant to men, I went
into the study hall backed by something more than knowledge. I
answered questions from understanding rather than from memory. I
wrote with an enthusiasm born of love. It mattered little that I won
the prize. It mattered a great deal that I knew that God had called
me to be one of His priests. No one had advised me. No one had
urged me. No attraction had been held out to me. Indeed it was
all the other way around. That afternoon of study, and the picture
it painted permanently on mind and heart sounded the unrefusable
call.

In September I left the island. Through the kindness of a bishop
I had found an opportunity in the little College of Chicoutimi

in the Province of Quebec. Small indeed was the college, and just beginning as a pioneer outpost of Laval University. For a short time each day I taught English to French boys, who, in turn, all unknown to themselves, taught me some French. I had a special class for myself in philosophy. I attended Scripture lectures given by Dr. Begin, future Cardinal-Archbishop of Quebec but then Bishop of Chicoutimi. Only the Superior and three or four persons in the school could speak any English and of course for months I spoke no French. I had to learn it to get along. Discouraged, I used to chum with one of the students who spoke a few words of English. One day the Superior called me to his room. "You, monsieur," he said, "must cease speaking English. You will go about in the future with those who do not speak it. That is an order."

"But," I protested, "what is the use? I should be dumb. I cannot understand them and they cannot understand me."

"No matter."—He was a ruler who knew how to handle his subjects.—"No matter. A language comes not through the study of books but through the ear. Listen to the conversations of your companions. What you hear will be for a long time only a succession of unintelligible sounds. Words and sentences will go in one ear and out the other. But soon some of them will stick. Gradually you will separate word from word and sentence from sentence. That is how you learned English. That is how you are going to learn French. It's all in the ear, monsieur. It's all in the ear."

I obeyed. One day six months later I was saying things not at all complimentary about that same rector, whose name, by the way, was Ambrose Fafard. I did not know that he was near enough to hear me till I felt a hand on my shoulder. I turned around to gaze into what I thought was a teasing smile. He was saying something to me in French. I understood it. I had just been saying something about him in the same language. He likewise had understood. But this was all he added, "Very good, monsieur, very good. You speak French quite intelligibly. What was it I told you six months ago, monsieur? That a language comes by the ear, n'est-ce pas? It's all in the ear, monsieur—all in the ear, monsieur."

The last words I heard only faintly. Father Fafard was on his way to his rooms. He never referred to the matter again, nor did I. After that I spoke French, not very well; only French of a kind. But I treasured a secret about learning a new language. "It's all in the ear, monsieur—all in the ear—in the ear—monsieur."

By the end of that year I knew some philosophy. I do not say that I had finished philosophy. Nowadays one has to put two years into the elementary textbooks of philosophy, and those two years are little enough. I had no two years to spare on my money, or rather on my lack of it, and one was then all that was required before entering on the study of theology. So I was as ready for the next step as one year of philosophy could make me. I went home to The Island to think about that.

When I dwell on my memory of Chicoutimi, and let it drift into later memories, it seems as if I have always been fated for pioneering. The college was an unfinished building of field stone. Only the first coat of rough plaster had been put upon the inside walls. There was no central heating plant, so we got on with wood-burning stoves. I had to light two of them in my turn at four-thirty in the winter mornings. There were neither baths nor bathrooms. The only running water we had was when we ran back with pitchers full from barrels placed at the end of the corridors. It was a two-day journey by open sleigh to the nearest railway after the ice bridge caught on the river and the Quebec steamer ceased coming. But the spring paid for it all. From my window I could see the Saguenay fighting for its freedom against the ice that, weakened by the sun, kept piling floes one on top the other in a last effort to hold its grip and keep the river in thrall. One day the hold would be broken and with a crash the mountains of ice would sweep across the bar below the *Bassin*, and down the dark river to St. Lawrence and the gulf. Then the saplings clinging to the sides of the eternal cliffs would laugh themselves into brightness and all the Saguenay—Bayard Taylor's "River of Death"—and all its mountain walls and barriers would become a picture to rival the finest earth could show.

On the way back home after ten months in the new north country I stopped at Chatham, New Brunswick, to see Bishop Rogers. It was he who in his kindness had found the place at Chicoutimi for me. He was awaiting me with a plan. I must jot something down about Bishop Rogers for he was well worth attention.

Never before or since have I met a man just like that Bishop of Chatham. In appearance not impressive, he certainly was "different." A small man in height, he was a big man in width, one of the few who almost fitted the description "as broad as long." His head was massive, with a large mouth that drooped at the ends, though he tried to keep them up by a semiperpetual air of good nature which suggested a smile even when there was none in sight. When he sat down he could barely put his hands on his knees; there was so little room. He prefaced almost every speech with a sort of blessing, "Glory be to God." Sometimes he said that two or three times before he got into action. Likewise he had a habit of ending with a hearty, "Hurray! Hurray!" This is how it was done: The smile expanded; the ends of the mouth came up; he drew back his head, puckered his lips and half-whistled out a puff of breath: "Glory be to God!—So here you are, back from the seminary.—Glad to see you.—Reports from your superiors quite satisfactory—I am pleased, very much pleased.—Hurray! Hurray!" And everybody listening was likewise pleased. When the Bishop said that he was pleased even those who had no interest in the case had to feel elated. They could not help it. The pleasure of the Bishop was catching.

Bishop Rogers was a generous man. I can illustrate it by his travel habits. In those days we were being introduced to the first Pullmans in Eastern Canada. When the Bishop traveled any long distance from Chatham at night—he had to catch the main line train at a junction point—he went straight to the Pullman. Sitting down he would call the porter to him and hand him a dollar. "That, sir," he would remark impressively, "is what is vulgarly called a tip.—I do not greatly approve the habit, but it seems to be a rather general one.—So I give you a tip.—I do not give the usual silver quarter.— When I give a tip I give a good tip, and I give it in advance so as to keep you from worrying.—Now then, Hurray! Hurray! and off you go to find the conductor.—I want to pay for a berth."

He was like that with his students. He wrote to each one of them regularly and always in his own hand. There would be a five or ten dollar bill folded in an epistle of fatherly advice, encouragement, and sometimes gentle reproof. It is a misfortune that copies of the Bishop's letters to students were not kept. A selection of them in book form would be well worth while as human documents. They all ran from grave to gay, or from gay to grave, as circumstances demanded. It was hard for the Bishop not to be happy with the young. If he thought an admonition was in order, the letter for the case would begin gaily enough, but end with the unwelcome task well done. His gift was designed, I used to think, to take the sting out of his touches of severity. Nothing that concerned the welfare of the young men was excluded. I remember receiving a letter, though I was a stranger, every word set down in his own handwriting and four pages long, with advice on the kind of underwear I should buy for the severe northern winter. "It's not the weight of the overcoat that is important," he wrote, "but the thickness of what is under it. I double my own underwear whenever I take long winter journeys around by Caraquet and the coast where the chilly blasts can get at me as I ride in an open sleigh. I'll tell you some day about these trips. Once I went through the ice and got a ducking. But of that later. Be sure to listen well to the new bishop if he comes to lecture at the seminary. He is a very learned man, God bless him. I am glad to know that he gave you a copy of his book. And, by the way, how are you progressing with your philosophy? Do you realize how fortunate you are to be a class all by yourself? Brush up your Latin too. Remember what I said about your having given too much cultivation to your imagination in St. Dunstan's! We can use only a few poets, but a host of practical men." So it went. No month without its letter. And I was only one of the many in whom he took such fatherly interest.

Bishop Rogers had the unusual distinction of never having studied in an ecclesiastical seminary. Early in his boyhood he had been taken into the house of Bishop Connolly of St. John, afterward Archbishop of Halifax. The future Archbishop and Father of the Vatican Council was a man of solid learning as well as a born teacher. He loved to teach, and practiced on young Rogers who received his full classical, philosophical, and theological training at first hand from his bishop; and never himself forgot how good it had been for him. Perhaps Bishop Rogers was thinking of it when he unfolded to me his plan for the coming year.

He proposed that I should spend that year in his house, nominally to assist his sick secretary, really to be under his own tutelage. I had suspected that this would be the plan, for one of his priests had warned me that the Bishop had the habit of keeping a student with him. He told me also of some of the Bishop's methods of instruction and training. "It will be worth any three years of your life," he said, "but as lonesome as the desert."

He was right on both counts. It was as lonesome as the desert and worse, but it was worth at least any five years of my life. Besides, it was interesting as a return to the days when students for the priesthood were trained under the episcopal eye and in the episcopal house. Bishop Rogers was following the lead of no less a person than St. Augustine. I gave little thought to that, however, seeing only a chance to advance at no cost in cash. I literally grabbed for it. For one year I was sorry that I had. For more than forty-five years I have been glad, very, very glad.

The Bishop's plan of instruction and training did not immediately disclose its mysteries. He was busy with his pastoral visitations and confirmations. They were soon over, however, and I knew that I was "in for it." Scarcely ever did I get far from the grounds. My daily recreation was a walk in solitude along a nearby railroad track. The first lesson of each day was given just before the Bishop's Mass, in the sacristy of the temporary cathedral. Any book, like any port in a storm, would do. Many times he did not get beyond the Ordo. Aquinas, Augustine, Dominic, Alphonsus or Ignatius meant beginning Mass close to the noon hour. It was not only comments on their lives and the works they had founded that I heard. There were lectures on systems, teachings, influences, heresies, characters. Hours might pass with both of us still standing at the vestment case in the sacristy. I had to interfere once when the clock was about to strike one. Confusing? It was at first, but awakening too. Many were the times I hurried from the sacristy to look up some interesting point upon which the Bishop had only touched in passing. I knew that he would come back to it next day, and it was good sport to be ahead of him.

In the afternoon the work was more orderly, and I was left alone for a few hours to do it. Four o'clock brought a summons back to school. The Bishop was ready for me with some book. Ostensibly it was only reading time; I being the reader and he the listener. But we never got beyond a few pages in two hours. The reference books which he had in plenty, were always conveniently near my chair. "Look it up, sir, look it up," was the order I heard oftenest. Everything, literally everything, had to be looked up. Before six I was a solitary island completely surrounded by reference books, with a smiling fat Bishop gazing at me over the waves of them like a lighthouse over a stormy sea. Nothing light or trivial had a chance to look in. We were at work, real work and no play, the hardest but the most profitable work of all my student years.

Nevertheless I am no advocate of such a harking back to the days of St. Augustine. He could do it. Archbishop Connolly could do it. Bishop Rogers could do it. I could not do it, and few bishops I know would dare try to do it, even if they had the time. The old method works well in exceptional cases, and happily mine was one of them, but it is hard on the teacher and harder on the student. After a month of grind, with the Bishop turning the crank of the stone to which my nose was firmly held, I longed for the relief, the comfort, and the comparative ease of a regular ecclesiastical seminary.

More and more do I look back to that year with the Bishop as the outstanding one of my life. Others I have more than half-forgotten. That one I shall never forget. When, later, I went to a seminary it seemed as if the Bishop had lectured to me on about everything I had to study there. He had covered more than the first year of theology. I had been dipped into three others. He had taught me no little Scripture. He had shown me how to preach, though not by example, for Bishop Rogers was the sorriest preacher I ever heard. For the pulpit he was only great in precept. No man could be more irregular than he when it came to keeping to a schedule. He worked sometimes up to daylight at his desk, fell asleep and came out for his Mass at eleven. Sometimes he slept twelve hours a day and sometimes only two. A "five minute sermon" by him was likely to take thirty minutes. I was present when he preached for two and a half hours, not a soul hearing more than a tenth of what he said. Time for the Bishop was nothing to worry about. His meditation might run to two hours. His meals, except breakfast, he had to take by the clock; the Rector of the cathedral saw to that. But if the Bishop missed a meal he did not seem to mind. One day, talking to me on monasticism, he praised regularity. He must have seen a smile in my eye for he chided me. "I know what you are thinking about, you young rascal," he said, "it is that

I don't practice what I preach. But I do. I am regular. In fact I am
regularly irregular. That's the one form of regularity which fits me."

There was no task he would not put on me. Once, when he had
returned from preaching a sermon at the opening of the University
of Ottawa, he called me to his room, and, looking, I thought, a bit
ashamed of the job he was about to give me, said, "Glory be to
God, Mr. Kelley!—Here we are again.—Back from Ottawa.—New
university.—Good.—I preached.—Now the university wants to print
my sermon.—I have only the notes." He showed me a small bit of
paper with some writing in pencil on it. "You know how busy I
am.—Here's a test of your ability to rise to an occasion.—Take the
notes and see what you can do.—Write the sermon, sir.—There'll
be no four o'clock reading till you have finished.—Off you go,
sir—Hurray! Hurray!"

I knew better than to hesitate. With the notes in hand I went
sadly back to my room. Three days later I gave the Bishop his sermon. I never heard of it again till I read it in *The Owl*, a monthly
published by the university. I have a copy of that number, given
me by the president of the university five years ago. October-
November, 1889, it was. I should have been given a Doctorate in
Emergencies for that sermon, but I got nothing out of the misery
of writing it except an order from the Bishop to read it to him.
He criticized it unmercifully and told me to do better next time.
Happily there was no next time while I was with him.

Bishop Rogers had the kindest of hearts. He climbed up to my
room right under the roof one day when I failed to answer the bell
because I was in bed with a cold and neglected by the servants.
He tried to light a fire in the cold stove for me. It was funny to see
the little man on his knees raking down the ashes and putting in
the sticks. His cassock got in the way of his feet, and his pectoral
cross kept getting in the way of his hands. He could not make the
fire and rang for the housekeeper. There was fire of another kind
then, and I was looked after a little better for a while.

Of course the Bishop is long since dead. Already he has had two
successors. The older clergy of his diocese still tell stories about him,
and always with a note of affection running through them. I saw
him twice after my year under his teaching. When I was going
away the last time he said, "Glory be to God, Mr. Kelley!—Off you

go—God bless you.—Here is a letter for your bishop about you—a little exaggerated perhaps, for I called you a *juvenis optimus.*—You won't make a liar out of an old man, will you now?—I gave you something to live up to anyway.—Hurray! Hurray!"

I was joining the diocese of Detroit and going to the Seminary of Nicolet, back to the Laval influence. But to this day I bless that one year with Bishop Rogers, the one year that I know to have been worth five. Glory be to God for it. Hurray! Hurray!

≈§ 4 ê≈

GETTING ON

HOW I became a student for the diocese of Detroit is a story all by itself. I knew little about Detroit until I had been a distant subject of its Bishop for over a month. It was too far away from Boston to be a real city for an islander. Bishop Rogers it was who, without knowing, rather pushed me into the complication that ended in Michigan.

I have admitted already that I had acquired the state, if not the virtue, of poverty. Determined to be a priest, I had no money with which to pay my way. The good old Bishop offered to find a place for me where I should not have to pay. Without bothering to say another word to me about it, he arranged with St. Francis Xavier College in Nova Scotia to put me on its teaching staff, half-time, with board and instruction in theology for salary. I was worried for I wanted a regular seminary, no matter how small, with as little teaching work on the side as possible. Not knowing what my epis-copal friend was doing, I had struck out for myself and found gold. Nicolet in Quebec had a regular diocesan seminary. The college department wanted an assistant in English. One hour a day of actual teaching would answer all requirements. There was instruc-tion, with board, room, and forty dollars a year for small expenses as recompense. I had already a very, very modest market for my writings, which disgraceful imposition on the reading public may come in for later attention. Bishop Rogers did not know all that. He wrote an enthusiastic letter to me about the place he had found for me in Nova Scotia, said that he was coming to the island and would expect to find me all ready to leave for my new duties. That was the only unwelcome word I ever received from him, since it left me in a quandary. I had accepted the post at Nicolet. Bishop

45

Rogers knew that I could not stand the damp winters of his diocese any more than those of the island. But I could not reject his kind offices without hurting him.

Here I shall have to explain. I had inherited what has since been classed by some as a weakness, when, especially later in life, I was given the responsibility of authority. I mean, a great reluctance to hurt the feelings of others. In a superior that may be a handicap, especially if carried to the extent of my father's unswerving devotion to the human virtue of common courtesy, as well as to the spiritual virtue of charity unfeigned. Every time I am tempted to say a harsh word or do an unkind thing I seem to see him standing before me, significantly touching his lips with a warning finger. When duty forces me to speak to others with severity I must do it in spite of him, gritting my teeth and setting my jaw. I can do that only because I learned, in Bishop Rogers' house, "to take it." I knew that he sympathized with me over certain petty persecutions I had to endure, yet he never, except on the one occasion already mentioned, tried to save me from them. Perhaps he knew that they would do good by helping to develop in me the virtue of patience. I had known good examples of that virtue. Never once had I seen either of my parents show the slightest sign of discourtesy toward others. My father could be actually unjust to himself rather than exhibit resentment even in the face of a wrong done him. My mother, as the daughter of irascible old Andrew Murphy, might well have been excused for a few biting words under provocation, but never needed the excuse. Unfailing courtesy seemed a fixed family entail. Is it hard to see why I could not do anything that I felt might hurt Bishop Rogers?

Fate disguised as another fat man intervened. An islander who had not seen his birthplace for perhaps thirty years came home on a visit. He was Father Thomas J. Broydrick, pastor of St. Martin's Church in Baltimore. I was detailed to show him around.

Up to this time I had met only two American priests. One day in Chicoutimi I saw them, in long coats and silk hats, toiling up the hill toward the seminary. I knew that they were tourists from the Saguenay steamer which had just arrived. They would have an hour or two for a stroll. I was stopped to answer questions about the seminary. The visitors seemed surprised when I answered in Eng-

lish. One was Father Harty, then Rector of the Cathedral of Hart-
ford, and the other Father Shahan of the same diocese. Father
Harty told me, in a whisper, that his companion was soon to leave
for Europe to prepare himself for the Chair of History in the recently established Catholic University at Washington. I thought
that Father Shahan looked me over with a slight show of curiosity
and I could not blame him. I was wearing a borrowed cassock much
too short for me, spoke no French in a French town, and looked
young enough to be no more than an altar boy. He knew only in
later years that the funny appearing youngster he met on the
seminary hill in Chicoutimi in 1888 would, in 1929, come near—
so near that he actually was elected—being his successor as Rector
of that same University. Father Broydrick was the third American
priest I met.

One day during his visit he noticed that I was worried and asked
the reason. I plucked up sufficient courage to tell him—and, behold,
a new vision was opened up for me.

"Don't you know," he queried, "that almost any American bishop
would send you to a regular seminary and pay for you there if you
joined his diocese?" I knew nothing of the kind. "Do you want to
study for an American diocese?"

I did, and further explained that Bishop Rogers knew that I had
a sinus trouble which made it imperative for me to get out of the
cold damp North.

"I see no difficulty," said my new friend. "Follow this plan:
meet Bishop Rogers at the train when he arrives. Serve his Mass
next morning. He will probably talk to you after Mass. Tell him
that I am arranging for your admittance into the Archdiocese of
Baltimore, but that, as the time is now short, I want you to go to
Nicolet until Cardinal Gibbons decides where you are to continue
your studies. The Bishop seems to be your friend. He will be glad
to hear of your good fortune. About the money for incidentals,
can you get it from home?"

I had to confess that I hated to take anything from home at that
time. There were others in the family, and my father, once com-
fortably well off, was now in hard financial circumstances.

"I see," said the Baltimore pastor kindly. "Well, we may forget
about that. I'll lend you what money you need for incidentals."

He said that as if it were all in a day's work and seemed to resent even a modest expression of thanks.

Everything went according to plan as far as Bishop Rogers was concerned. He offered me a place in his diocese, but warmly congratulated me on finding such a friend as Father Broydrick. He waxed enthusiastic at the thought that he had helped prepare a priest for Cardinal Gibbons. I went to Nicolet with his blessing and an old-time "Hurray! Hurray!" for good-by.

Things did not go quite so well on the Baltimore end. When Cardinal Gibbons was approached on the subject of my incardination he decided that his diocese already had students enough for its needs. Father Broydrick was slightly miffed, for he was, as he told me later, selecting in me a future assistant. It was nearly two months before I knew what had happened down South. Then I got word that my papers had been handed over to Father Broydrick's former pastor and friend, Bishop Foley of Detroit. I was to continue at Nicolet, and, incidentally, get all the French I could absorb. Though I had nothing to say about the arrangement I was perfectly satisfied. It all looked so much like Providence taking care of me—and so it turned out to be.

One year later I met the Cardinal, in fact I went fishing with him. Father Broydrick brought him to the island and again my services were requisitioned. An amusing incident brought me to His Eminence's notice. When the Bishop of Charlottetown had outside visitors at his table he always invited the ecclesiastical students on vacation who had received any orders. I had at least been "tonsured," so I was present at a luncheon given in honor of the Cardinal at the palace. Going upstairs after the luncheon, His Eminence asked who "that very young looking priest" was. Father Broydrick was prompt to break in with a telling shot, "He is not a priest, Your Eminence. He is the student I offered you a year ago and whom you turned down."

The Cardinal stopped and looked down over the rail at me. "You are Mr. Kelley?"

"Yes, Your Eminence."

"Well, my son, I never buy a pig in a poke nor accept a student till I have seen him. Come up to my room and have a chat with me."

Father Broydrick answered for me, "It's too late now, Your Eminence." There was a twinkle in his eye as he added, "He has a better ——"

"Bishop?" queried the Cardinal in mock severity.

"Well, it wouldn't be safe to go quite that far, Your Eminence," replied Broydrick. "Let us say—diocese."

"What is the diocese?"

"Detroit."

The Cardinal seemed pleased. Before he started climbing the other steps he said, "Very good. I'll not steal a student from my best friend, and that exactly is what the Bishop of Detroit is. You will be happy in your work with him, Mr. Kelley."

Two days later came the fishing party. The Cardinal went out to my native parish of Vernon River to stay with the wit of the diocese, Father Doyle, successor to Father James. Wherever Father Doyle was stories grew up in abundance, and it was a fine thing about Father Doyle that he liked to tell them on himself. He was a great pastor for visiting his parishioners. There was an old lady in a former parish, a widow, to whom he had given a little pig. She called it after the donor, but did not tell him of the honor conferred. Doyle the porker grew up with a certain freedom of movement not ordinarily accorded small pigs. He was a pet and in consequence fell into evil ways. One of them was that of stealing the pies which the widow set out on the window sill to cool. Now it happened that Father Doyle liked pie, and used to stop, in his afternoon round of visits, at certain farms where the lady of the house had a reputation for good pie baking, and where, consequently, there might be a slice of pie with a glass of fresh milk for him. Every pie expert in the parish knew that Father Doyle's afternoon walk might lead him to her door and was prepared. One day he came to visit the home he had endowed with the pig. Instead of knocking he made a noise outside with his stick. From within came the widow's plaint, "Git out of that, Doyle. It's the pies ye're afther. I've got them put away high enough this time. Devil a bit of wan ye'll git." It took long explaining to right herself with the generous Father Doyle. But the story was too good to keep. I heard him tell it to the Cardinal.

Every stream on the island has speckled trout in it, and they can be caught easily at the mill dams. The Cardinal decided to try fishing for them in the easy way, at the Ross mill not far from the rectory. I went along. His Eminence got one small fish, but it had to be thrown back, "to its mother," he said. "We won't take advantage of rash little children." He called me to walk back with him.

"You ought to go to Baltimore or to Rome," he advised. "Of course I know that you will find good teaching and excellent training in Nicolet, but you will have no circle of American friends when you come out. I shall say a word to Bishop Foley about that."

I stayed on at Nicolet, however. Evidently the Bishop of Detroit saw greater value in my acquiring French than in making new friends. But he arranged to save me from teaching, a relief I appreciated.

I saw Cardinal Gibbons many times after and had at least one or two intimate chats with him. I read everything he wrote and followed his public utterances with the greatest interest. He was in appearance an ascetic who never seemed to grow old.

"I think Your Eminence must have discovered the Fountain of Youth," I remarked to him once.

"No, Father," he answered, "I have only discovered that short eating goes a long way in the important business of keeping one's health. When I was a young priest like you I had a fortunate stomach weakness which forbade me to eat much. I got into the habit of only picking at meals, and walking every day. There is scarcely enough flesh on me now for a disease to grip."

I wish I had taken the hint so diplomatically offered.

Cardinal Gibbons did not have the profound learning of a specialist, but he had what many a more learned man lacked, a splendid balance wheel in his head. It went on working in the same old way no matter what happened. He knew well how to use everything his intellect possessed to the best advantage. He knew his Scripture, not as a critic but as a preacher and writer, and used it with telling effect. A deeply learned theologian could not have written "The Faith of Our Fathers." He could not even have selected such a winning title for it. The Cardinal's strength as a writer and speaker was in knowing how to carry his message in plain language and in the most effective way right where he wanted it to go. He was, too, an expert swimmer in troubled waters, if never a deep-sea diver. No watcher on the shore ever lost sight of his little red *zucchetta* or got far from the sound of his splashing. He was a prince of applied prudence in his public utterances, as well as a master repair mechanic. I cannot vouch for the truth of the story, but one I heard about him is characteristic. Loaded with heavy pontifical vestments on a hot autumn day, he went down into the excavation for the basement of the shrine at the Catholic University to lay its cornerstone. "It's a shame," said a young bishop present, "a burning shame to send such a feeble old man down into that hole in this oppressive weather."

An older bishop nearby heard the remark, "Don't you worry about that feeble old man," he said. "It's not the first hole he got into and climbed out of in triumph."

Cardinal Gibbons enjoyed no society more than that of the witty Archbishop Ryan of Philadelphia, who loved to joke with him, even in public. When the Cardinal complained over "a touch of insomnia," the Archbishop recommended reading in bed till sleep came.

"And what book would you advise me to use?" asked His Eminence.

"None better," replied his friend, "than one called *The Faith of Our Fathers.*"

At a banquet given on the occasion of an episcopal consecration the Archbishop remarked on the advantage of a bishop over a cardinal. "A bishop is consecrated," he said, "but a cardinal is created, and creation means making something out of nothing."

No one present laughed as heartily as did Cardinal Gibbons over that thrust at his dignity.

There was no repressing the flow of wit and humor that came out of Philadelphia in those days. To a young priest who said that the site of the Archbishop's house had been used for hangings in colonial times, the Archbishop pointedly remarked that "there were some *suspensions* there still." A suspension in clerical parlance usually means the drastic and seldom inflicted punishment of a temporary removal of ecclesiastical faculties. But the Archbishop did not confine his humor to clerical circles. When the general counsel of the Pennsylvania Railroad humorously suggested that the president might be persuaded to exchange an annual pass over the system for a pass to the Kingdom of Heaven, the Archbishop assured him that the idea had occurred to him, but that he had hesitated because of "the danger of separating the president from his counsel." The temptation to go on chatting about Archbishop Ryan is great, but the charm of him is pulling me ahead of my story.

Before he left the island Bishop Rogers made a most impressive summing-up of my chief scholastic weaknesses, while trying to show me how to profit by such compensating gifts as he thought I had. Many a time, as an editor, I remembered that excellent homily in connection with some absolutely perfect public statement by Cardinal Gibbons. Please listen to one wise old man addressing one very unwise young one, "Glory be to God, Mr. Kelley!—Read books that apply the principles and deductions of philosophy to the errors of the day.—You may bring that imagination of yours to light the road for the march of reason.—That's why you have it.—You are going to be a fairly good writer, but you are not going to be as good a writer as you would have been had you paid more attention to the mental gymnastics that mathematics would have put you through."

Confound mathematics! He simply would not stop referring to them, but he did not add, "Hurray! Hurray!" to his warning, which was nice of him.

One reason I liked Cardinal Gibbons was that I thought some wise old man might have said something like that to him when he was young. Without knowing what the Cardinal thought of mathematics, or what he knew about them, I somehow got the impression that he never loved them. A cold mathematical Gibbons never would have made the impression on the American public that the warm, diplomatic, and polished Gibbons made. And that really would have been too bad. The American public learned a lot about things it did not know from James Cardinal Gibbons.

5

UNDER THE SHADOW OF THE PINES

AT THE end of a long wide avenue lined with great trees and pretty gardens stands the old stone building of the Seminary and College of Nicolet. Alongside the street out of which one turns into the avenue runs the Nicolet River, a tributary stream of the St. Lawrence. A half hour's walk to the right, past the cathedral and bishop's palace, is rewarded by a view of the Lake of St. Peter, which is not really a lake but a widening out of the great river. This is the lake so many admirers of the French-Canadian "Habitant" have heard of through Drummond's famous bit of humor in verse, "The Wreck of the Julie Plante," when

> "De win' she blow lak' hurricane,
> Bimeby she blow some more,
> An' de skow bus' up on Lac St. Pierre,
> Wan arpent from de shore."

To the left of the long street, always as one faces the river, there used to be a clump of pine trees, grown to an extraordinary height. Louis Frechette, one of the first of the French-Canadian poets and an alumnus of the college, sang their praises. More fearful about venturing into the land of literature, but stung to action by the need of loose change, I wrote a legend about the trees and called it "Under the Shadow of the Pines." It brought some loose change, but the puzzled local historians wanted to know where I had dug up the legend. I thought it better to be reticent. Quebec lends herself delightfully to the manufacturing of old legends.

The seminary itself was founded in 1803 by Letters Patent from King George IV. They provide for its direction by a Board of Trustees officially known as *les Messieurs du Seminaire de Nicolet*. The Gentlemen of the Seminary of Nicolet still flourish. They own the seminary, govern it, and teach in it. All of them are diocesan priests who consecrated themselves from ordination to the work of education. They form the administrative council and select colleagues and successors out of their graduating classes. Those selected are asked if they wish to stay. If they accept, some are sent abroad for special study. As the Gentlemen of the Seminary pass on, their places are filled from the ranks of these younger men. Thus it is that they live and die in the harness of educators, remain always in one place and are never out of a job. The only Catholic college I know in the United States which is organized on that plan, a common one in Quebec, is Mount St. Mary's in Emmitsburg, Maryland.

The main college building in Nicolet was erected in the old days. Its stone walls are as thick as those of a fortress. Its corridors are long and wide, its furniture old and strong. Behind the building there is now a new chapel, far from being as good architecturally as the college; and behind the chapel is a small forest with leaf-shaded paths on which students have worked for over a hundred years, and which used to contain two tiny but lovely artificial lakes. Throughout the woods are cleared spaces, recalling the old Greek groves of learning. In these the students' academies and societies meet, weather permitting, and to them the musicians come for practice. Right in the center of the woods is "Versailles," a cottage built by the old-time "theologians," and by tradition always the treasured possession of their successors. No priest-professor comes to "Versailles" except as an occasional visitor. As a club it is one of the most exclusive. When one becomes a Gentleman of the Seminary he passes around "Versailles," but, respecting the tradition, enters not. Here in this old Seminary and College some of the greatest men of the French-Canadian race were educated; poets and novelists, bishops, governors both in Canada and in the United States, cabinet ministers, senators, judges, and members of Parliament. Even some not of the French-Canadian race have profited educationally by that ancient foundation.

There are really two distinct institutions under the charge of the Gentlemen of the Seminary, a college and a theological school. I was in the latter, but for awhile gave a little time daily to teaching English in the college. I liked the diversion well enough, but liking is not the name for my feeling for the whole place. Peace hovers over it. Quiet reigns in the woods around "Versailles." The Gentlemen of the Seminary were and are gentlemen in spirit and in truth, and models as well. The discipline was strict but sensible. There was an atmosphere not only of study and piety but also of sincere goodness all about. I still envy *les Messieurs du Seminaire de Nicolet.* They have no money and they do not mind. They work for board and enough extra to afford the very smallest luxuries; perhaps a vacation, if not in too far distant a place, once every few years. They get pleasure out of little things like a new plant in the garden or an improvement in the electric lamps, but for the French-Canadian race and nation they did and are doing great things.

Higher education in the Province of Quebec is represented for the major part by some twenty-five institutions such as that of Nicolet. They are the colleges of the people in every sense. Their endowment is scant and chiefly in land; but what it produces goes to keeping down the costs of education and not to fads. Any boy in Quebec who really wants to go through college can do so. His parish priest keeps in touch with his diocesan seminary, and that influence means reductions when reductions are necessary. The food he gets is plentiful and wholesome, and there are no luxuries. All the students of my day in Nicolet, except those in the theological wing, slept in common dormitories and brought their own bedding. They stayed on the grounds during the months of study and had no freedom of the village. The little town of Nicolet was as quiet as any self-respecting country town ought to be. There were no student "cuttings-up" to trouble its peace; no dances, no fraternities, no football.

The course of study was mapped out long ago by the University of Laval, to which all classical colleges in the province were then affiliated. There are now two Catholic universities, Laval and Montreal. In my day there was only Laval. Students live and work in their own colleges, while examinations and degrees are given by the university.

These colleges and universities are encouraged, but not supported, by the provincial government, which now and then makes small appropriations for them. They are not, however, state institutions, and are no strain on the purse of the taxpayer. In fact, they depend for the most part on themselves. They furnish instruction plus discipline for all who want them, at as low a rate as possible. It is by no means inferior education. If the old Greeks could look on their orators, rhetoricians, and philosophers as their highest and best, by that test the French-Canadians are justified in keeping their system of higher education. I never heard better orators. They handle French beautifully. They reason well. Without cultural attainments there would be no orators, rhetoricians or philosophers.

An American friend, Bishop Boyle of Pittsburgh, traveled with me part of a summer in Quebec. We did not go to the cities except to pass quickly through them. The Bishop had been a school superintendent. He summed up Quebec thus: "A charming country, a good people. They ought to put a wall around the province to keep us out or we'll spoil them."

The course of studies in these classical colleges is a rigid one. There are no electives if one is going up for a degree; and the degree is a legal necessity for entrance into professional schools. No one may begin the study of law or medicine, for example, without graduation from a classical college. The aim of the Quebec educator is to develop a mind and cultivate a heart to ornament it. He neglects nothing that the experience of centuries testifies is needed to produce that result. Hence the professional man goes through exactly the same cultural course as the priest. (Perhaps that fact explains French-Canadian unity.) Religion and philosophy are essential parts of it. Discipline is not neglected. In fact, with Sydney Smith, the French-Canadian educator holds that essentially education is discipline, the discipline of the whole man.

The system is a co-ordinated one. It is built around a tested philosophy of education and ends in two years of scholastic philosophy, Aristotelian and Thomistic. Juniors and Seniors are "The Philosophers," and by tradition the aristocrats of the student body, who arrive at their distinction only after passing through the classes of rhetoric and belles-lettres. Students may enter from the grade school or as soon as they are ready to take up Latin. They never leave Latin, for, even when they become Junior Philosophers, much of the class work is done in that language. Examinations test their knowledge at frequent intervals, even as often as once a month. The great examinations come at the end of rhetoric, our Sophomore year, and at the end of senior philosophy, our Senior year. There is no such thing as our system of credit hours. There are no standardizing agencies, since all the colleges are part of one of the two universities, which set the standards. To insure uniformity of tests, as well as to respect the rights and freedom of the colleges, each of them prepares a full set of questions on all examinations for degrees. The test papers to be used for all are then selected by lot. A student may find that in one subject his examination was prepared at a college far away, another by his own professors, another by the university faculty. Degrees are never given in the name of a college. All are from the universities. Thus, one may study at the college nearest home, but the diploma will be the same as that given by another fifty miles away. The graduate is a Bachelor of the University of Laval or of the University of Montreal. In my day there were no women's colleges. There are several now, all affiliated with one or other of the two universities.

The primary and secondary educational system of Quebec is most interesting. Schools are either Protestant or Catholic. The citizen pays taxes to the board he elects. The only "School Question" in Quebec is how to improve education without having recourse to experiments and fads. There is no "institutional bloc" in the legislature of the province. In Quebec one finds a religious minority treated with fairness, justice, and consideration.

The day is coming fast when such an example as that of Quebec will be needed to give a disillusioned world encouragement for a new start. The next decade in that world's history is likely to be marked by wholesale rejections of many governmental, social, and religious ideas hitherto considered as having the binding force of accepted doctrines. The age of the theorist, the experimenter, is not past, but it is coming rapidly to an inglorious end. To such a world I recommend a study of Quebec. There are signs that, in its largest city at least, the people are not safe from the destructive ideas that flow everywhere from one source. There is, however, too much good sense, too much solid happiness, too many strong traditions in rural Quebec to permit it to weaken a religious and racial foundation that has made a nation out of a handful of people deserted by its homeland and given over to the rule of an enemy; now pretty well turned into a friend because he well knows that his greatest strength in his most important colony is the recognition by the French-Canadian that he has been allowed to live his own life and mould his own destiny.

What individuals stand out in my memories of Nicolet? The bishop, of course. I have a not quite inexplicable habit of talking about bishops. They always did interest, and sometimes worry me. The bishop I found in Nicolet was the one who later ordained me, Elphege Gravel. I saw little of him at first, except when I went to the cathedral on Sundays to assist in the ceremonies. A day came, however, when that bishop took the center of my stage.

It all happened over the ambitious project of a handful of queer "Irish" determined on celebrating St. Patrick's Day. To get the full force of the story you must know that the French-Canadian divides the population of the world immediately surrounding him into three racial categories about as follows: if you are a Catholic and speak French you are "*Canadien*"; if you are a Protestant and speak English you are "*Anglais*"; if you are a Catholic and speak English you are "*Irlandais*." Registration is now complete. The books are closed. Scots, Jews, Yankees, etc., must be classified in one or another of the three main groups. Only as a matter of formal politeness may they be taken for what they really are.

So it happened that when, in 1890, an agitation to celebrate St. Patrick's Day shook Nicolet, it was no trouble at all for us to put up a united front in favor of the move. A St. Patrick's Society was formed. The president was an Irish Protestant, classed of course as English. The vice-president was one O'Shaughnessy who spoke no English at all but was a Catholic and therefore officially "Canadien." For festival purpose only, he was Irish. The treasurer was a convert Jew who had married a French-Canadian wife and whose children all spoke French. Officially he was Irish. The chaplain was myself, clearly indicated as Irish. The one member, that is the only one without any office, was a fellow seminarian from Boston whose name was O'Hara. There could be no question about him.

We were determined about the celebration in all its details. Nothing would be acceptable but the best: a Solemn Mass in the cathedral, a sermon in English, and a crowded congregation. We called on the Bishop. He agreed to everything, but pointedly asked where

we were going to find a preacher. The committee felt the sting.
What to do? The Bishop came to the rescue. He would preach in
English. Never before had a sermon in English been announced for
the cathedral pulpit. The whole population of the town turned
out to hear it, though there were not even a baker's dozen who
would understand ten words of it. The Solemn Mass *Coram
Episcopo* went on. No trouble, for there is no nationality about the
Mass. The Bishop stood up on his throne, faced the people, and
made the Sign of the Cross, speaking the words in English. His
flock gasped and looked with admiring eyes on their chief pastor.
Here was a bishop indeed, one who could not be bluffed by the
Irish, but could deliver his thoughts even in their barbarous adopted
tongue. I have never forgotten the humor, which I learned later
was of the essence of good diplomacy, with which the Bishop entered upon his task of preaching to a congregation of some twelve
hundred who did not understand him, and, perhaps—I am stretching
a point—fifteen who did.

"Why should I be preaching to you here on St. Patrick's Day?"
he began. "You are asking yourselves that question, my brethren.
thinking that I am not Irish, and, therefore, a poor interpreter of
the sentiments of the Irish people. But though I am not Irish in
blood I have a right to speak on St. Patrick's Day, for I am the
uncle of all the Irish. 'What?' you exclaim, 'you, a Canadien, you
the uncle of all the Irish? *Comment?* How can that be?' I shall
answer you. I was consecrated bishop in the chapel of the Irish
College at Rome. My consecrator was the Irish Cardinal Moran of
Sydney, with two assisting bishops from Ireland. And another Irish
bishop was consecrated with me. He was Dr. Walsh, Archbishop
of Dublin. After breakfast the Irish College students came to me
saying, 'Give us your blessing, Uncle.' 'Uncle? Uncle? How am I
your uncle?' I asked. And this was their answer: 'Having been consecrated with the Primate of Ireland, our spiritual father, you are
his spiritual brother, and therefore our spiritual uncle.' And that,
my brethren, is how I became the uncle of all the Irish."

St. Patrick's Society flourished like a very young cedar of Lebanon
for three years. Before it passed away I had the honor of preaching
its last sermon. When I say that there have been none since, I intend no disrespect to the preacher. It was not his sermon that

killed the society. I do not think that there is today one person in Nicolet who could, even for politeness' sake, qualify as Irish. I was called to deaconship ahead of time to preach that sermon. When I presented myself before Bishop Gravel for his blessing after the ceremony, he stepped back and, with a twinkle in his eye, impressively remarked, "You are now all ready to celebrate St. Patrick's Day." I claim to be the only deacon ever ordained expressly to honor St. Patrick.

It was my first sermon. I had worked hard on it. Several of the Gentlemen of the Seminary came to hear it. I got no compliments from any of them. Compliments are not good for youngsters. All they did was to nod their wise heads up and down a few times, as if to say, "Not so bad. Not so bad. At least not quite as bad as we expected. Later on we shall see—what we shall see."

But down on the Main Street of the village one Monsieur Beauchemin kept a grocery store of which I was a valued patron for such food as could conveniently be warmed up over a lamp and made to supplement and complement the more or less monotonous servings of the seminary dining hall. My purchases ran mostly in the direction of baked beans, which could easily be made an agreeable dish for improvised banquets. It is said that the real secret of French cooking is the sauce, but no French sauce that I have tasted equaled the sauce of secrecy poured over a can of beans, with one eye on the door and the other on a smoking lamp. Through the beans I was in good standing with M. Beauchemin. I dropped in to see him a few days after my first pulpit oration.

"It appears," he said gravely, "that you preach well."

"Thank you," I replied, with a proper show of modesty. "What makes you think so?"

"I was in the cathedral on St. Patrick's Day to hear you," he answered, "and it appears that you preach exactly like Monseigneur."

Now to preach "exactly like Monseigneur," the Bishop, was to reach the summit of absolute oratorical perfection. I was duly set up. "Did you understand my sermon?" I asked, hoping to prolong so agreeable a conversation, and for the nonce forgetting that the object of my call was the acquisition of one can of Boston baked beans.

"I understand very well your text," he said.

I did not press the subject farther. To preach "exactly like Monseigneur" was glory enough for one day. On my way back, however, it dawned upon me that the only compliment I had received for my first sermon came from a diplomatic grocer, prejudiced in favor of a regular customer, who had understood only the familiar few words of the Latin text.

The Superior of the Seminary and College in my day was Father Moise Georges Proulx. He spoke English quite well, for his mother was Scotch. French was his language, however, and he was therefore an accepted "Canadien." But he was all Scotch when it came to business, and wisely had the financial affairs of the institution been entrusted to him. In appearance he resembled Leo XIII, the Pope then reigning. In his room were many queer things all settled in peace together: packets of seeds, for example, keeping company with packets of textbooks. In the inner sanctum were boxes of pills and bottles of medicine. When a student developed some slight ailment he had recourse first to Father Proulx. If the malady was in the nature of a cold, one might hope for a generous and agreeable dose from an unlabeled bottle, strong enough to discourage, if not dislodge, any ordinary cold microbe. Some of my companions developed slight colds quite frequently.

"What do you think of that medicine, sir?" Father Proulx asked an applicant for relief one day—in English, for he knew that the man was a private pupil of mine and he saw an opportunity to test the results of my teaching.

My pupil basely betrayed me, "Bully!" he said, "it had whiskers on it."

"Whisky in it? What do you mean, sir? It's medicine."

The misunderstanding was straightened out. I was called on the carpet by the Superior. "What sort of English are you teaching those companions of yours?" he snapped, "and what is meant by saying that a thing has whiskers on it? Eh?"

I explained with a few apologetic coughs some of the advanced expressions of modern English.

"You are getting a cold," he interrupted.

I assured him that some cold symptoms were appearing, looking hopefully toward the open door of the inner sanctum. But the

Superior did not rise from his seat. "I'll tell the doctor to give you some quinine for it," he assured me, "something without whiskers on it," he added meaningly; "it's my personal opinion that the symptoms I have noted in you and your friends indicate over-eating of hearty food between meals, such as—let us say—baked beans."

That was my first introduction to humor of the French-Scotch brand.

I was ordained priest in the seminary chapel on the Feast of St. Bartholomew, August 24th, 1893. My class had been ordained in June, but I had to wait two months to reach the proper age, though given advantage of all the time allowed by dispensation.

My ordination was made one of the exercises of the annual retreat of the clergy of the diocese. The seminary chapel was, consequently, full of priests who, in observance of the prescriptions of the Liturgy, all imposed hands on my head. I was going out with an abundance of blessings. It was unusual, at least, that the whole priestly body of a diocese should impose hands on a young brother, and it made my ordination not only most solemn and inspiring to others but left a deep and lasting impression on my heart. The new chapel of the seminary has the dignity and almost the proportions of a cathedral, but I regret the loss of the old one, now a library. It smiled with me and prayed with me on the happiest day of my life.

I went back to the island for my First Mass and a few weeks' vacation before setting out for Detroit to open the mysterious casket that is called Life, the key to which for me was the priesthood. I had struggled hard to secure it, and wondered why I was not more excited now that it was in my hand. The truth is that I was frightened. The key meant exile in a land I did not know, new faces and new people, new work, and the making of new friends. Above all was there an uneasy feeling that something different from what I had learned in theory about priestly duties would be required of me. That feeling had been in me from the day of my "mysterious enlightenment" on the campus of St. Dunstan's. My struggle had been unusually difficult. How had I managed it at all? Poverty, loneliness, a feeling of inferiority, more than ordinary labor; they were all there. Why had the easy way been kept so long hidden from me? Had I known of it I might even have gone to Rome. It was Cardinal Gibbons who told me that, but too late, for I was not equipped for Rome. I had been forced by circumstances to take a different and a harder road. Now I had to give up thinking about what I had missed and console myself with the hope that I had done my best for the greater part at least. The future was in God's hands. He knew what He wanted of me and would make it known at the proper time and in His own way. When I left for Detroit the worry was over—for a while.

≈§ 6 §≈

DETROIT

THE Detroit I saw in September, 1893, was a city of less than three hundred thousand population. To bring it up to date a million at least should now be added. I had to visit Assumption College in Sandwich, on the Canadian side of the river, so I left the train at Windsor. Visit and business over, I crossed to the American side by ferry, and walked up from the dock toward the Campus Martius. In front of the old Russell House I hesitated and glanced about for a policeman to direct me to the residence of the bishop on Washington Avenue, which, I had been told at the college, was not far from the City Hall. Two men stood on the corner conversing. One of them seemed to be looking me over with some curiosity. He was a short, rather stout man, wearing a black frock coat. A striking but not handsome black mustache dropped its ends low on each side of his mouth. He appeared surprised that he could not recognize me. Evidently he was one who knew well the wearers of clerical collars. I felt sure that he would have spoken had his attention not been claimed at the moment. He was the first citizen of Michigan to receive particular notice from that happy state's newest resident. When I was introduced later to the Hon. William C. Maybury, and we became friends, I recognized him at once. Later he was elected Mayor of Detroit. There is a bronze statue reproducing the short stout figure, the drooping mustache, and the frock coat, now standing in a park only a few blocks away from the spot on which I first saw "Billy Maybury" in life.

Maybury was one of America's most ready and finished public speakers. He had all the natural oratorical gifts except personal pulchritude, but he made up for that defect by a fund of humor and a well-stocked mind. In these days Detroit was the great Conven-

64

tion City. Mayor Maybury helped Detroit win that distinction, since he knew better than any other man in it how to make a convention feel at home. His short, witty addresses of welcome to delegates were famous; always astonishing the listeners by the speaker's knowledge of their own specialty. For lawyers he went to the roots of all the known codes. Physicians he led back to Hippocrates. Professors learned from "Mayor Billy" things that they had never known before about Plato, Aristotle, and Plotinus. Undertakers were urged to take credit for the wonders of Egyptian embalming. Mechanics saw, under the magic of his speech, lathes turning in ancient Carthage. Labor unions were surprised to know that there had been walking delegates in Babylon. Billy Maybury was gold and rubies for Detroit.

The city itself was beautiful. It had tree-lined avenues and a wonderful island park. Belle Isle is still there, but the fine streets downtown are now no more. Old Woodward is just two lines of shops. Jefferson looks run-down at the heel. Detroit is full of people, full of factories, full of bustle, but no longer the queen she once was. Worse still, Detroit has now only a bronze Billy Maybury sitting silent on his hard chair not far from an equally silent bronze Potato Pingree who had preceded him as Mayor and to the cemetery. The bronze forbids them to look natural. To be that, both should be talking: Pingree about himself and Maybury about history, cattle, banking, liberty, books, shoes, St. Patrick, William Tell, Mr. Pickwick, Cicero, and—everything that ever was and everybody who ever had been. Detroit, for those who knew the city forty years ago, is built around these two statues recalling other days.

It was almost in front of the bishop's residence on Washington Avenue that Henry Ford tinkered with his first car. He made it run from one end of that street to the other, much to the delight of the urchins, and to doubtful shakes of the head by wise adults speculating on the sanity of its inventor. Away up Woodward, "on the other side of the tracks," Henry later turned out what once were plain Lizzies, but are now quite beautiful Elizabeths, by the thousands. His new factories and his palace, however, are in what was then the far-away village of Dearborn; today a city as businesslike as its once beautiful mother.

I rang the bell of 33 Washington Avenue and in a few moments saw the Bishop of Detroit, my Ordinary. His name was John Samuel Foley. He was, like the city, then strikingly handsome. Alas! again like the city, he changed, for he lived long and faded with the years. A transplanted Baltimorian, he flourished in the cold North but never learned how to pronounce the name of his adopted state. It was always, even to the day of his passing, "Mitchigan" to him.

There were about twenty-seven or twenty-eight Catholic parish churches in Detroit when I arrived. There are now over a hundred. One converted Protestant church, changed into St. Aloysius, was neatly tucked away under the shadow of the old Cadillac Hotel, later the modern Book-Cadillac. That old church building is gone. Where the little frame rectory of St. Aloysius stood there is an office building, the chancery of the diocese. There is also a new St. Aloysius, a sort of wonder church, with tiers of galleries half-circling a glorious altar. The old church had a scion of one of Detroit's most aristocratic families as pastor, Father Ernest Van Dyke. He tolerated and was kind to me; that is to say he once invited me to dinner and he also came once to take dinner with me. He had the coziest library I had ever seen. I was jealous of his possession of it. Father Van Dyke told stories of old Detroit with a distinguishing lisp and a smile just as aristocratic. When he sat in that library, on a leather chair trained by long use to enclose him softly, and expatiated to his guests on history and art, he was a most satisfying picture of what a scholarly and dignified, but none too energetic, cleric should be. Never, never, would he have fitted into the modern steel and stone building which now occupies the site of his former rectory, nor yet into the background of colored marbles in the sanctuary of the new St. Aloysius.

Out of Michigan Avenue ran Porter Street, leading to "Corktown" and the Church of the Most Holy Trinity, its center and its pride. Over the parish of Corktown presided a thin ascetic named James Savage, with long hair and a genial heart. He had a hobby befitting his name—collecting Indian relics. Arrowheads, axes, flint knives, spear points, stone pestles and mortars, and all such related wild things, took gradual possession of Trinity Rectory. At Dean Savage's house one could meet collectors as strange as himself; men who knew why obsidian made the best knife, and the difference between the arrows of all the Stone Age tribes. When Dean Savage began to dig up weapons of tempered copper his house became a veritable museum.

There was one great difference between the clerical guests who visited Father Van Dyke and those who visited Dean Savage. The former, very few in number, were selected by their host; the latter selected themselves. Trinity Rectory was the property of its visitors. The beds were for the first who found them. The table always had room for a few extra chairs. No one sent word in advance of his coming. One just came, whether before meals or during meals or after meals mattered little. The box of "Mild and Pleasant," best of five-cent cigars, was never empty. There was rarely any spoken welcome or good-by, except for distinguished visitors from a distance. Even bishops drifted in now and then. The grave Archbishop Elder of Cincinnati, whose ascetic face alone would seem to forbid joking, was heard, after a visit to Trinity in summer, to refer to the sun-warmed seat of his cab as a "base burner." It almost brought on a rain, that unlooked-for pleasantry. John Hennessy, the Bishop *from* Wichita, as some wags suggested because of his many travels, but also the Bishop who *made* Wichita—its first bishop—always dropped in if passing through Detroit. There was a frequent priest-visitor from Chicago, Father Pope Hodnett, pastor of St. Malachy's, an orator without terminal facilities. He brought down the house at Dean Savage's silver jubilee by beginning his sixth speech with the proclamation: "I come from the Windy City."

A man much more interesting to me than any of the collectors visiting Trinity Rectory was Captain Henry Reaney, once of "Old Ironsides," and a retired officer of the United States Navy. In his stories he brought the smell of the sea with him to Trinity. The captain's courtesy was unfailing. "Sir" was one of the most employed words in his vocabulary. Never did I hear him fail to say "Your Reverence" when he addressed a priest, even a very young one. When the war with Spain broke out, the old captain's predictions as to the place and triumph of the Navy in it were almost uncanny in their accuracy. He had a son no less interesting than himself, Father William Henry Ironsides Reaney, chaplain on the "Olympia" under Dewey. Torn between a love for the sea and a vocation to the priesthood, young Reaney managed a fine compromise by becoming a "Sky Pilot" in the Navy. He reached his father's rank before he died, thus giving Trinity Rectory the distinction of having had two Captains Reaney on its visiting list. I preached the funeral sermon of the second, returning to Detroit from Chicago for the purpose.

When Chaplain Reaney returned home from his service in Manila a few of his clerical friends gave him a dinner over which I presided as toastmaster. On that occasion he told a worth-while story. I do not think it has ever been put into print before, or even committed to writing. Here it is: When the American troops were preparing for the attack on Manila the thought occurred to Chaplain William McKinnon of the First California—by the way he was born on The Island—that something might be done to save bloodshed and secure the city peacefully through the Archbishop of Manila. He consulted Chaplain Reaney of the Navy and Chaplain Doherty, later of the Army but then an unofficial addition to the staff of General Merrett, suggesting that if the Spanish Captain-General in command behind the walls knew how hopeless was his case, he might agree to a peaceful capitulation. The other chaplains offered to join McKinnon in an attempt to see Archbishop Nozelada and ask him to suggest to the Captain-General an honorable surrender in the face of certain loss and much bloodshed. McKinnon learned that the chaplains would be permitted by the Spaniards to enter the city for a visit to the Archbishop. General Merrett and Colonel Smith agreed to let their own chaplains go. Admiral Dewey also was willing to allow Reaney to go, but the captain of the "Olympia," Lamberton, refused his consent. Reaney had to remain on shipboard.

At an appointed time McKinnon and Doherty left the American lines to enter Manila, but something went wrong and they were fired upon. They took cover and, after waiting awhile in ambush, tried again. This time they succeeded in reaching the city gate, where they were blindfolded and driven to the Archbishop's palace. There His Grace was waiting with the Captain-General in person. The latter agreed that his position was hopeless but would not agree to surrender the city without a stand for Spanish honor.

The upshot of the affair was our capture of the city after a short show of resistance and with few casualties on either side. Somewhere in San Francisco there is a bronze statue to the memory of McKinnon. Reaney it was who took the initiative in collecting the money for it. McKinnon was the first American superintendent of education in the city of Manila—the first in the Philippines for that matter. His colonel became their first American Governor-General.

The diocesan clergy who frequented Trinity were mostly of now vanished types. There was Frank O'Rourke, who never got on a train without a Cicero, Virgil, or Horace in his pocket for company. He was a great bulk of handsome manhood plus an artistic temperament; a musician who might get out of bed at any hour of the night to play on his piano. Stricken down before forty with peritonitis, he came out of a coma to see his relatives weeping around his bed. "What's all this about?" he asked of his mother.

"You are very, very sick, Frank," she answered.

He had marked her tears. "Am I going to die? Tell me the truth."

She knew that he would press that question till he got the answer, so she told him. He seemed dazed for a moment. "Must I die?" he murmured, "Must I die?" No one spoke. Then over his face ran a cheerful accepting smile. "All right," he said, "All right. Send for my confessor." That was how he looked into the face of the Destroyer.

Then there was Peter Loughran, who still read his old textbooks of philosophy at home and teased Dean Savage when he came to town. A younger priest than myself adopted Trinity about as soon as he was ordained. He read the Latin Fathers and always managed to bring the conversation around to the one he had dipped into the day before. Smart is the word! John Ryan never bothered about discussions but managed to keep the discussers pleasantly irritated and going. George Clarson was a learned Maynooth graduate, frequently called upon to pass judgments. William Kilroy was a cynic with an enthusiastic appetite. Old Dr. Gauthier used to try his hand at squelching Dr. Charles Ormond Reilly. Both wore doctorial rings which they hammered on the well-scratched arm rests of the Dean's chairs. Reilly could talk faster than Gauthier and usually won, rings down. He was a most interesting character who had been national treasurer of the Irish Land League in America, and a suspect in English governmental circles. With joy and pride he would tell how Scotland Yard used to follow him around when he visited England. He had a crop of long white hair which he tossed about as he talked, and was a marvelous public speaker, not only because of a musical voice and a steady flow of liquid speech, but also by virtue of a memory like a vise. More than once, for pure love of testing that memory, I would contrive to ask him about some passage in Darras' six-volume *History of the Church*. I needed only to quote the opening of any paragraph. "That is on page so and so," he would state at once, and go on to finish the paragraph from memory. Never could I stick the Doctor on any book he had studied.

There was another trick that I used to play on the Doctor to save work for myself. When I had a sermon to prepare for any special occasion I always sought him out, but knew better than to ask for information by the direct route. He was impatient of contradiction and I knew it. The right plan was to lead the conversation to the desired subject and then suggest the suspicious side of it. In an instant the old lion was roaring at me. "Young ass!" was the mildest epithet I could expect from the Doctor then. Into the defense he would tear, shaking back his shaggy mane while striding up and down in front of me and now and then pausing to shake a threatening finger under my nose. In half an hour I had all the material I needed. Once I had to get up a lecture on volunteers and wanted a historical opening. I got the Doctor started by praising professional soldiers and regular armies. He dove right into the Old Testament. In five minutes I was annihilated, but I had my historical opening. He heard the lecture a year later and complimented me on it. God bless his good old heart, he did not remember that he had contributed to it. The Doctor was a bit of a wit, too. When he came to visit me later in my little country parish, a non-Catholic lady told him that she could find no scriptural warrant for an unmarried clergy. "Not a direct but certainly an implied warrant, madam," he assured her.

"Implied?" she queried. "Where in Scripture is the implication?"

"In the narrative of Christ healing the mother-in-law of Peter."

Detroit

"I don't see your point."

"Madam," he said with gravity, "if Our Lord wanted a married clergy do you think he would have *healed* her?"

"Charlie Reilly?" said Abbé Magnien, the president of St. Mary's Seminary in Baltimore. "Charlie Reilly was the smartest man who passed through this house, and one of the very few who took a doctor's diploma out of it with him."

Reilly was a genius who flared up for a moment, lit part of the sky brilliantly, and dropped back to level again, disappointed and perhaps disillusioned. What happened to this man with his great store of knowledge and abundance of natural gifts, who seemed destined to be a steady and lasting light rather than a momentary flash? I think the answer is found in the inspired Word: "No man can serve two masters." In Dr. Reilly's day the Land League agitation had become an intensive interest for people of Irish birth or descent all over America. It was looking for the very kind of man Reilly was. So a political cause absorbed him during the best years of his life, and a side issue became the main issue with him before he knew it. In fact he never did know it. Every genius has his blind side. The Church could have had a great leader in Dr. Reilly. But it must be admitted that in those days there were few places for such as he—more's the pity. Better than any other scholar I had ever known, Reilly was a master of applied knowledge. Everything in his head was for instant use. Every intellectual tool in his kit was polished and kept sharp by an active mind. At the time I knew him he was awaiting assignment to a parish after a few years of retirement and rest. His books were still packed away. But the Doctor did not need books to keep himself mentally alert and up-to-date. He found all the intellectual exercise he needed in the debates at Trinity Rectory.

It was in Detroit, a short time after meeting Dr. Reilly, that I was inspired to check up on the contents of my own intellectual and spiritual kit of tools. Dr. Reilly, without knowing, was responsible for that. He filled me with despair because I saw by comparison how small was my store. As far as I could see I had only one intellectual advantage over him, my knowledge of French. His was not even passable. Mine was sufficient not only for conversation but for study. French was a key I already had discovered and

71

intended to use. In everything else I was intellectually an infant compared with the Doctor, and I knew how unlikely it was that I should ever win an opportunity to get back to ordered study. Bishops were not then training specialists as some of them, including myself, are now doing.

I looked at the Doctor with an appraising eye. What could I get out of him? He was a man easily flattered, but one did not have to desert truth to flatter him. He liked to feel the deference of the young and see a touch of admiration on their faces for him. I gave him what he loved, but gave it as his right. The Doctor became a sort of graduate school for me as a consequence. I always knew where to find my unsuspecting professor. I knew how to start him going, for he needed only the priming of contradiction. It was safe enough to contradict him once, but once was good for at least an hour of hard lecturing. He did not mind being interrupted by questions. In fact, a question seemed to freshen and please him. He reminded me in some respects of Bishop Rogers. The lectures of the Doctor were, however, less interrupted by references to books than those of the Bishop. But Bishop Rogers knew that he was teaching, while Dr. Reilly thought he was only amusing himself with a young brother who happened to be fair company for the nonce. From the Doctor I learned a lot. There was one thing he could not teach me because, as with French, I had more of it than he. It was something I had picked up in French Canada—sympathy. The Doctor was no great admirer of the human race. I was then a sort of enthusiast about it. Alas! each year of my life after thirty seems to have lessened that enthusiasm.

We of English speech and influence neither use the word sympathy as do the Latins, nor do we understand the meaning they attach to it. People to them are simpatico or else outside the pale. What they mean by simpatico really is what we call charm. But no American, Celt or Saxon, likes to call a man charming. The word is feminine with us. So I should not say that I had learned to be simpatico. What I had learned was a bit of understanding—sympathetic understanding let us call it. I had met and lived with another people than my own. I had noted their virtues and had drawn the cover of charity over their faults. I had gotten to feel myself at times an intimate part of their life. No one can sit down in the quiet room that is the heart of another people, and not forever drop the thought of racial superiority. The trouble with most of us is that we know only one language and therefore know only ourselves—our race, our nation, our ideas of government, our systems. One of the saddest spectacles the world ever saw was that of a tongue-tied President trying in Paris to divide a world according to the affinities of the colors on the map. But softly—softly—that too might be another story.

What is sympathetic understanding? If you want a definition turn to Newman's portrait of a gentleman. If you want models I must admit that nowadays they are hard to find. Newman was perhaps too sensitive to be himself an absolutely perfect model. I thought Cardinal Begin of Quebec very close to perfection. I was sure of my Superior in the grand seminary at Nicolet, Father Gelinas. Later in life I found a near-perfect model in Cardinal Mercier, though he lacked something in the understanding of his Flemish fellow countrymen. I can name one perfect model, the late Cardinal Hayes of New York. The living can wait for appreciation. An outstanding model amongst the dead I remember—a Pope. Some day the Holy See may declare Pius X a saint. When that happens, as I hope it does, it will be plain that saint and gentleman really mean the same thing. Does anyone wonder why I speak of my having acquired only a very little bit of sympathetic understanding? But even a very little bit goes a long way. What I really had was no more than the recognition of its value and a desire to possess it. That I still have, but I am yet far, very far away from the goal.

A priest's success in his vocation depends largely upon at least a desire to reach sympathetic understanding. A headstrong pedant has scarcely any of it. It is nearly always absent in a genius. St. Ignatius knew that, hence the Exercises. Those who think they were born to rule, the very self-centered "conquerors," ordinarily have little thought of the rights of others. They may win admiration but, at least in life, never affection. Much about them must be forgotten before their work can be judged with fairness, for time has to relegate their faults into oblivion before their own real value to the world can be recognized. The decade after their passing is the hardest on their fame. It goes without saying that sympathetic understanding and vanity simply cannot inhabit the same house.

The vain man has not a grain of it, and pomposity is a sign of spiritual poverty. Sympathetic understanding makes up for many defects, as charity covers a multitude of sins. Being a product of humility, sympathy is a well-laid foundation for the greatest of the virtues, which always remains charity.

In my kit I found much with which I was far from satisfied—studies to be made up, enthusiasms to be checked, ideas of the world, now that I was in it, to be revised. But I had had good example, the teacher of teachers. So, looking ahead with hope and pleasure, I laid what I had of sympathy on the very top of my poor little stock of spiritual possessions. Of temporal possessions I had of course none.

7

STARTING

A GOOD habit for an old man to cultivate is that of looking back over his life to find justification for laughing at himself. He will, of course, also find some quite valid reasons for crying over the same person. These too will do him good, but the laugh producing interludes will do him more good if he follows the impulse. Above all other virtues for the aged is the virtue of humility. To take a kindly laugh at one's self is a triumph of humility, and the triumph is cheaply gained when laugher and laughee are one and the same person.

Take for example my youthful dream of the life I expected to lead as a pastor. It did my "cultivated imagination"—as Bishop Rogers used to put it—great credit. Once I jotted the dream down to remind me to laugh over it often. The temptation now to copy the jotting is too strong to be overcome: "There was the world— my world. It was bounded on the north, south, east, and west by green hedges (there is no such season as winter in student dreams). The hedges shut in the church and home away from the noise of the world outside. No one ever came within these green hedges but myself, a privileged gardener, a housekeeper, and, now and then, a parishioner to whirl the dreamer away to a quick round of duty, and then back again to his retreat. Within the rectory I could see only one room in the dream. There were others, but the dreamer was not interested in them. How could he be when he had that library? (He has it now, but somehow, alas, though it *looks* like the one in the dream, it is not quite the same.) Books, books, more books, here and there a painting and a bit of sculpture, and a deep window recess. Oh yes, there was also a sun parlor with plants, but so arranged that it could be shut off with curtains when His

Reverence wanted dim religious light and meditative solitude. The dream church was Gothic. It had towers, not steeples. There were bells that chimed in one of them. There was ivy to climb up and over both of the towers and the gables of stone. Inside was the idea of vastness, even within small compass, a deep-toned pipe organ, statues from Carrara, and—ever so many other beautiful things." Passing strange it is that a lot of all this came true, but when it did the dreamer had to leave it.

My first parish was not a bit like that. I made a pen picture of what it was. Let's have a look at that one too: "The grass was dead on the lawns. The poor, narrow house was set back from the walk, but alas! there was no garden and therefore no hedges. An unpainted black barn occupied a corner with its unsightly bulk. Across a street that nobody ever seemed to know existed was the dry-goods box of a church. There was no sacristy; but there were smoky coal stoves, a horrible reed organ, and pews that were a penance; no pulpit, no statues, no stained glass windows; but there were dirty vestments, and none of certain colors at all. Grim, dire church poverty we had, the worst kind of poverty because it so often speaks of cold calculating indifference to God, and smug self-satisfaction in the things that are of this earth."

It was not a bit fair to the people of my first parish to write that last sentence, for it was not their fault, as will be seen, that the picture was so unattractive. They were a good people and I have never stopped loving them, even though most of them have preceded me to the Kingdom—of Heaven I hope. When they were given the chance they made the dream picture almost come true. Sometime in your summer wanderings stop at Lapeer in the State of Michigan and see for yourself. When you do, please give my love to the "ivy-mantled tower" of the stone church and the flowering lawn and garden of the rectory. Listen to the chime from the tower if Ireton Jackson is still there to play it for you.

It is not uncommon in France for writers to weave tales, even romantic ones, with the country *curé* as inspiration. Some forty years ago everybody read Halevy's *Abbé Constantin*. Recently we have had a translation of Bernanos' remorseless probing of the soul of a country priest. Whether friendly or antagonistic the literary Frenchman finds it hard to keep away from the *presbytère*.

American writers get inspiration elsewhere. They have had little contact with the Catholic clergy and think they find too many Elmer Gantrys in their own. They are, perhaps, also a bit inclined to pity an educated celibate buried in a small town, with only a pittance for bread and butter and no hope for the future but advancement to a charge that will add to his burdens and not to the purse. No fuel for the fire of a modern problem novel there. Such a study as Bernardos made is out of the range of possibility for our novelists. Even the anti-clerical Frenchman knows what faith is and what can come out of its loss or its gain. For him there is no battlefield of the spirit more likely to make literature than the one on which he suspects a country priest is fighting for his soul. But apart even from all that, there is a charm around the *presbytère* that invites attention. I felt it in the first one I occupied.

The only practical training I had for pastoral work was gained in Lansing where for two weeks I took over his Sunday duties from a pastor down with a bad cold. That meant preaching. No trouble was to be anticipated over at least one sermon. I had a sermon, just one, but a sermon. I had lost the Nicolet effort. The new sermon had been written and committed to memory during my ordination retreat in a Dominican monastery. Appropriately, since done in such an atmosphere, the subject was "The Rosary." I preached it in the cathedral on The Island, and again on the Patronal Feast of the Parish of Our Lady of the Rosary in Detroit. I could preach it in Lansing.

It was the Rosary sermon that had attracted the attention of Dr. Reilly when he heard it in Detroit. There was in it a striking paragraph from Lacordaire which the Doctor mistakenly thought was my own. He remarked that *he* should have thought of the heart-throb in the Rosary "instead of a youngster who had not yet learned how to preach without committing pages to memory." But the fact that the thought was Lacordaire's and not mine consoled him. The paragraph ran as follows: "Rationalism laughs to see pass by ranks continually repeating the same word; but he who is illumined by a better light knows that love has but one word which, though ever spoken, is never repeated." Again I felt the sting Monsieur Beauchemin had so unwittingly given me in Nicolet when I remembered that the compliment he had offered came from one who had not understood a word I uttered. Now the compliment was based on a thought not my own.

Lansing heard the Rosary sermon in the morning. But, when I saw the sick pastor after High Mass, the terrible news that another sermon was expected for that evening shocked me. I had no other sermon. I begged and pleaded to be let off but the pastor was adamant. There was always an evening service with sermon in his church on Sundays, and I had to preach it this time. "You might as well learn early how to do it," he said. "From now on you'll have to extemporize often enough. You have the whole afternoon for preparation." There being no way out, I accepted the inevitable and went into his library to work, consoled by the thought that the pastor would be too sick to come over to the church and hear me making a fool of myself. But when I entered the sacristy after the sermon there he was, bundled up in a heavy overcoat and wearing a grin of satisfaction. "Some day you'll thank me for forcing that on you, young man," he said. I thanked him next morning.

Two weeks later I had my appointment to Lapeer and Missions.

The pastor of Lapeer, Father William Sinn, was sick at the home of his parents in Detroit. I called on him there. When he entered the little parlor I was shocked to see a man still young, with death's call written on his wasted face. Lapeer had been his only charge and he had had it for less than two years. Like most tubercular cases, he was quite sure that he was suffering from nothing worse than a stubborn cold and would soon return to duty. I knew that he would never be well again and made up my mind quickly to make things easy for him by allowing him to think that I was going to Lapeer as his assistant. At once he brightened and offered to come up the following Sunday and introduce me to the congregation. He came at the risk of his life. But that was nothing, for he had lost his life already by an act of devotion. The winter before he had risen from a sickbed to go on a fourteen-mile call through a snow storm, had been pitched out of the sleigh into a drift, walked two miles through the storm in thin shoes, and dropped exhausted on the floor of a farmer's house. He gave the last sacraments to the farmer's dying wife with half-frozen hands. While he preached to his old flock on that first Sunday of mine in Lapeer I noted, under the lace of the surplice falling down over the poor hands as he held tight to the sanctuary rail, how thin and frail they were. When he said good-by next morning he spoke of coming back, but he never came back.

Before going to Lapeer I went to call on Father Van Antwerp in whose church I had delivered my first Detroit sermon, and who had been very kind and cordial in welcoming me. I told him that I had been appointed to Lapeer. He was by no means enthusiastic in expressing congratulations. "Lapeer? Surely not."

"Yes, it's Lapeer," I assured him. "What's wrong with Lapeer?"

"You will find a major trial and problem awaiting you there— and you are young and inexperienced. An older man should have been sent."

"What is the major problem?"

"A former pastor, the first. He is living there—in apostasy."

"One of those shouting ex-priests making a living by abusing his mother?" I asked, but added, "I can stand that."

"No. He is not of that kidney. The case is much more complicated. His difficulty is intellectual, or so he says. He went off the end of a springboard called Herbert Spencer. I don't know of a like case in the country. He will annoy you by his writings in the local papers, and you can't hit back."

"I can't hit back? Why can't I hit back?"

"For one good and sufficient reason, at least. Because the Bishop will not permit it. You will have enough to do anyhow without getting into a controversy. There is building work to be done in all three of your charges. You are going to a brick-and-mortar job, my boy. Better ignore the other problem if you want to stay. If you don't, then keep away from the brick-and-mortar. If you once get into that you'll remain until you finish and the good Lord alone knows when that will be. But no matter what else you do, leave that human problem alone. 'In all things charity,'" he quoted as a parting counsel.

When I had all the available facts about my Human Problem it turned out that he was less a problem to me than I was a problem to myself. I had never read the books that had destroyed his faith. I could not even afford to buy them. I had no time to devote to new studies. The brick-and-mortar prophecy was true. Then another truth flashed out at me. My seminary had given me a lot but it had not brought me down to date. There was at that time little news about Haeckel or Spencer or Huxley in French-Canadian seminaries. Darwin, of course, had a few mentions. But French-Canadian priests were educated and trained to become pastors of souls who cared nothing even for Mr. Darwin's opinions.

I should have fared little better had I been enrolled in an American seminary. It was not the book but the building age American priests had to prepare for then. The founders of the Catholic University were ahead of their time. Had I run across what the Abbé Hogan, a distinguished theologian and seminary director, wrote, I should have agreed with him. I found the quotation recently in Ward's *Insurrection versus Resurrection:* "We were taught the various philosophical positions as the 'right view' and if any of us did not find those positions convincing we were accounted heterodox. Thus philosophy which professed to prove the rational duty of accepting Theism and revelation was not really enforced by reason but by authority. It was really learnt by rote and by sheer memory. Those students were best thought of who learnt best by heart. Genuine philosophic thought annoyed our Professors. . . . A Catholic rightly surrenders himself in great measure to the recognized channels of authority; and the Church rightly guards philosophy from serious error; but the point which the mediaeval schoolmen felt so keenly, that reason must be convinced on fundamentals, is being in practice almost entirely lost sight of."

My Human Problem did not leave me alone. He began to nag as I fully expected him to do. He wrote nothing I could not answer, but I kept the peace—very unwillingly I admit. I had great respect for episcopal commands. It was not so easy with some of the intelligentsia of my flock. Bright boys and girls were coming out. It was one of them who detected the Spencerian note in his pastor's carefully read sermons. "Why don't you answer him, Father?" was a question I often heard. I could only fall back on old principles, but they sufficed for the nonce.

"All these gentlemen," I said, "are only bringing you back part way. They are careful not to go too far back. Their 'interaction of organism and environment,' their unexplained 'omnipotent force,' their 'all-creative atoms,' are only enlarging the puzzle they think exists. There is nothing to wonder at if the physical universe was of slow making. The Creator could do His creative work that way or any other way. Atoms have to be accounted for as well as men."

So I did what I could, began with the books I had and made practically all my sermons doctrinal. My Human Problem let me alone after a while. I had the congregation and he had the weekly paper. It was the congregation that mattered. So score one for the Bishop.

I know that I am going off the line a trifle, but it will be useful to quote a paragraph about Alfred Noyes' book, *The Unknown God*, even if it is only the publisher's: "Alfred Noyes sets the statement of a strikingly individual approach to God. 'I remember,' he writes, 'the cold sense of reality, and the deepening shadow of a new loneliness that crept into the mind and heart of one boy of seventeen who began to read Huxley in the last decade of the nineteenth century. Later generations can hardly even guess at the mental sufferings of the more thoughtful in that time of transition.' He was too honest a thinker to abandon agnosticism simply because it meant the impoverishment and destruction of life. But as he read on, he found that each of the great agnostics—Spencer, Darwin, Huxley, Haeckel—postulated one special thing, which could only mean God. In each it was a different thing. It never seemed part of the normal current of their thinking, but to be a demand made upon their minds by Reality itself. 'They gave an impression of feeling more than they could say, yet of saying more than they knew they were saying.' With this as clue, he read more widely—Swinburne, Goethe, Matthew Arnold, John Stuart Mill, Voltaire: and he found that the rule was invariable—ever and again the writer would assert, always with immense emphasis, one of the attributes of God—the Unknown God, worshipped unawares by every agnostic or atheist who could think at all."

At the end my Human Problem had a struggle with grace. He came back as far as prayer. But grace must have decided that it had waited long enough. Death closed the book of his life in silence and mystery. He did not die unmourned, for his old flock never lost a kindly feeling for him. Catholics are like that. For years before his removal from the parish, nine-tenths of his flock had ceased to attend church. They could not understand his sermons, copied word for word out of Spencer and read to them in his odd German accent. But they could have stood the sermons had there not been other doubts. The Christ they had known was never mentioned. The devotions they loved had been dropped one by one. The sacraments were given with obvious reluctance. No priestly visitor ever came to Lapeer. All the people knew was that a strange puzzle of a man was behind the rectory doors, poring over books he did not understand, and, on Sundays, trying hard to ease his pain by asking them to share it with him. I had to live for ten years with the third act of the tragedy under my eyes and the sounds of it always in my ears.

Life teaches us some strange lessons. Who, for example, is one's worst enemy? He who once was the best of friends. It seems often enough that implacable hatred must first have had the nourishment of a great love to give it strength. There is no greater hatred than that of brother for brother except the hatred of the apostate for his former faith. Sincerely was I sorry for "the man on the hill," for I knew that my every move to bring back those he had tried to drive away was hurting him. His immediate successor had begun by a mission, and two-thirds of the people attended it. The country wagons of the congregation around the packed church could be seen plainly from the ex-pastor's window. For twenty-eight years he had been the spiritual leader of those people, and now he knew that they were looking at him with pitying eyes. The parish he thought dead was reviving. Its people were coming back home. Richfield, a little country mission where his own mother tongue was spoken, moved its center to the neighboring town of Davison and took on new life with an increased church population. For Imlay City he had built a frame church hidden away in the fields. The people erected a new brick and stone church in the town. The Lapeer congregation left the sight of the house on the hill and secured a hill of its own in the best residential district. On it a stone church was soon under construction. A chime of ten bells was to be placed in one of its imposing towers. A fine pastoral residence was secured. The old days were being forgotten, and with them the sad old story. The Faith returned. Today there are three parishes where one struggled hard to keep alive in the face of the hardest of trials.

It was not long before I found an opportunity to test the value of my small bit of sympathetic understanding, but in an entirely different field from any that I had hitherto known. Quebec had given me the first opportunity to see and study a people different in blood and language from the one in which I had been born. Lapeer gave me the opportunity of doing the same amongst a people holding a different religious belief, or, harder still, a people who were religiously united only on the basis of opposing what I believed. The town was almost entirely non-Catholic. There were not more than, perhaps, thirty Catholic families in it. My flock for the greater part lived in the country. The population of the town was then about 3,500. On The Island, Protestants and Catholics got on fairly well together. Although there was not much mixing on the social plane, there was mutual respect for one another, and each group was large enough to live its own life. Besides, the islanders, both Catholic and Protestant, were a people of deep religious convictions. Protestants and Catholics had certain fundamental ideals in common, especially on the permanence of the marriage bond. Lapeer was quite different. The social plane was common to all. There was some religious bigotry based on a suspicion that there must be something wrong with the other fellow; else why was he not in all things like his neighbors? In Lapeer for a long time a priest was a mysterious person. Both my predecessors had fostered the growth of that idea; the first, by looking the part when people saw him on his solitary daily walk, with his tall, meager form encased in a long frock coat, a small and unbecoming hat on his head, and an umbrella carried on his shoulder like a gun; the second, because his illness and short tenure of office kept him a stranger within the gates.

I came to Lapeer with the influence of The Island still strong in me. I found myself without friends. I was lonesome, for I had not been used to any society save that of Catholics. Frankly, I did not know much about others and was afraid of them. It took me a couple of years to learn that they were afraid of me. I stood the lonesomeness as long as I could, running into Detroit when it became unbearable. Then, after three years, things suddenly seemed to change.

A private banker named Oliver Wattles helped to make the change. Oliver belonged to no church. Neither was he a generous man to the churches, or to anything else for that matter. But he had one great life affection. It was for a sister who had been stricken with tuberculosis a short time after I came to Lapeer. She was attracted by the beautiful church I was building and wanted to have bells in the tower. For her sake the brother presented chimes. When the bells arrived and the people heard them play they realized that Lapeer had acquired a special distinction, and I was welcome to all they could do for me. It was only then I found out that I would have been made welcome at any time. The people in Lapeer were fair. There were seven Catholic teachers in the public schools; one of them, Miss Emma Loughnane, was the principal of the high school. She was even then Lapeer's most beloved teacher, and her popularity increased as more and more of her pupils grew up to be leaders in the life of the state and the community. She herself became a fixture in the high school and in the affections of parents. Ministers came and went in the churches; graduates of the schools passed to universities and returned as professional men and women; mayor succeeded mayor in the City Hall, but Miss Loughnane kept her place and never seemed to change—even to grow older. She had a quiet dignity and poise all her own. Her ability as an instructor was far above the ordinary. She had no apologies to make and never invented any. When I look back over my early days in Lapeer I have to admit that perhaps Miss Loughnane, more than anyone else, and without even knowing or trying, had made my path easy with my neighbors.

The parish of Lapeer is a standing testimony to the miraculous vitality of the Faith, to the strength of the Crucified Christ's grip on hearts, to the fact that virtue can make fortresses out of seemingly defenseless souls. It came back just as soon as its Christ came back. I emphasize all this to point a lesson the whole world that calls itself Christian had better learn. Christ leaves souls only when they desert virtue. The elements seeking to substitute in the world a pagan for a Christian culture always begin by attempts to corrupt it. They know the only way. A society weakened by filthy books and pictures, a careless press, and an education that sneers at decency, is a society easily captured by the forces of destructive revolution. Those who fear it, and would save their world from it, need arguments far less than they need Christ. A clean people is a safe people. The danger lies in being deceived by speech and print, and then by a general letting down of the bars of morality. One by one these bars have been falling of late, and our saving ideals with them. Legal divorce was adopted against the will of the majority.

Religion was driven from public education by the trick of covering a rotten philosophy with the green moss of patriotism. There are always those who are willing to make money by exploiting vice. Fewer and fewer voices are raised today in protest against dishonesty in public life. Fewer and fewer are the attempts to keep the only human habitations in which Christ can live fit for His Presence. Christ alone can save us. But it is a cowardly lip-service that most men are giving Him today—love and a lie. The lie has meaning, terrible meaning. The love has none, for it is without substance; a tradition from the lost faith that made a great civilization and is now, for all too many, only an echo flung against the walls of the bare mountains of doubt and dying away in the desert and the waterless valleys of corruption.

An autobiography may be no place for even a short sermon, but surely an old pastor recalling his memories home has a right to slip back now and then into his pulpit. It would not be much of an autobiography if he did not. His preachings are as much a part of his life as his adventures.

8

STORMS OF 1896

POLITICALLY the year 1896 was one of the most interesting in the history of the nation, for it saw a campaign only a little less stirring than the one which sent Lincoln into the White House and the Civil War. That expert rememberer, Mark Sullivan, makes William Jennings Bryan its central political figure, but during the early part of the campaign at least Bryan was more. He was dominant as well as central. For a few months of 1896 the whole American political universe revolved around "The Boy Orator of the Platte." His political opponent, later his conqueror, William McKinley, was half-obscured during most of the fight. Little light shone from or upon him. He was not an orator. All he had was pictured in his physique, that of a stout, clean shaven, silent, and solid man; type of everything conservative. But it was the solidity, as well the genius of Mark Hanna in capitalizing it, that gave him the victory over one of the most picturesque and brilliant failures in American political history.

Perhaps I should not have said that about Bryan—calling him a failure without making a distinction. Bryan went far in American public life though not as far as his objective. It was by his own ambitious measuring tape that he fell short. By the one most men use it would not be true to say that a Warwick who elected one President and became himself Secretary of State fell far short. Then, one ought to go slow in passing judgments on men and their ambitions. Not only have their personal prejudices and acquired habits of thought to be considered, but something else much more important, those of the judge. There were about and in Bryan things most people did not like. A ministerial air in a layman blows a cold draft. I never felt a genial current issuing from Bryan even though I

did start by admiring him—at a safe distance. But I can thank him
for something. It was the rise of the Bryan star that awakened my
first interest in the American political scene. I was not of his party.
I had no party. But the dramatic incident of the Democratic Convention, when the unknown Nebraskan, as if by foreordination of
fate, swept from the darkness of the backstage full into the glare of a
single spotlight, proved too much for my calm.

I could not entirely agree with Bryan, but neither could I deny
him interest and admiration. Nothing I had ever experienced before could equal the wonder of it all. Here indeed was a country
in which anything could happen. So 1896 burst upon me "as the
dawn comes up like thunder outer China 'crost the bay." No one
asks when reading Kipling if any dawn anywhere really does that.
In fact none does. I did not question the thunderous dawn of that
campaign. I know more about it now, but at that time I heard only
the fearsome and wonderful noise it made.

Before that year Mark Hanna was only a rich Clevelander and
William McKinley only the author of a tariff bill. There was a
young recovered consumptive whose name was Theodore Roosevelt
doing fair police service in New York. He was so insistent on talking that already the Republican bosses were hoping he would talk
himself to death. There was one Richard Bland of Colorado shouting about the free coinage of silver at the ratio of sixteen to one
into unlistening ears in Washington. Radicals had been born but
had not been baptized. Anybody who was not a Republican could
easily be charged with radicalism—and generally was. The people
did not want radicals. Democracy as a plan of government was accepted as a permanent and unquestioned success. Anything else
was simply unthinkable. The United States of America was called
a first-rate world power only for reasons of diplomatic politeness.

Bryan's speech in Chicago changed the political scene at home
in the flash of the spotlight that fell upon him. A handsome enough
looking man the light showed: coal black hair worn fairly long, as
became a statesman of that day, clean-cut features, a wide forensic
mouth, expressive hands, and fire-darting eyes. He caught more
than the Convention. At any time within three months after his
nomination it seemed as if he would be swept into the Presidency
on a tidal wave of votes.

I heard him speak in Detroit. Easily he was one of the best. Before him a young fellow from Chicago, James Hamilton Lewis, was introduced. He was dwarfed by Bryan that night, but in truth he was Bryan's superior as an all-around public speaker. He had what Bryan had not, the arts and crafts of the polished and "well-read man." Bryan had the presence, the voice, the sincerity, the roll of rotund thunder. He did not keep them. When I heard him, some ten years later, deliver his lecture "The Prince of Peace" he had deteriorated. The voice was there; the sincerity was there; but the tones and inflections were those of a practiced evangelist. The ministerial air had got him. He had been trying to paint the lily. I said that he was still sincere, but one who had not heard him as the Boy Orator of the Platte might have doubted the fact. Bryan was never anything but sincere. He might conceivably fail to win his audience. He never failed to win himself.

How little did I dream as I sat, enthralled but only half-convinced, listening to the Bryan of 1896, that after long years a day would come for that man and me to face each other in bitterness. But softly—softly again. That certainly *is* another story.

A storm had been going on in Church circles for some time—really two storms that met and united: the Cahensly and the Faribault-Stillwater school questions. The good Herr Cahensly, head of a German society interested in aiding immigrants, was supposed to be leading a movement to divide the hierarchy of the United States along nationalistic lines: German bishops for Germans, Polish bishops for Poles, and so on down the racial list. I followed the controversy as closely as I could, but never was able to satisfy myself that Herr Cahensly had been so very busy about it, though I knew that he had proposed such an arrangement. It was foolish to think that the Holy See would countenance a plan so much at variance with her old and well-tested policy. True, the great number of foreign immigrants entering the United States from Catholic countries made our situation somewhat exceptional, but Rome would be sure to see that the exceptional under such circumstances was also the temporary. There was not the slightest reason to believe that the Vatican would decide to handle a passing phase by a permanent departure from accepted tradition, and by an arrangement which certainly could not fail to be displeasing to the vast majority of the American people. The Vatican was too wise to make such a blunder.

The importance given the Faribault-Stillwater school question puzzled me. It was Archbishop Ireland of St. Paul, pleased with an arrangement made with two public school boards to take over the parochial schools in their cities under an agreement satisfactory to both parties, who threw out the suggestion that in some such arrangement a solution might be found for the religious education problem then troubling us. The very nature of the Minnesota compromise indicated its purely local character. There was little reason to believe that the plan would prove generally acceptable or generally workable, though it had been used effectively in some cases. In the diocese of my birth it actually was working when I was a schoolboy, and is still in use there, even with its scope extended. There was nothing strange about it that I could see, excepting the row stirred up by suggesting that it might prove a universal cureall. The Holy See settled the trouble in two words, *Tolerari Potest;* which mean, in a strict translation, "It may be tolerated," but which actually were intended to say: "it is not the ideal, but there are circumstances of time, place, and population when and where, and for whom, guarding well the principle, you must do the best you can." Thinking of the dangers faced by religious education now, I fear that the suggestion of Archbishop Ireland was dismissed with too little thought of what problems the future might bring. It never pays to take a question requiring cool discussion into a tropical atmosphere.

The time was yet to come when I should know Archbishop Ireland better. He was a man well worth knowing, an Empire Builder, even if his ecclesiastical office forbade him to be a match for his friend James J. Hill. Ireland was as great in vision as Cecil Rhodes, of South Africa. He thought and planned on a wide scale. That was one reason, and the chief reason, for mistakes made on a smaller one. They should be attributed to the fact that he was better fitted for the great things than for the small. He never really reached, nor, because of his office, ever could reach, the world plane of usefulness upon which his powers could deploy. John Ireland was a ten-thousand horsepower dynamo driving a thousand horsepower plant. He persistently kept trying to use the reserve nine thousand,

and failed because there was nothing on which he could use them. It was said that he grasped at national prohibition and played with politics, but it was individual total abstinence he advocated, not prohibition, and when he found no place for an honest man in politics he eased himself out. His success was bound, in the end, to be a home success. In truth there is no place but home for a bishop, at least while he lives. If he becomes a national character it is in history. That will be the fate of John Ireland, and perhaps his real usefulness, for stilled hands have been known to build. When the news of Ireland's death reached Rome I was with Archbishop Cerretti, later Cardinal, who was then Under-Secretary of State. He immediately told me that the Pope had decided on Ireland's elevation to the cardinalate. The Archbishop missed that ambition by only a few weeks, but what good would a cardinal's hat have been to a tired and dying old man?

Archbishop Corrigan of New York, supposed to be the great antagonist of Ireland, was as different from him as a zephyr is different from a gale. He was gentle and retiring, but persistent and uncompromising. He was generous and kind, but he could be firm and, when he felt that he had to be, was. I met him in his own home one day during the Spanish-American War when I came up North on a mission from my commanding officer to the Secretary of War. The Archbishop asked only about the welfare of one of his priests serving near me as a chaplain, Father William J. B. Daly, and news of the Sixty-ninth, a New York City regiment of Catholic soldiers. He had the most winning of smiles. In truth Corrigan was a most attractive personality.

When I look back to catch again in memory a glimpse of these two, I wonder how it came about that they never really knew each other. Both were understanding souls who could have made generous allowances for differences in character. No one could make Ireland over, but a gentle yet firm character like Corrigan could have made him a friend, and Ireland too was generous. This I have always found to be true when leaders dispute: the big fighting is done by volunteer supporters who contribute most of the noise and acrimony. Their advice, persistently offered, goes on enlarging and strengthening the thought of their assumed personal responsibility. Two wise men who knew their principles could have sat down alone and settled the school question as far as Catholics were concerned. Rome settled it in two words. But what chance had they to be alone together? The volunteers were never off guard.

Chief of these volunteers was the strong and energetic Bishop of Rochester, Bernard McQuaid. Someone said of him: "He is the only bishop in the American hierarchy who will still be found governing his diocese twenty-five years after his death." I was told that he even said it himself, and so he might. One look at the bronze face of his statue in the grounds of the splendid seminary he founded in Rochester will force agreement with that judgment, even from those who never knew Bishop McQuaid in life. The Bishop of Rochester had no opinions; what he had were convictions, and his convictions were dogmas only a little below those of the Faith. When a fellow student of mine heard of the death of Archbishop Lynch, of Toronto, he said: "I can hear his first remark in Heaven: 'My! My! How quick I went off; but how will Canada get along without me at all, at all?'" It is significant perhaps that the Rochester of Bishop McQuaid was just across the Lake from the Toronto of Archbishop Lynch. Both Canada and Rochester have gotten on without their strong-willed prelates of other days, but Rochester especially has no reason to be sorry that it once had a McQuaid. Few public men I have known had less need of a memorial in bronze. Byron might lament over fallen Greece that "soul was wanting there." Over the dead founder of the Diocese of Rochester no poet will ever sing that. The McQuaid soul does not pass so easily from the scene of its labors.

I am going to devote more space to Bishop McQuaid than to the two ostensible leaders in the Ireland-Corrigan controversy. He was and is interesting as a bishop of an old school, and there are none like him today. His was the horny hand that worked on foundations.

The school question was never to my mind important enough, at bottom, to stir up such excitement, except that there were those who feared that Ireland wanted to grant the state a right over the child to which it was not entitled. But the Faribault school idea was, as I said, not new, having been in operation in the State of New York as well as in Canada. The true issue was something else: the rights of a bishop within the limits of his own diocese. McQuaid was no ecclesiastical federalist. He would have been as emphatic as was one Pope in rejecting anyone's right to the title of "Universal Bishop," while loyal beyond criticism to the See of Peter. For him it was Rome and Rochester, with Rome in front. He knew why Rome called Rochester "Brother" and not "Son"; and he knew why Rochester called Rome "Peter" and not just "one of the Twelve." All this, coupled with a resolute and masterful character, meant a Keep Off sign on the front lawn. It meant likewise that his sidewalk was intended for pedestrians and not for public speakers. It was all right for anyone to walk by on it, but not to use it for orations. And the old lion happened to be right. But he stumbled, by not recognizing the fact that the good God has so endowed some men that their influence simply has to radiate, and all for His own purposes. The Bishop mistook a radio voice—though there were none then of the kind we now know—for that of an intruder on his grounds. He resented the newspaper interviews of Archbishop Ireland. He resented his offering advice outside of St. Paul. Bishop McQuaid could tolerate Cardinal Gibbons' diplomatic national utterances because the kind diplomacy of them softened the offense but, at bottom, even these must sometimes have been semianathema to him.

There may be a metal so hard that a blow-torch will not melt it, but personally I have never seen it. There may be characters stubborn enough to resist generosity, but I have only heard of them. Perhaps, even on these, not quite enough compressed good will is used. I hold fast to the faith that generosity is a sort of miracle worker when it comes to making a hole in stubbornness. But it simply won't work at a distance. There has to be close contact. So it turned out to be in the great controversy, for when the contact was made all was well.

When good Catholics quarrel over principles, the dove of charity is always hovering around. It is hard to escape the beloved virtue of the Apostle to the Gentiles. I shall let one who saw the dove welcomed and fed tell the story of the end, by quoting from a letter of Monsignor Hartley, former president of Bishop McQuaid's seminary: "The reconciliation of the two Bishops is of the greatest importance to them now. It happened that Bishop McQuaid, as spiritual director of the L. C. B. A., had occasion to visit different cities where the Catholic ladies held a convention. Before visiting

St. Paul he no doubt wrote to the Chancery according to the usual courtesies and received an answer that his visit would be acceptable. While there he was invited to preach in the Cathedral and accepted, returning home highly gratified with his visit. A year or two later Archbishop Ireland and Bishop McGolrick came to Rochester and spent three days as the guests of Bishop McQuaid, appearing in his Cathedral and visiting different institutions of the city. They all took dinner at the Seminary the evening of December 3, 1905, and the Archbishop was the life of the party from the very first to the close. Toward the end he rose to make a speech, beginning with a reference to the construction of the Suez Canal, which gave engineers concern as to the possible result if it were found that the great bodies of water at either end had a different water level. 'I have discovered on this visit,' he said, 'that St. Paul and Rochester are on the same level.' A characteristic incident happened on their first sitting down to table, when Archbishop Ireland reached out at once and took a piece of cake. Whereupon Bishop McQuaid turned and said: 'Your Grace, just a minute, the domestic will bring in the food presently.' Instantly the Archbishop put the cake back, folded his arms and looked like a mischief-making boy, thus setting the table in a roar. Many years previously a sister of the Archbishop, a nun, came to Rochester to visit the schools, and during her stay she received special courtesy and attentions from Bishop McQuaid; which induced her, it is said, to beg her brother later on not to allow the good old Bishop to die unreconciled to him—an instance of *dux femina facti.* In his last illness Bishop McQuaid mentioned to certain priests: 'I believe I can now say that in the various controversies I have had I always tried to fight for a principle and not to be swayed by personal feeling.' Archbishop Ireland in making the first approach to reconciliation manifested a noble spirit of self-conquest and Christian charity."

The seminary in Rochester was the core of the McQuaid heart, the easy road to reconciliation. It had even a valid claim on the cores of other episcopal hearts, for it marked an advance step in the training of the American clergy. It was "up to date" for its day, and the spirit of the old warrior has never deserted it. How could it? Choice among the stories that flew over the country about Bishop McQuaid was the post mortem one of his putting St. Peter in his place when the Gate Keeper insisted on showing the newly arrived Bishop of Rochester the glories he guarded and was stopped by the question, "But did Your Holiness ever see St. Bernard's Seminary?"

Please do not think I was all this time absorbed in watching storms. I was building churches as well as trying hard to get my flock back around their pastor, and succeeding fairly well. When the churches were finished I began "Catholic Evidence" lectures in them. Converts were few, but even one soul is worth the universe. I consoled myself with that thought.

An amusing incident occurred while the stonework of the façade of the church at the mission of Imlay City was being erected. It was my custom to visit the new buildings on the pretense of superintending construction. One day I found great excitement among the workmen and quite a knot of my parishioners around sharing it. Something had happened. When the crowd saw me the excitement increased. "Come and see what's going to happen to you, Father," said the contractor as he led me to a place from which I could see the half-built wall of the façade being erected out of the hard glacier-rolled stones found on every farm in the neighborhood, "Look at that stone."

"What stone?"

"The big one to the right."

"What about it?"

"Don't you see the shape it took when we split it?"

"Yes. It's a sort of triangle."

"Triangle? That's no triangle. It's a miter. You're going to be a bishop, Father Kelley."

From that day on no one could persuade the folks at Imlay City that I was not destined to become a bishop.

"It's superstition," I told them.

"Mebbe so, Father. But it'll work out just the same; you'll see."

When I did become a bishop there were many who said, "I told you so," in Imlay City. Someone suggested that the date of the fulfillment of the prophecy ought to be carved on the stone. But the big boulder was hard enough to make the job too difficult for a country-town artist.

My thirteen years as a country pastor were years of peace and poverty, but the honey of one sweetened the hard bread of the other. The time was coming near when the honey was to be taken from me and the bread changed into—but let the next chapter tell its own story.

❧ 9 ☙

WAR

I T WAS Mars who broke my peace. He met me one fine spring
day in Detroit, reined up his horse for a moment, spoke a single
pregnant sentence, and passed on. A week or two later he came
back holding a yellow envelope containing a telegraphic order from
the Bishop in his hand. He beckoned and I followed. All that
happened in 1898.

No one could hate the thought of war more than I did, and still
do. No one could have had a stronger conviction that the war with
Spain was not only unnecessary but unjust. Nevertheless, I went to
that war—to a war I abominated. Had I stayed home one lonesome
day instead of seeking relief in Detroit, I should not have had to
face the consequences of meeting Mars. The seemingly small incident of a major stopping his horse to exchange a word with two
young priests standing on a corner, watching his battalion go by,
became an incident important enough to turn the current of my
life into channels uncharted and unknown.

Newspapers made our war with Spain. President McKinley and
his advisers were against it. The remote cause, which was the Cuban
rebellion, was none of our business. The immediate cause, the blow-
ing up of the battleship "Maine," was never proved against the
Spaniards. The Queen Regent of Spain had, at the instance of the
Pope, agreed to all that we legitimately could ask; but, alas, too late.
The war itself, with its misery and expense, as well as the sin it
could not fail to produce, might have been avoided without loss
of that queer thing governments call honor.

For another reason it was a crime to enter that war. We were
risking too much. All we had was a Navy and, till it proved its
prowess, we were not any too sure of that. Our Regular Army was,

on the face of things, altogether too small. Our National Guard units were for the greater part summer camping clubs, without artillery, armed with obsolete rifles, and in some cases, perhaps in most, even without proper uniforms. There were whole regiments without rifles. I am not writing this on hearsay. I saw it.

The war with Spain called for service in the tropics. What equipment the Army had was unfitted for such service. Every bit of clothing the government could issue was made of wool, and none too light at that. Such clothes were a menace to the health as well as the mobility of the men. We had no well-organized medical corps for a large army. We knew little about camp sanitation. Even in maneuvers we were, at best, good only on parade. I do not write from camp gossip. I saw it.

Even the commissary was as bad as it could be. Only half-effective railroad transportation reached Tampa, where the first invading army had to gather and train. The training was superficial. There were not even half-good country roads in Florida to take over a part of the supply problem. It was near the rainy season when we went South, which was a guarantee of sinks of mud on the roads from the railway yards to the camps. The Florida rainy season meant tropical downpours alternating, often hourly, with broiling sunshine. The meat arriving in Tampa for the camps would be tainted between the yards and the cook shanties. The papers up North went wild with rage over canned "embalmed beef." It was not canned embalmed beef that bothered us but tainted fresh beef. No one was needed to tell me that. I ate it.

Two pieces of good fortune gave us victory: the Navy and the exhausted Spanish soldiers. Had we tackled these latter a year or two earlier, fresh from their training and as yet untouched by tropical sicknesses and discontent, they might have beaten us on land. But it would have done them no good, for our Navy tore up their salty road home. But we would have paid a higher price for the Cuba that we neither wanted nor got.

It was my heart that put me into that war. While I was looking at the Detroit Battalion of the First Michigan Infantry parading to the train, Major Tom Reynolds saw me with a young priest friend, Father John Crowe, and rode over to the curb. "Why is it," he asked, "that there is no priest coming with us?" Neither of us knew, but, when the procession had passed, I went straight to the Bishop's house to tell him what the major had said, and offered to go if needed. I emphasized *needed*. The Bishop thought no priest would be needed from Michigan, but a few weeks later I was sent. I had plenty to do in my parish. I had no desire to leave it. I had just talked too much for my own peace, but strange as it may seem, I was not really sorry that I had.

One possible blessing, I thought, was in sight: I might force the war to finish the church in Lapeer for me. Work had stopped on it for lack of funds, but the completion of that church meant everything in the remaking of the parish. I decided that one life was not too much to give for that. I went into the war with a joy hard to explain. I had insured my life for the amount needed to finish the building and I could not very well lose, whatever happened. I was quite certain that it would be the worst.

The war with Spain was, of course, a very tame military affair. For five months I lived under canvas, most of the time in a tent pitched under a burning sun, and a refuge for mosquitoes and flies. Now and then there were snakes too, as well as one lone alligator which was taken prisoner. I had to learn everything, even to ride a horse. How I learned that may show how I learned everything else needed in the process of turning a peace-loving cleric into a soldier for a day.

My colonel was one of those to whom the title "soldier by nature" rightfully could be applied. His qualifications began with his appearance. He looked like Napoleon III. From youth he had been attracted by military life, had served as private and officer in the National Guard, had studied soldiering—and his name was McGurrin. He promised to teach me to ride a horse, but kept the promise in his own way. It took five minutes or less of his time to do the job effectively and for me most distressingly.

One day the regimental staff was ordered to mount and enter a nearby palmetto grove to pose for a photograph. I borrowed the colonel's second horse, "Monte Cristo." I was not nervous, since the grove was just across the parade ground and the horses would have no chance to break into a run. If they did I was lost. The photograph was taken and we returned as far as the level parade. I was about to dismount when a thought of mischief entered the colonel's head. He gave orders to the staff to line up for drill. That worried me, but things went off fairly well, with only "Column Right"—"Column Left"—"Fours Right"—"Fours Left"—"Twos Right"—"Twos Left"—to obey. Then came the fatal moment. The colonel snapped out the order "Charge." "Monte Cristo" knew his master's habits and loved a race. Appalled, I saw the horse thrust out his head, and set back his ears. I felt all the muscles of his body gathering their forces together beneath me. In a second he was off, headed for the other end of that quarter-mile stretch of smooth parade. I lost the reins. I lost the stirrups. Desperately I hunched down holding on to the racer's mane. I prayed that my inevitable fall might be on a soft spot. The whole regiment was on the side lines. I heard shouts of laughter as I just missed an army wagon crossing the field. My face was redder from shame than from the heat. We neared the end of the parade ground. "Monte Cristo's" nose reached out till it was on a line with the flanks of the colonel's new horse. The colonel swung around and saw me. "Hello, Father," he said. "What brought you here?"

I looked a reproach.

"Hang it," the colonel added, "I had intended keeping you and Dr. Weed out of it. I guess I forgot."

I walked "Monte Cristo" back toward my tent. My "striker," Jim Hinchey, a policeman in civil life, was waiting. He took the horse away and I heard him chuckling as he went along to the corral. What I did was to go into the tent to hide my shame. In a few minutes Jim came back and sat down. "Ye did foine, Father," he remarked.

"Don't rub it in, Jim," I pleaded.

Jim looked surprised. "What's the matter wid ye, Father?"

"Matter! Matter!" I said bitterly. "I didn't know how to ride. I lost the reins and the stirrups. I grabbed the mane. What else ——?"

"Just a minute, Father," put in Jim, "when ye passed me like a flash of black lightnin'—if there's such a thing, and there is for its name is 'Monte Cristo'—ye had yer head down like a jockey and, I swear to hiven, ye had the spurs driv into him half an inch. Father, the bhoys are proud of ye. The colonel had three horse-lengths on ye at the start and 'Monte Cristo' wad have passed that new horse of his in another second. Ye are a grand chaplain from this day on. Ye won that race."

It was only then that I learned what everybody else seemed long to have known: that "Monte Cristo" had been a racer. But I still had an argument to offer. "Why were the boys laughing at me, Jim?"

"Laffin' at ye? Sure it was not ye they were laffin' at. Major Knowles fell into that army wagon ye missed and they had to pull him out av the sthraw."

That settled it. I went down the line to the tent of Major Knowles, our chief surgeon, who was applying arnica to his many scrapes. He was a very fleshy man who should not have been expected to furnish a merry lot of soldiers with an imitation of John Gilpin. When he saw me smiling before his tent, he said something that sounded like a violation of army regulations. It was a whole day before he got over his propensity for using such language. The colonel had taught me in record time and in a painful way how to ride a horse. I got most things in life like that.

The boat which was to take the Thirty-second Michigan to Cuba with General Shafter was rammed in Tampa Bay and we were left behind. It began to be lonesome waiting for action. Then one day relief marched into camp and occupied the vacant ground next to us. The Sixty-ninth New York it was, and there was no more gloom.

I knew it was the Sixty-ninth because of what I heard next morning. Often our band began the day at reveille with "Dixie," and the Floridans or Georgians down the line would answer with shouts and "Yankee Doodle." North and South were getting together; one good thing that came out of the war with Spain. But the Sixty-ninth had an awakening musical selection they considered to be of a more all-embracing character. I woke up quickly the first dawn after their arrival to the tune of "St. Patrick's Day in the Mornin'."

There was fun wherever the Sixty-niners went. Our regiment had officially been listed as the Thirty-second Michigan Volunteer Infantry. The Sixty-ninth, perhaps for good reasons, I won't commit myself on the point, gave us a new name, "The Thirsty-seconds." One of their wags even suggested "The Half-Minutes," on the ground that thirty seconds made half a minute. The two regiments became the best of friends. When a fight broke out amongst soldiers of different units off duty, the law for these two was the same: learn if the other was in it, join the combat on that side, and ask what it was all about when the battle was over and done with.

An incident leading into a most interesting story had occurred when I accompanied Colonel McGurrin to report our regiment's arrival to General Shafter at his Tampa Bay Hotel headquarters. We remained at the hotel for dinner after seeing the fattest general on earth, and then joined the brilliant gathering of uniforms in the lobby. Many nations were represented by military observers, all with finer trappings than even our generals could muster. An Englishman named Paget outshone all. I doubt if I ever saw him in exactly the same uniform twice. But I was especially attracted by a fine-looking captain of our own Regular Army who bore himself with genuine distinction, a gentleman if ever there was one. I asked a Regular Army chaplain who he was. His answer was to seize my arm, bring me over and introduce me to Captain Ord. I chatted with the captain for quite a long time that evening. When news of the Battle at San Juan Hill began to come back to Tampa I inquired anxiously about my new friend. He had been killed. In command of a battalion when the fight ended and the hilltop was taken, he had pointed with his sword to a wounded Spanish soldier sitting on a box with a rifle across his knees, bleeding. The captain called for someone to "take care of that wounded man." The Spanish soldier, mistaking the gesture with the sword and the order snapped out in a language he did not understand, thought he was to be killed. He shot Ord in the face.

Thirty-five years later, with Archbishop Orozco y Jiminez of Guadalajara, Mexico, I called on a lady, Mrs. Rebecca Peshine, in Santa Barbara, California. She had a beautiful home built in Spanish style with a lovely chapel. She spoke Spanish to the Archbishop and English to me, both languages equally well. Behind the altar of the chapel I noted an American regimental flag, and in the parlor a painting in oils of an American general. I asked her who he was.

"My father," she answered, a bit proudly, "we are a military family. That is General Ord."

"I knew a Captain Ord who was killed in the Spanish War," I said.

"My nephew," she answered, "see, here is a photograph of him." It was my Captain Ord.

Now comes the strangest part of the story, apropos of another picture in oils on the wall, that of a man in royal robes. "Is he too an Ord?" I asked with a smile.

"He is my ancestor, King George the Fourth of England," she answered. "The Ords are descended from him and his lawfully wedded wife who was called Mrs. Fitzherbert. The Ords came from England to the United States via Mexico."

The Archbishop had caught the thread of the conversation. At this point he became thoroughly interested and broke in: "Ord? King? Mexico? England?—Ha! I have heard something. Let me think— Yes, I have it. In the archives of my diocese in Mexico there is a letter about that son of King George who came to Mexico. When the question of selecting an emperor was discussed, before Maximilian was chosen by Napoleon the Third, it was suggested by a British official in Mexico, in private, of course, that Mexico might do well by choosing that son of the King as emperor. Assurance was given of his legitimacy, his religion, and of the interest of the British royal family in him. Wonderful! He might have become Emperor of Mexico but for Napoleon."

Later the Archbishop sent me a copy of the document which he had ordered mailed to him from Guadalajara.

After Shafter's Fifth Army Corps sailed we were transferred to the Seventh, under General Lee, which was to take Havana, and sent to a new headquarters in Fernandina, Florida, near the sea. But before we left, indeed before Shafter left, a new figure arrived in camp. General Miles burst upon us like a rising sun and outshone even Colonel Paget. The chaplains had been complaining about their uniforms and we knew that Miles was the man to understand our complaint. In the Regular Army at the time a chaplain's uniform differed in nothing from the ordinary dress of a clergyman. It was "of black cloth without welt, stripe, or cord . . . nine black buttons down the front . . . a falling collar." There was also a black hat, without ornament. Chaplains had been constantly mistaken for civilians when called to other camps than their own. I never left mine for a night sick call without the thought that dawn might find me in some guardhouse. We had to provide a better means of identifying ourselves as army men than a black coat with "nine black buttons," etc. Sentries could not be expected to count buttons. National Guard units had, however, some chaplains fearfully and wonderfully gotten up. All of us ranked as captains, but a Florida regiment had a chaplain who wore the gold maple-leaf shoulder straps of a major, but had to content himself with the pay of a captain. Some of the National Guard chaplains adopted crossed silver shepherd crooks on a black ground for shoulder straps, but the boys referred to the emblem as the "scissors" or suggested that the chaplain was the regimental tailor. We sent a delegation to General Miles. He it was who issued the order that, in the future, chaplains in the field should dress as other officers, and change the crooks on the shoulder straps for a Latin cross. He retired from the Army soon after and headed an anti-Catholic political party. When I heard of that activity I wondered if he remembered that it was he who had selected a Latin cross as a distinctive religious emblem on the uniforms of American army chaplains.

We stayed in Fernandina only long enough for most of us to get typhoid-malarial fever. Nine-tenths of the regiment was stricken with the disease, and "those in the know" were well aware of the fact that some cases of "yellow jack" also had appeared. There was a Sisters' Academy in Fernandina with a large exhibition hall. The nuns kindly turned it over to me for our sick, who were thus given better shelter than tents, as well as better care. Then came an order for the regiment to move to Huntsville, Alabama, transferred to the Fourth Army Corps under General Coppinger.

In Huntsville I met General Coppinger, one of the most interesting personalities in the Army, now rarely spoken of. He was to head the Porto Rican expedition, but Miles worked himself into its command on the ground that Coppinger was near the age of retirement. Coppinger was an old and experienced soldier who had begun his fighting with the Papal Zouaves in defending Rome against the House of Savoy. He had a bad saber cut on the side of his face, which was disfiguring when he wore civilian clothes, but went well with his military uniform. The general used to come over to my Mass every Sunday with his staff because he had heard that I never preached longer than twenty minutes. But he hated the new chaplains' uniform. "A clergyman," he insisted, "should dress like a clergyman." I asked him if he had ever spent the night in a guardhouse. He saw the point but never really became reconciled to the idea of a chaplain looking like a soldier. Even the Latin cross did not make the old Papal Zouave think any better of the new uniform. Perhaps the fact that it was General Miles' idea helped fix the prejudice. Miles was after his command and Coppinger knew it. Close to Coppinger was Major Clarence Edwards, his adjutant, a splendid type—efficient, courteous, wise. Of course Edwards went high in the service after the war. That was where he belonged.

We knew nothing about the general strategy worked out in Washington for the conduct of the war, but it became plain enough after our changes of corps. We had passed from Shafter's, through Lee's, to Coppinger's. Evidently the strategy was for Shafter to reduce Santiago and march overland on Havana, joining Lee there while Coppinger was taking Porto Rico. The Navy's victory over Admiral Cervera, and the Spanish surrender at Santiago, made all that unnecessary. There was no longer need for experienced soldiers like Coppinger, so the rest of the active service of the war became nothing more than a political race for command and, perhaps, for a small place in history. But no one ever benefited much, if we except Colonels Wood and Roosevelt. I saw the latter in Tampa with his Rough Riders. They looked like good fighters but were not nearly as experienced in campaigning as the regulars. It was with them that Wood, a physician, got his start as a soldier. Later he became a general, while Roosevelt attained the Presidency. "Teddy" was not a great military commander, but he had the "something" in him that wins. Was it destiny? Who knows? It seems to set the goal for those it patronizes, but neglects to tell them what and where the goal is. So from triumph to triumph they pass and never think of stopping. But most of them do stop— with a crash. The "something" has a bad habit of abandoning its favorites. It abandoned a real personage and a great man when it left Theodore Roosevelt.

I still hate war, but I am no pacifist. War is sometimes justified, though not often; because not often is there a right side and a wrong side in war. Mostly there are only two wrong sides. Its consequences to those who fight in it are decidedly bad from many points of view. War cultivates the destructive spirit. The most expensive things become cheap and common to soldiers in the field. Who bothers about an airplane that cost the price of two farms when it fails to rise because of a mendable defect? Who bothers about an army truck with engine trouble when it is vital to get supplies to the front? It goes into the ditch. France was left with abandoned American army supplies scattered all over it when the Great War was done. This careless waste had its psychological effect on those who saw it and helped make it. Nor is there any idealism left in soldiering. One could at least imagine it in the clash of sword on armor, but what is idealistic about a tank? Can poetry come out of a gas mask? When war becomes a matter of retorts and test tubes, and it is fast coming to that, the last vestige of idealism will have disappeared from it. The scientist is killing war, for he is preparing to make it so horrible and loathsome that mankind is bound to sicken of it and vomit it out of its mouth—pray God, forever.

Alas! By the time the scientist has done away with war we may— I fear we shall—find that he likewise has done away with human liberty. In other days it was always possible for an oppressed people to free itself from the yoke of tyranny through an appeal to arms. That day seems to have passed. A small minority with the new artillery, with airplanes and machine guns, can now impose its will on a whole nation. Mexico, where all fundamental rights are denied to fifteen millions of unarmed people by a minority not even reaching half a million, is one of the saddest examples of that in contemporary history. Russia is another. The days of the Arnold Winkelrieds and the George Washingtons have passed, perhaps forever; and with them will pass the songs that lifted tribes into nations and slaves into freemen. The spirit of liberty, warmed into life and action by music, could defend a heritage of freedom in the old days until the plowshares could be beaten into swords. Plowshares cannot be beaten into machine guns. The "Pibroch of Donal Dhu" has given place to the ghastly rat-tat-tat of scientific death-making. Even the Star Spangled Banner will wave only as long as the laboratories decide to keep its eagle-topped staff higher than the smokestack.

✑§ 10 §✑

POST-BELLUM

LIFE insurance one part and war one part failed as a prescription for finishing a church. The second ingredient never effervesced into the foam of battle. When I returned to my parish it was to plan some surer way to secure enough money for plaster, paint, and pews. By this time I had become as accustomed to the unusual as a Californian, and had a Micawber-like confidence that something would turn up. It did. I discovered a strange thing: there were funny people who actually would pay me for talking to them. I liked so much to talk to people, and so often was lonesome, that, had I the money, I think there were days when I should have been glad to pay them to listen to me. The idea of making money by such a form of simple enjoyment as lecturing appealed as a new and wonderful Yankee notion.

I learned about Lyceum lecturing through a gentleman from the neighboring city of Flint, Charles Maines. He was present when I gave a talk on the Spanish War to the people of my mission in Davison and came backstage to find out if I cared to polish up and expand the chat into a regular lecture. He thought, the good man, that a few audiences might be found willing to give me as much as fifteen or twenty dollars to hear it. In fact he was quite sure about that, for he was himself the manager of a lecture bureau. For a while I thought that Mr. Maines was romancing, but soon found that he really meant what he said. Had he put his offer to music it could not have sounded better to a man naturally talkative, who had a church to finish, and had just failed to collect on a life insurance policy destined to that good end. I snapped up the offer of Mr. Maines, after, of course, telling the Bishop about it and securing the help I needed for the parish during my wanderings over the small towns of the state. The winter following, that was the winter of 1899, I ventured into other states. In 1900 still others were included in my travels. I made money, not much, but enough to save me from the necessity of begging all the time for what was needed to finish the church. Each succeeding year my fee went up a little higher. What the money actually meant to me was the assurance of a living while all the revenues of the parish were being used for building.

When Gladstone was asked by a visitor to England the best way to see London, his answer was, "From the top of a bus, sir—from the top of a bus." Should a visitor to the United States of America have asked me, before the days of movies, the very best way to see the whole nation, I should unhesitatingly have answered: "Become a lecturer, sir—a Lyceum lecturer." But I could not have promised him even the chill comfort of the top of a London bus.

Amongst the strange ways by which people made a living in the Nineties, I am sure the strangest was by giving Lyceum lectures. My experience with what turned out to be a form of torture covered the period between 1899 and 1906. It was not so bad in 1899 because I was then beginning with only a few "dates." It was not so bad in 1906 because I was then easing out. But the intervening years planted my memory plentifully with seeds of misery: missed trains, long buggy rides in the mud of the worst of roads, hotels of horror, "opry houses" over stores, small boys throwing peanut shells, sparking youth eating popcorn in the front row, old ladies who looked disapproval at the first Catholic priest they had ever seen while wondering how he concealed his horns so cleverly, committees searching for an excuse to defer payment, storms to prevent reaching the next "date" on time, being "entertained" by a family of six to save expense for the lecture committee, blizzards in the Dakotas, snows and stalled trains in the Adirondacks, catching colds and keeping at work in spite of them. There's more, but isn't that enough?

Nevertheless, it was not all misery. I saw the country as no one in any other business could have seen it. A traveling salesman has only a limited territory to cover. My territory was the whole nation. An actor could not very well go to towns that had no theaters. I could deliver my stock-in-trade in a cross roads "meetin' house,"

a little red schoolhouse, or even a vacant shop. In the summer the
Chautauqua circuits offered tents, and on the grounds camped an
audience that even pelting rain could not keep away; but when
that rain rattled down on the canvas and started all the babies in a
determined effort also to be heard, it was no fun for the lecturer.
Loud-speakers had not then been invented, but babies had, and
they were plenty and flourishing in the Nineties. They still flourish
but not in such plenty.

It was a rare event to meet a fellow-lecturer, but not rare to hear
what people thought of him. Such criticisms were usually held over
until the "next number" came along. That system served to keep
down the conceit and the fees of "talent" wise enough to guess
that they might be on the gridiron themselves a month later. If
Bob La Follette or William Jennings Bryan could have heard what
I heard about them they would either have reduced their fees or
their good opinion of themselves.

Why did the lecturers stick so persistently to the road? Most of
them could have made a living in less painful ways. American
scenery is beautiful in spots and at certain seasons, but a Lyceum
lecturer saw the glory of the mountains only when they were
covered with snow, and the fields when it was slushy underfoot.
His sight of the prairies in the Chautauqua season was when the
August sun had burned them brown, but he saw them, and that
was something. He likewise saw people, people the like of whom
he had never known, people who could be sorted and pigeonholed
by localities. The New Englander, who had started this Lyceum
lecture idea, was quite unlike the rural New Yorker, and nothing
at all like the Nebraskan or the Kentuckian. These in turn differed
from the people who came to lectures in the far South. When I
lectured in Oklahoma I feared for my silk hat. Oklahomans at that
time could stand only "so much," while Kansas tested oratory by
the Jerry Simpson sample. One had to be flowery and scriptural in
the vast kingdom of Bryan.

The early Lyceum as New England founded it had been a serious
affair. Lectures were all of it then. Later came bell ringers, con-
cert troupers, magicians, whistlers, bands, and dancers. Redpath
was the great bureau for courses; Major Pond the first to handle
celebrities for single dates. I think it was Pond who started the

plague of overseas poet and novelist speakers in America. They were good enough except for the fact that few of them could talk. They are still coming over, by the way, and the new generation of them is no notable improvement on the old. The regular "talent" presented by the bureaus in my day might be called professional. They knew how to hold an audience, for long experience had told them what a Lyceum crowd wanted. The concoction usually consisted of a catchy title, a little information, a few flights of oratory, many witticisms, a bit of preaching, and at least three funny stories which need not of necessity be new. The most typical of the Lyceum lecturers I heard was Robert McIntyre, who later became a Methodist bishop but did not even then stop lecturing. His specialty was word painting, which he did superbly. Dr. Quayle and Dr. Hughes also talked themselves up that high in Methodism. A lawyer named George Wendling could hold any audience, even though he never cracked a joke; he read from a manuscript, and his specialty was history. DeWitt Miller was a collector whose lecturing travels brought him into every secondhand bookshop in America. I used to meet him occasionally at railway junction points. He always carried a number of valises full of books and had stacks of them strapped together on the seat beside him, his latest acquisitions. Lou Beauchamp kept his audience in good humor the better to preach to them. The most talked-of Lyceum lecture was Russell Conwell's "Acres of Diamonds." This lecture founded Temple University in Philadelphia. Thomas Dixon waded through the Northern snow and slush he hated into the permanent job of a successful story writer. The funniest lecturer I ever heard was Sam Jones. His drawl alone made an old joke new. He died as he lived—on a train.

There were a few priests on the platform. Perhaps the best as a speaker was the late Father Joseph Nugent of Des Moines. He was an exception in that, like Wendling, he had no humor to offer. Yet he could make any audience, city or rural, large or small, educated or ordinary, want him to continue. He always stopped too soon for his hearers. Though he served up philosophy and theology to all, he would nevertheless be asked to return with more. Nugent was an impressive figure on the platform, in size, in gravity, in speech. His voice was rich and expressive. He was a millionaire in homely metaphors. A listener was kept in constant expectation of a burst of oratory from him that would raise the roof, but it never came. His best and most popular subject was "The Philosophy of Civilization"; but even such a title never frightened away anyone who had once heard him. Nugent had a great reputation all over the Middle West.

Father Lawrence Vaughan became for a few years the most popular of all Lyceum lecturers, a greater drawing card than even Bryan. He had been an actor before entering the seminary, and as a lecturer continued to be an excellent one. There was little meat in his talks, but that little was made attractive by being presented with the best sauce of the stage. Vaughan made a great deal of money on the platform and spent it freely on charity and good works. He died at the height of his popularity. Off the platform he was a quiet and a rather humble man. On the platform he knew his business and was quite the opposite. His specialty was Shakespeare who, if he had heard himself interpreted in the Vaughanesque way, would have been surprised at least.

Vaughan's former pastor, Father Dunne of Eau Claire, Wisconsin, used to step on and off the platform. He had a good Wisconsin reputation, but I think that he disliked the work. Father Cleary of Minneapolis was often in demand, and answered with temperance addresses, when he could spare the time. But, one by one the priest-lecturers left the Lyceum. In truth the Lyceum was leaving them. The old-time lecture was in decay. Soon there was only a shred of its garments left. But before it began the decline it did the West, especially, the favor of showing thousands of people that a priest did not really conceal horns under his hair or use shoes to cover cloven hoofs.

The history of the American Lyceum movement tells a rather sad and humiliating story. At the beginning it was the answer to a call on the best minds of the country for an extension of their educational influence into the smaller cities, the towns, and the rural villages. So thoroughly educational were the lecture courses then that philanthropists encouraged them by gifts; some, like Peabody in New England, even by foundations. I am quite sure that the courses founded by Peabody still exist. In the early years of the Lyceum the lecture course committees had to do real fishing to

secure their "talent." The fees were not high, but the lecturers cared
not over much for remuneration. They felt like educators, for they
were doing educators' work. The best people of each small community were lecture course patrons. There was nothing political
about the courses then, and little business side to the booking.
That first act, however, was not much more than a prologue. Business stepped in and was welcomed by committees glad to have
a bureau take the major part of the work of securing "talent" off
their hands. Organization on business lines did not at first hurt
the movement. Lecture bureaus and their branches spread all
over the country, and the West outstripped the East in the number
of them. A demand for new "talent" was quickly answered. Bureau managers became ambitious. Why not provide entertainment
as well as information? The lecture was all very well and good, but
a little music, a laugh now and then, or a specialty not often seen
in villages, would increase profits and make the courses attractive
to a larger number of people. Lecture bureau management became
a recognized line of business. The modest circulars of the "talent"
blossomed out into triumphs of the advertising and printing arts.
In a lecture course of six numbers, costing around six hundred
dollars, an orchestra or band got three hundred, a noted political
speaker one hundred and fifty. The rest might be divided unequally
between a reader and two lecturers who paid the managers twenty
per cent of their fees, as well as their own traveling and hotel expenses. The next step in organization followed quite naturally.
The bureaus bought "time" in blocks of a week, a month, or a
whole season. The "talent" had more work but less money for
each "date." Savings were effected by making the "jumps" smaller
and cutting out the vacant date problem. On the whole the
"talent" liked it; but more and more the lecture was ignored or
pushed out of the picture altogether in favor of entertainment.
The Lyceum that heard Emerson and Wendell Phillips was no
more.

The saddest part of the story, however, was not the tragedy of
the discarded lecturer who had taken up the work as a profession
as honorable as that of the teacher. It was the discouraging lesson
the tragedy taught. When the lecture courses began, high schools
were not as plentiful as they now are. The lectures made up in

part, at least amongst adults, for the lack of them, by helping those who had only a little advanced schooling. The patrons often saw and listened to men and women whose very presence in their communities brought with them an atmosphere of culture and refinement. One naturally would say that the increase of high schools and their products should have had the effect of raising the standards of the lectures and the courses. Nothing of the kind happened. The more schools and schooling, the lighter became the lectures. When the movies arrived audiences were ready for them. They had prepared for mediocrity by the steady deterioration of the Lyceum from an educational movement to a show enterprise.

Worse than all was the sad fact that the story of this once educational movement is only a scene in a tragedy much more general. Schools are everywhere now. Standards have been worked out for them, accepted, and put into operation. More and more in the way of training and equipment is being demanded of teachers. High schools are much commoner in the small towns than were simple grade schools fifty years ago. There are libraries at nearly every door. But our taste for "the true, the beautiful, and the good" has not been bettered. People no longer seem hungry for the improvement of mind and heart. Every little village can see "She Done Him Wrong," but not even those with a high-school that possesses a hundred-thousand-dollar auditorium over a tiled swimming pool want to hear anything about "The Philosophy of Civilization."

Nevertheless, the Lyceum worked out for me as a benefit never expected, for not only did it give me a job that finished my beloved church, but, by sending me out amongst the scattered people and into the churchless places, gave me also the inspiration for a dream that became the central interest in my life. The dream took form and being on the 18th day of October, 1905, after a year of planning and preparation. For twenty years it was almost my only thought. Though the story of it was set down and told in another book, I am quite certain that its name and deeds will run like golden threads through the warp and woof of all the rest of this one.

11

THE DREAM

IN CATHOLIC clerical life the hour of passing from youth to age depends more on geographical location than on advancing years. While a priest remains a curate, or assistant, he is young. When, with a smile of satisfaction, he reads the bishop's letter appointing him to a pastorate, he has in his hands an official diploma of admission into the academy of venerables. In, say, Boston, Chicago, or New York, a sacerdotal youth may have white hairs. In Oklahoma he may officially become a venerable without the slightest change in their color. In the Detroit of my day a young priest was fortunate, even blessed, if he did not step from recruit to veteran standing in a month.

This situation was, however, recognized even then as unusual, and allowance was made for it, but the allowance produced a new difficulty. When was a pastor obviously too young to be considered out of his teeth-cutting period? It was a real difficulty and hard to solve, but there was a sort of common understanding that, when admittedly old pastors began to listen to a junior with some slight show of respect for his opinions, the end of the first period was in sight for him. The Academy might then be assumed to be only a short way ahead. But no one ever decided how long the short way should be. For me it came to a sudden end when I was already thirteen years a pastor.

Now a young priest is always very, very young to his presumed elders and is supposed to know it, which means that he is expected to do his work as well as his inexperience will permit and not occupy his mind overmuch with what is obviously none of his business. He may, of course, dream of other things, but telling his dream in the presence of his seniors is considered by them something akin to the indiscretion of Joseph telling his to his brethren. What I mean is that the adage "children should be seen and not heard" is in high favor with the venerables. It used to be in particularly high favor with bishops. It was in super-particularly high favor with mine. But out of the lecturing episode of my clerical youth came a dream that somehow I could not help telling. My peaceful war experience had not made me a hero, but I claim a hero's crown for telling that dream; yes, and another for having had the audacity to write and publish it.

The dream? It had been growing on me from the day when I read a letter of appeal for the Society for the Propagation of the Faith sent out by Abbé Magnien; the same whose tribute to Dr. Reilly I quoted a short way back. I was then too poor to help but hopeful enough to promise that some day I should. I felt as I read the Abbé's circular that the whole Church in America ought to help. It was not gratitude for what the great Society had done for the Church of America that moved me, but the thought that we had a duty to vindicate our Catholicity in missionary action within and even beyond our borders. There was for me an effective lecture on that particular mark of the Church in the appeal of the Grand Old Man of Baltimore.

Then came travel and lecturing. I saw America, not the America of the great cities but the real America which feeds and sustains the other—the America of the small towns, villages, and countryside. In the West and South I ran into many small groups of Catholics threatened with being swallowed up by indifference, pastorless people as well as churchless people. And the conviction came to me that our leaders had missed something great because they had been overwhelmed by numbers pouring out of ships into the cities. We had, I thought, been forced to neglect the minority that had gone to the little places. But these were the hope of the cities of the future, the fathers and mothers of the next and succeeding generations of city dwellers. Could we afford to lose them? I was sure we could not.

There is something substantial behind every dream no matter how fantasy may distort it. Dreams are the plays of the subconscious memory. The substantial behind mine was the Catholicity of the Church. So deep-rooted became my desire to help the rural places that I felt no discouragement would prevent me from planting a seed in soil I hoped would be fertile enough to give it strength and growth.

There came to Trinity Rectory one evening when I was there a stern, dignified, and aloof-appearing man whose name has already been mentioned. He was John Hennessy, Bishop of Wichita. His bearing did not invite confidences—even conversation for that matter. But young men with dreams are not afraid. I talked of mine in his presence. He showed interest. To the Dean's astonishment he even invited me to pay him a visit if my lecturing brought me near Wichita. I thanked him for the invitation without determining to accept it. I was afraid to accept it. But when I did actually find myself near Wichita I recalled it and paid him a visit. He questioned me closely about the thing that was interesting me. I was launched into the subject of home missions before I knew it, because I was soon aware of the fact that I had a sympathetic listener. To my surprise the Bishop took up the discussion when and where I left off and suggested that I should make an effort to found a Society dedicated to the work.

"What we need first of all," he said, "is financial help to put up chapels for small groups scattered here and there all over the West. Someone like you must make a study of the situation and begin the work."

When I suggested that I was too unimportant a person to do more than make the study, he answered, "For some good purpose of Divine Providence you have been forced out to see conditions from one end of the country to the other. Learn all you can about home mission societies elsewhere and write on the subject. That is the way to begin."

I did make the study but remained doubtful that I was indicated as the founder of such a work. Then something else happened, and again in Kansas. I visited Ellsworth to lecture for the high school of the town and there met the pastor, Father Arthur Luckey. What happened to me in Ellsworth was read by thousands when the appeal I felt forced to write was published in the *Ecclesiastical Review* of Philadelphia and reprinted many times in pamphlet form. For years after the Church Extension was founded that appeal was known as the "Little Shanty Story" because it began:

"I know a little 'shanty' in the West, patched and desolate, through whose creaks and cracks the blizzard moans and chills, cellarless, stairless, and dreary. Built on low prairie land, the excuse for a garden about it floods with water when the rains come, so that the tumbling old fence, with its network of weeds, falling, fails to hide the heart-breaking desolation. The 'shanty' has three rooms; the first a combination of office, library, and bedroom. In one corner is a folding bed; in another a desk; in another, curtained off with cheap print, is an improvised wardrobe. Against a wall stands a poor bookcase, while a few chairs are scattered about. The next room is also a combination, for eating and sleeping. A table is near the wall, a bed in the corner, and close by are a washstand and a few chairs. Back of all is the third room, kitchen, coal bin, utility, and—what not.

"Whose shanty is it? Who lives here?

"A pioneer on the vast plains, advance guard of civilization, trying in a sod hut to compromise between the longings within him and the wilderness that overwhelms by its lonely savagery without?

"No!

"The hut of a negro huddled away on the outskirts of a great city?

"No!

"A squatter on the railroad right-of-way?

"No!

"It is the rectory of a Catholic parish in a town of two thousand inhabitants, in a well-settled state of the Union. And today it is the home of an educated, cultured gentleman, a priest, who has left his wordly chances behind him—for this!

"Across the street stands a shaky, once white building surmounted by a cross, the only sign of its high and holy mission. Outside it is as ugly as the gargoyles of Notre Dame, without the artistic beauty that surrounds them, to make it all magnificent by contrast. The steps shake as you mount them. The floor trembles at your tread. The rough, unsightly pews are the acme of discomfort, and a house painter's desecrating brush has touched the altar and the Holy of Holies. No vestry. The confessional is literally a box. The vestments are few and tattered. Not a footstep sounds from fortnight to fortnight across the threshold of the Hidden God but His priest's, as alone he comes daily to offer up the mighty redeeming Sacrifice, or steals before the altar, to watch and pray, and perchance—who could blame him?—to sob down his discouragement before this tawdry throne of his Master.

"Why alone?

"Because his people do not care. The decades of neglect, when neglect was the only thing possible, have left the scattered few unmindful. Do not think, gentle reader, that I am drawing with rough charcoal and tinting with pigments from my imagination. I am drawing with a well-tempered pen, and using the colors of fact.

"One priest died in this place a short year before this priest came, died of a fever bred by malarial surroundings, died while his sister was speeding from cultured Boston to share his exile, only to find that she had passed her brother's body on his last journey home. Other priests followed; none of them stayed long enough to die except this one. He will stay. The timid, shrinking eye fights to master the determined expression of a Western mouth and jaw, and they win. He is working, and working hard, against the odds of indifference and irreligion, working to save for the children the inestimable gift of Faith which the parents have forgotten how to appreciate. Yes, he will win as surely as God reigns and His grace lives."

That Little Shanty Story founded The Catholic Church Extension Society both in the United States and Canada because it played a sympathy if not a symphony on the heartstrings of many people. In the spring of 1905 nothing was wanting for the founding of the society but a distinguished sponsor, definitely the archbishop of one of the large metropolitan sees of the United States. I wanted to go out searching for one but had no money to pay my way around. To my rescue came a group of the Knights of Columbus in Michigan and Ohio. They gave me a one hour job and paid well for it. I was invited to preach on my hobby at their summer outing at Cedar Point, Ohio, with the collection as recompense. That collection netted me about two hundred dollars. I could travel as far as that sum would carry me.

Naturally New York was my first objective. I wanted Archbishop Farley to be the honorary head of the society. His refusal was kindly expressed but clearly definite. I tried Archbishop Ryan of Philadelphia. His refusal, too, was kind and to it he added the saving bit of humor that was expected of the Episcopal wit of the day. But it too was definite. Archbishop Bourgade of Santa Fe was willing to help but did not think himself important enough to lead. Archbishop Williams of Boston was growing old. I knew that he would not consider adding burdens to the great one he already was carrying. I felt the same about Cardinal Gibbons. While I was hesitating about approaching Archbishop Ireland of St. Paul I learned that the "Little Shanty Story" had met with the approbation of Archbishop Quigley of Chicago. Why not Chicago? It was the very gateway to the whole home mission field. At the suggestion of Archbishop Bourgade I put all my hopes on Chicago.

It was at the University of Notre Dame that I met Archbishop Quigley for the first time. He was seated on a rear veranda of the presbytery chatting with President Morrissey and Dr. Zahm, the scientist, when I was presented by the future president, Dr. Cavanaugh. The sun was setting, but for yet a little while I had a chance to study the face of the Archbishop. It was a good face to look at because it seemed to be set in quiet repose. One had the feeling that its owner was a tranquil man who might let his heart's influence count. He had keen measuring eyes, both dark and deep; one did not know how deep they might be. His movements were slow and purposeful. His hand went out toward an ash tray now and then, for when I arrived he was enjoying an after-dinner cigar, but they did not move at all when he spoke. He was a good listener, like a judge hearing a case and anxious to follow and check the points of law involved in it, or an Oxford examiner intent on finding out from the way the student handles himself, rather than from a display of technical learning, if he really merits the honors he seeks. I got the impression that my arguments would count with the Archbishop much less than my personality. That worried me, for my confidence was all in the arguments. Truth was that the Archbishop knew them as well as I did, since for years he had had the same thought on the subject which in me was only developing. But what I had seen in my travels around the West and South interested him, and it was plain that he loved a story with a lesson to end it. The strong impression I got from watching and hearing him was that he was a man of wide vision. His title and dignity meant little, but his object, and the means to attain it, meant everything. He was not one from whom to expect such trifles as personal favors, and certainly not one who would ever expect to receive any; a man who could not be flattered or moved by such things. I must admit that he frightened me. But I knew that here was a personality and a protector well worth winning. He proved easy to win, not because I had winning ways but because he himself had been over the ground. When the light faded and a bell called him to the chapel for the opening of the retreat he was there to attend, his mind was made up and he said so. I had found my protector and knew that if I lost him later it would not be because he failed to stick but because I failed to make good.

All my dealings with Archbishop Quigley, up to his last illness, confirmed my first impressions. I had his confidence in one matter only, the special business he had taken up to do with me. In that I had it to the full. In all the other things which pertained to his office I was an outsider. I spent at least one evening a week alone with him. Business always came first in these visits. He would not even offer me a cigar until I had said "that's all" to the business part of the discussion. Then he would rise from his chair, walk over to a humidor on a side table, hand me a cigar and say, "Very well. We'll have a smoke now."

My evenings with Archbishop Quigley are now very happy memories. I think of him as a friend who gave nothing to me personally but whose friendship was all the better because it included me in something greater. James Edward Quigley was the finest, the strongest, and the noblest influence in my life save that of the stern father who resembled him in so many ways and the saintly mother who contributed to my life what none but mothers can give.

The Catholic Church Extension Society was founded in Archbishop Quigley's house in Chicago on the 18th of October, 1905. I was given mountains to climb. I knew well what was on the other side of them but I never expected to see it. Yet I think that, through a narrow pass high up on the most desolate part of one of them, perhaps I caught a glimpse of it. Cryptic? No! I am only thinking of the advance guard of a new generation of priests, imitating the poor man of Assisi in a modern world; or, if you will, imitating the Apostle to the Gentiles in his own good way—priests of the highways and hedges.

It was, however, one thing to have a plan in mind or on paper and quite another to put it into active operation. At a preliminary meeting in Chicago I had secured a few men to advise with, and, if success came later, to become directors of the work. But I knew that in the beginning both burden and responsibility would be mine and mine alone. I was ready to face the fact that if failure did result, it would find me stripped of all defense except the melancholy excuse of good intentions. The thing to do was to imitate Cortez and destroy my ships. I made ready to do it. But before I did, I took a rapid glance over my defenses against possible, perhaps even probable, failure.

My first and greatest defense was the cause itself. I might be condemned for unskillful planning or over-confident generalship, but no one to whom I intended to appeal could logically condemn the objective. That much was certain.

My second defense was the interest of Archbishop Quigley, as well as his fine reputation for saneness of outlook and sterling good sense. No one ever thought of *him* as a dreamer. But, on the other hand, I had in him picked a future superior, and I could look back uneasily over incidents which showed a certain lack of skill in dealing with superiors. There was, I felt, something in my character or personality that made such relations all the more difficult because there was nothing outwardly wanting in them of absolute correctness. I felt that to superiors I was a sort of problem, too obviously real to be cast aside but just as obviously too complicated to solve. Knowledge of the handicap first dawned upon me in the Army. My colonel told me one day that General Coppinger did not like me. "It's about that new chaplains' uniform," he said. "The general thinks you were the one responsible for its adoption."

"But I was not," I answered, a bit warmly. "I was not even one of the committee that called on General Miles to ask for it."

"Yes, I know that," he said. "But you were the first chaplain the general saw wearing it, and when he said that he didn't like it you defended it. Yesterday he came over here for Mass and saw you wearing it before you put on your cassock."

"Of course I was wearing it," I answered. "It's regulation. Of course I defended it. It's right. But I was not responsible for its adoption. Why is it that I always seem to get in bad with some people?"

"You don't get in bad with me," the colonel consoled, "but I'm not a general. Better keep away from generals."

I was a bit blue over the matter. "I wonder what's really wrong with me?" I said, "I like and admire General Coppinger."

"Ever see a king snake?" the colonel asked.

"No. Why?"

"Nothing. I was just thinking about them. They look like ugly customers to folks who don't know them. But there are always a few who do know and who let them go ahead quietly attending to their business of exterminating rats and rattlers. Changing old customs and getting down to work hard at it is always a business of exterminating something—maybe only a prejudice. By the way, the general's coming over to dine at our mess tomorrow. What are you going to wear?"

"This uniform," I answered promptly.

"I thought so." He shook his head. "Well, I guess that's about what you ought to do. Better right than President, eh? But it ain't always comfortable, this business of being right. So long!"

Suppose Archbishop Quigley turned out to be just another general? I could take the chance safely enough at the beginning, but what might happen later? I decided that I had to take all the chances, and was not sorry later that I did. The Archbishop turned out to be the happy exception to prove an unhappy rule because he was an almost perfect imitation of the Church herself, careful neither to give too much nor to inquire too little, but when inquiry was over and done with, and the gift made, to follow them both with the unquestioning confidence that awakens loyalty and stimulates courage. Just the same I knew that I had in myself a complicated personal problem. I was afraid of myself, afraid that I might fail to win confidence, afraid of my impetuous nature, afraid of the test that had come of my ability to make good. I knew that I had to be a founder, an executive, an editor, an advertiser, a diplomat, all in one. My friends warned me. They were a discouraging lot. I almost blew out the torch I had lighted to destroy my ships. But the dream returned, stood between my friends and me, and blotted them out with all their fears and all their misgivings. This thing was God's, not mine. If He wanted a fool or a child to do it, that was His business. He had His way of picking poor material and working it over to suit His purposes. I was quite sure that I was poor material, but why worry? The skeleton of a failure often marks the beginning of the right trail.

"I can't understand you priests," said a business friend as he shook hands in farewell when I was leaving Lapeer for Chicago. "Here you are abandoning your new church and your fine new home almost the day after you got into them, to start all over again in a Chicago flat with nothing but a dream and not much of a dream at that."

A dream? The man did not know the compelling force and persistent glory of a dream. While I am now, as a bishop, committed to a dislike for dreamers, only yesterday a mother, my own sister, pouring out of her artist soul a prayer of resignation over her afflicted son, brought tears acknowledging the truth and power of a dream from my eyes. She called her poem, "Pilgrim of Shadows."

> "As petals fold the fragrance of a rose
> Till burgeoning, so did he hold the Dream
> Within his heart; and never garden close
> Held bud of sweeter promise. It would seem
> That all his days were fashioned to attain
> One gracious goal: for this his cloistered years,
> His exile, and his deep bewildered pain
> In lonely, seeking hours; perhaps his tears,
> Glimpsing the glory he had failed to win.
> And dare we say he failed, whose chalice waits
> The touch of priestly fingers? Nay, within
> His soul, unstained, the vision compensates;
> Always for him pale altar candles gleam;
> Always he keeps inviolate—the Dream."

Had I been leaving for a promotion few would have thought or expressed any wonderment. But the business that has to wait for eternity to pay its dividend is another matter. Those who follow the red-gold lure of the Cross are mysterious, even to some who ought to understand.

I had a friend in Detroit, Edward H. Doyle, who would have his joke. He was one of those who thought I was risking too much by the burning of my ships.

"Did you ever hear the definition for a promoter made by my unusual friend, Marcus Pollasky?" he asked when I called at his office in the Majestic Building to say good-by.

"Never. What is it?"

"He was on the witness stand in a court case. The examining lawyer asked his name and his business. Marcus gave his name and said that his business was that of a promoter."

"What is your definition of a promoter, Mr. Pollasky?"

"A promoter? Why, a promoter is a man who has nothing to sell and who sells it to a man who doesn't want to buy it."

I saw the point and tried to explain what my kind of promoter was and what he had to sell. My friend listened politely for awhile. Really I was only trying to give him information, not to "sell him" anything. "That will do. That will do," he interrupted. "Before you go you ought to meet my friend Marcus. He was right. But I'll buy it."

Buy it expensively he did. In him I landed my first big fish. It weighed ten thousand dollars.

The society stayed only one year in Lapeer. Then it was moved to Chicago and I had to go with it. The Bishop of Detroit granted me the usual *Exeat* transferring me to the archdiocese of Chicago. I must admit that he seemed to take his loss in a spirit of resignation.

12

CHICAGO

THE Chicago of 1906 was not the Chicago of today. For one thing it was far from being as beautiful. When I looked out over the lake front I could think of an old story told by one of my Lyceum friends. "Why do you place the good apples on the top of your basket, Uncle, while you have the scrawny ones on the bottom?" was asked of an old negro fruit seller. "Fo' de same reason, sar, that de front of your house is marble and de back mos'ly ash barrel, sar." But Chicago was different; the ash barrels were in the front yard. But the possibilities were not to be hidden. That wonderful thirty-mile shore front was even then pleading to be changed into what it is today, the longest line of civic beauty in the whole world.

I knew little about the city and few of its citizens when I came to live there. True, I had seen something of Chicago during the first World's Fair, but only that part immediately surrounding Jackson Park. One look at it was enough. The fair was a ruby set in a tin ring. Later, on my lecture tours, quite often I had to stay overnight in the city. That, however, gave me sight of nothing more than the Great Northern Hotel, the railway stations, and old St. Mary's. I had taken up a few collections for the society in Chicago churches while still living in Lapeer and had met their pastors, but I scarcely knew Chicago's clergy. Even after I came to live there it was a long time before I knew them. Surrounded by millions I was almost as lonesome as I had been during that year of blessing spent in the house of Bishop Rogers. Naturally, Chicago did not stir herself to offer me any sort of welcome. Richmond Dean, general manager of the Pullman Company, the first lay friend I met after the decision to come to Chicago, arranged for an office and paid the year's rent of it to help me to a start. I needed that kind of start pretty badly. There was little money in the treasury.

It was one of Chicago's youngest priests who, I think, really broke the ice of reserve and permitted me to move the ship around a little. A red-headed lump of good will he was when, without warning, he entered my office one day and introduced himself as the William David O'Brien who had been one of the first to answer an appeal for the cause with ten dollars. He dropped in, he said, to leave another ten and tell me that, so far as he was concerned at least, I had his sympathy. That visit was for him the beginning of a career which no Chicago curate at the time would have dared anticipate. Father O'Brien came again a few months later to the office, and this time he stayed. He likewise became in turn diocesan director, general secretary, vice-president, president, and well—he now signs after his name Bishop of Calinda and Auxiliary of Chicago. His start was an unexpected glimpse of the society's name on the side of the door at 20 Adams Street, a generous thought, and the determination to follow an impulse. It's a way life has of opening up the right gate.

Father O'Brien's first attempt to interest the clergy of Chicago was his first battle—and he lost it. He presented himself before one of the hard-headed old clerical tyrants of the day, showed him a letter of introduction from the Archbishop, and humbly asked permission to place the cause of home missions before his congregation. The old man read the letter with great deliberation, looked a severe rebuke at the timid petitioner, folded the sheet, put it back in its envelope, returned it, and said, "Go back to your archbishop, sir, and tell him—No!" Father O'Brien did not go back to his archbishop with that masterpiece of laconic impudence. He came to me.

That old pastor was a nearly perfect picture of Chicago, civil— or uncivil?—and religious, at the time. It was new, uncouth, unmannerly, deeply resentful of all the rest of the world because all the rest of the world was abusing it. But Chicago had its saving graces. William R. Stead had made a mockery of its morals in his book *If Christ Came to Chicago*. But they were no worse than the morals of his own London, and far more superficial. Chicago had the frankness, even against itself, of an overgrown country boy too busy planting potatoes to give anyone a civil answer, too anxious to get the job done to listen to the school bell. "Dear, dirty Chicago," the first Bishop of Rockford called it when it showered him with blessings and gifts as he was departing for his new diocese. He described it well. It was dirty, but just as dear to those who knew it as a healthy boy with a guilty conscience and a smudged face is to a father looking for the disciplinary rod, which, though a pledge of pain, is also one of anxious affection. Catholic Chicago was even then wondering why its new archbishop kept one hand behind his back and one eye on the door leading to the woodshed. The apostolic chastener was not to live to see the boy grow into splendid manhood. But he had a successor who did, even before the woodshed days were over and done with. I do not believe that there is in all the world today a more generous and kindly body of people than those of Chicago.

What a timely opportunity I have here to say something that ought to be said, that must be said, somewhere in this book. I know that it will have readers other than Catholics; and some of them are sure to bring to its perusal certain age-old, inherited misunderstandings. They may wonder, for example, how a priest could dare do what that really good old fellow did with his archbishop's letter. They may wonder more when they read on and learn of, to them, still stranger happenings. They have been taught to think of the Catholic Church as an excellent model for the making of dictators; as an institution which rules with a rod of iron; as a government admitting no free speech, no free action, no discussion of any kind. They are simply mistaken. Nowhere on earth is there so much real liberty of discussion, of speech, of independent action, as is found in the Catholic Church on the matters which concern her human side. No institution relies more on study and discussion, dispute if you will, to prove the wisdom or unwisdom of what it is proposed she should do. On the divine side, which guards the deposit of the Faith confided to her, she is stern and changeless, because Christ's teachings are stern and changeless. There she has all the holy intolerance of truth. But she knows she is dealing with man, fallen man, and that she cannot escape his weaknesses. She ought to know him. Has he not sat even on her seats of the mighty? Does he not preach her Gospel, offer her Sacrifice, dispense her Sacraments? She treats him as that kind of man, whether he be pope, cardinal, bishop, priest, layman, monk, nun, king, subject, scholar, ignoramus, rich, pauper, saint or sinner. For all there is one law, one road to salvation, one life of righteousness. But she did not censure Dante for placing popes in hell, though she knew that one of those he so placed, Celestine, she herself was likely to canonize and did. She could see behind the anger of the Florentine poet-politician, likewise theologian, the eternal truth that a man might be a pope and yet lose his soul. Her canon law is the simplest of all codes, her legal procedure the fairest and clearest of all procedures in dealing with evidence. She has a government that tries hard to avoid too much governing. She is merciful in dealing with human weaknesses, while stern in dealing with the pride of intellect which paves the way to . error. Her every act is intelligible when once her principles are understood, and they are plain enough and logical enough for even the most ignorant to grasp the essentials of them.

I beg my readers not to be surprised then when they look with me over my sea of troubles, nor wonder why I was not saved from them. Perhaps the worst that could have happened to me would have been a quick triumph. Never yet has the lasting thing been spared its primary testing. Grasp the distinction between the divine and the human side of the Church, manifest even in the Apostles selected by Christ, and you have the explanation of seeming mysteries in the history of the dealings of that Church with men. Her servants may sometimes seem unjust and unreasonable. Quite often they are. Some of them were, I thought, unjust and unreasonable in dealing with me. But I understand now and I understood then.

Thoughtless and unsuspecting, I myself invited the first open conflict, giving the doubters the tremendous advantage of appearing to oppose only an individual. They were quick to take advantage, especially so because everything about the movement seemed to depend entirely on the one who had left himself open to attack.

On the morning of November 15th, 1908, at the call of the society, the First American Catholic Missionary Congress opened in Chicago. It was planned to give wide expression to the full meaning of the movement. It was not therefore simply a home missions affair. Foreign missions were allotted the place of honor on the program, and no missionary activity in America, no matter how small, was overlooked. No charge of selfishness could be made against the Congress with any hope of finding sympathy from those who read the call or even glanced over the plans. It was not diplomacy that dictated all that. It was appreciation of the fact that the objective was bigger than the work. Neither Archbishop Quigley nor I had ever dreamed of preserving the society for one day after its period of usefulness ended. But the cause of missions would not have an end as long as the world lasted. The program of the Congress then was made as wide as the world need.

The opening of the Congress in Holy Name Cathedral was an advance promise of success. The gathering was, perhaps, the most brilliant ever held under Catholic auspices up to that time in the history of North America. The Holy See had named the Papal Delegate, Archbishop Falconio, its special Legate to the Congress. Some sixty members of the hierarchy of the United States and Canada entered the cathedral that morning, with priests and laity from all over the land. Historically, it was the first really great Catholic convention in America. The sermon of Archbishop Blenk of New Orleans struck the keynote. He was one of those who understood the significance of it all. Each day's work had been planned. The closing meeting was to hear Bourke Cockran, at that time America's greatest forensic orator, as well as the late Bishop Donohue of Wheeling, the most winning speaker in the hierarchy; a lawyer as well as a prelate. No one doubted, after seeing the purple line in the procession on Sunday, that to the end there would be smooth sailing. The background was a perfect setting, the first act a triumph of promise.

That was Sunday. On Monday the second act opened in the First Regiment Armory. I heard little of it for I was here, there, and everywhere. I had to send a messenger to my office for my own address when I was reminded that I had one to deliver. I had not written it for the Congress. It was an article done before even the work of planning the Congress had started and, following habit, I had set it aside for revision; which consisted usually of correction and merciless excision. It was my way to dictate or write as I felt at the hour, put the script away and go over it later as the gardener, pruning knife in hand, goes over his hedges. This paper had not had any such attention. The address on Home Missions had been assigned to Father Michael Fallon, then of Buffalo and Provincial of the Oblate Fathers, but who died Bishop of London, Ontario. He had sent word that he could not keep his engagement. Archbishop Quigley told me not to invite another but, since I knew what was wanted, to deliver the address myself. I thought I could make the paper, cooling off in a drawer of my desk, do. Then I forgot all about it, buried as I was in management details, until the Press Committee's chairman, a former newspaper man who never failed to live up to his training, demanded "copy" in advance. Thoughtlessly I sent word to my office to give him the paper. It was in the hands of the press before the Congress opened. No reporter missed the paragraphs that could best be played up, and all played them, in spite of the fact that I tried to do some trimming as I read.

What did I say? I pitched into the seminaries and I pitched into the seminarians. The first I charged with a seeming lack of interest in the chief work of the Church, missions; the second as lacking in the missionary spirit. I hinted even at an absence of courage to face trials, hardships, and especially poverty. Not all was on the surface of the paper, but I was speaking, by voice and through the press, to men who could see below the surface. And that was not all. I paid unwelcome attention to the custom of allowing collectors from abroad to appeal in American churches for religious luxuries in Europe while so many emigrants here in America were without the religious necessities. That was an unforgivable blow at a custom approved of by patriotism. Even such devotional societies as cultivated piety but forgot sacrifice were not spared. Today little of what I charged would be true, but it was all true enough then. Every diocese was then a stranger to every other diocese. Each kept its own needs jealously before its people. We were Catholic in faith but not in corporate action. Protestantism had no unity of faith, but each sect had decided unity in its missionary activity. I did not fail to say that.

When I left the platform I was met by my old friend Bishop Hennessy, one of "The Original Nineteen" founder members of the society. "My son, my son," he wailed, "why did you make such a speech?"

"You did not like it?" I stammered.

He shook his head sadly.

"But," I urged, "it was all true and had to be said sooner or later. You know that."

"Of course, but why by you?"

"No one else would say it."

He left me without another word.

He was not the only one who left me. Some considerate critics said: "A bit imprudent," while others of them remarked: "He meant well." Now one of the most cutting things that can be said of anyone is that he meant well, and of an ecclesiastic that he was a bit imprudent. A layman could outlive that latter—a priest never. The work of the Church calls for prudence, since the whole world is eternally looking for flaws in it. That was always so. It is still so. One imprudent slip by a priest and not alone he, but all he stands for, suffers. No one could call me "a bit imprudent" and not raise a welt on my soul. The worst of it was that I had been imprudent—for the time.

Today I can jot all that down with a smile, for, as Dr. Shannon, editor of the Chicago *New World*, wrote later: "Dr. Kelley made a *faux pas* into a fashion by that speech." "Divine indiscretion" he called it when, after the passing of the years, the results could be studied. Today there are no more devoted foreign missionaries than the American. The missionary cause has its American martyrs. It was not my speech that changed things, but I hope it sparked out the first shock of realization. I can smile over my imprudence now, though the same witty editor remarked, "It almost cost Oklahoma a bishop." I suspect on good evidence that it may have saved a bishop for Oklahoma. The Papal Legate had been a missionary himself and must have sympathized with much that I said, but he was a prudent man, and prudent men as a rule are patient men. Perhaps, if my speech had the effect indicated, it was because the Lord wanted me to stay where I was till Oklahoma was ready. Besides, since I had no thought of anything but the job on hand, what I might have lost did not worry me. But other things did.

One week after the close of the Congress I was nearer to a complete physical collapse than I had ever been before or have been since. Every word of the criticisms that poured in upon me I read. It was like the torture of dripping water, and, tired out by overwork and anxiety, I was in no condition to bear it. My friends pushed me out and into a rest at Hot Springs, Arkansas. I could not stay there. My carefully built house seemed to be tumbling down like a child's stack of blocks. I came back. A single day of work and I was worse than before.

One evening, seated at a dinner I was giving to those who helped me with the Congress, a messenger arrived from Archbishop Quigley. He called me from my place and said, "His Grace wishes you to go away; not only because you need a change and the rest you will get from an ocean voyage, but because there is business to do in Rome for the Society. He will tell you about it tomorrow evening and asks you to come to his house then. But he told me to say that you must not worry any longer about your address at the Congress. What you said was what he himself would have felt justified in saying. He is allowing the criticisms to go on for a good reason. When they cease to be useful His Grace himself will, if necessary, speak out and take the responsibility for every word you uttered."

It was only from a vantage point in the after years that I saw all the reasons why Archbishop Quigley sent me to Rome. The adverse criticisms of my speech had uncovered the weaknesses of the movement. It was by far too much a private affair for one thing. It lacked the foundation of official approval by the highest authority; though that authority had given a letter of encouragement. The Archbishop realized that my speech had brought the work into the arena where it might be hurt, perhaps fatally. He wanted no such combat. I was sent to Rome for exhibition and a more complete pontifical approval for the society in the form of an Apostolic Brief of recognition. The Archbishop did not tell me all that at the time, but he did tell me enough to make me a determined petitioner. The society was scarcely old enough to merit what he wanted for it, but I was to ask for it nevertheless. Custom said that the testing period should be much longer than our little three years of activity. But we had at least a third of the American bishops on our side. We had organized in Canada. Fortifying letters were gathered, and I was almost ready to take the road to Rome. But not yet am I ready to jot down the story of that and other visits.

13

CRUCIBLE

HAD Lazarus appeared at the rich man's gate in perfumed silks he might have been invited in to dinner. When he came in cotton rags and hungry, the only welcome he got was from the dogs who licked his sores. I do not remember the name of the friendly humorist who offered me that unique form of consolation when I returned to face the storms, but never shall I forget his wisdom. The critics had been busy. I was charged with extravagance. "This?" remarked an episcopal visitor to the office, "This is not a missionary society's quarters. It is a bank." And all that because I had been putting the best foot forward and had accepted for use gifts of good carpets and furniture. The office did, I admit, appear to reflect a prosperity more apparent than real. I was collecting more criticisms than money—though the money made the criticisms bearable—very.

In the North, Archbishop Ireland was incredulous; Archbishop Keane of Dubuque not overly friendly; two influential editors decidedly against us, Father Gannon of the *True Voice* in Omaha, and Dr. Phelan of *The Western Watchman* in St. Louis. Besides, the editors of the German papers were as a rule somewhat doubtful, though their most learned and most trusted lay friend, as well as their most outspoken and conservative colleague, Dr. Arthur Preuss of *The Fortnightly Review*, was on our Board of Governors. We had to choose between him and Archbishop Keane, for Dr. Preuss was an editor of the old school who said his say when he felt called upon to do so and had been critical of Archbishop Keane as well as of Archbishop Ireland. Neither Archbishop Quigley nor I felt that the society could afford to take note of dead issues. We needed a staunch and able German-American on the board and selected

Dr. Preuss. "Time," said Archbishop Quigley, "will heal all these pin-pricks." Time, with courtesy and patience, did actually heal them, but while time was doing it the storm clouds became blacker. Neither Dr. Phelan nor Father Gannon lost any opportunities of throwing editorial javelins our way. They hurt, not only because of sensitive skin, but because, by encouraging others to do likewise, they increased the number afraid of our "innovation." Someone, I have forgotten who it was, struck a rich vein of opposition by calling attention to the fact that the Society did not publish financial reports. That was the very thing we did not want to do right at the moment; in fact the board had determined not to do it, and for an excellent reason: we were spending what our critics would be sure to say was too much money. In fact they said it, on a chance that they were guessing right. The guess was accurate enough for their purposes, but we were not spending more money than the exigencies of the case demanded. We could reach the people only through correspondence, circularizing, advertising, and travel, all of which were expensive. Salaries were reasonable enough, but post and printer took heavy toll. It could not be otherwise. It was too early to take the public into our confidence. We needed time and patience until the problem of methods could be worked out. We tried explanations, but they did not seem to explain. The whole Middle West was seeded down with suspicions, and the crops kept growing abundantly. Soon I knew that a part of the Far West was added to the "dark territory." That made little difference as far as donations were concerned, for we were expecting to give to the West rather than to receive from it.

It was Archbishop John J. Keane who dismissed us with the remark about the likeness of our office to a bank. It all looked quite too much like promotion for a man who dwelt like a saint in two rooms of his cathedral rectory, gave away all he had, and died as poor as he had lived. I used to be doubtful myself, if my advisers were not. There was Father Kelley—"Father Ed" as he was called by all Chicago, the Father Kelley of Mr. Dooley fame—who had a decided opinion on the matter. "Your business," he advised, "is the education of Catholics to give according to their means. Our rich seldom do that. Go after the thousand dollar fellow in the thousand dollar way. He knows no other." It was the late Mr. Edward Carry—afterwards president of the Pullman Company—who remarked: "A tramp can be put off with a sandwich or a nickel, but one would be ashamed to offer a sandwich or a nickel to a beggar wearing spats."

It was encouraging to hear talk like that, but there were sores that would have welcomed the kind attention of even a friendly dog under my habiliments of grandeur. I wasn't enjoying at all the consequences of being made over from a poor country pastor, glad to find three dollars and fifty cents in the Sunday offering box, into a Lazarus in a silk gabardine with an eye on the gold goblets of the rich man's table.

I mentioned my one or two evenings a week with Archbishop Quigley. After fifteen minutes or so of talk over business he got to directing the conversation into more cheerful channels; his student days at Innsbruck or Rome, vacation tramps through the Tyrol, or the interesting people he had known in his youth. I began to suspect that, while his face never changed its placid expression, inside he was laughing at me. I could see nothing to laugh at.

It occurred to me one day that I had never met the two leaders of the Western attack. All I knew of them was what their writings told me. If I were to judge Dr. Phelan by his, I should have to conclude that he was not a very pleasant person to meet unless one liked a fight for the very fun of it. His paper was gotten up in what we today would call the tabloid form, but without illustrations. Only two pages of it were much read: the two he wrote himself. No one ever missed his editorials, and few passed over the report of his last Sunday's sermon. For clerical readers, at least, the rest was just printing. Father Gannon was not so terrifying. He had a real weekly newspaper and a good one. He was a frank and outspoken writer and not, as a rule, an unjust one. I made up my mind to meet him and, in preparation for the encounter, began to ask about him from my Western visitors. All praised him highly. I sent one of my assistants, Father Edward Roe, on a Western mission with the suggestion that he stop off in Omaha and have a chat with the editor of the *True Voice*. When he sent me a report of the conversation I felt that a frank and full statement of the case in letter form might result in better understanding. It did.

Extracts from two long letters will show how effectively the oil of good nature and frankness may be used to calm troubled waters. I wrote: "All I ask is fair play. I have a hard job and I am doing it as best I can, according to the poor lights that have been given me. I have gone through, recently, a period which has left me pretty nearly a nervous wreck . . . I believe that if you visited Chicago and went through our offices with me, you would feel that what I am saying to you is absolutely true. I do not ask any favors at all for myself; not even for the work. I ask only an honest judgment upon it. The men who are working with me, Fathers Ledvina, Roe, O'Brien and Landry are square, decent, good men, and ideal priests. They are trying to do their work well. The Society is not stingy with them, but gives them an honest compensation for honest work. They are generous in returning to the work whatever they can afford. I know that one man gave, last year, more than half of what he got. I wish that we could live without being obliged to take a penny . . . I hope you will pardon this long letter; but I think the occasion warrants it and I wanted to give you the facts fully and at the length demanded by their importance."

An answer came promptly—a good answer. It wound up as follows: "Where the people are poor the priests must be content to suffer hardship and to take what they consider good enough for them. That is one of the reasons why I never believed much in the chapel car. It is liable to turn some away with the idea that the priest is 'too grand' for them. If the priest cannot be one of them— as it were—all the wealth in the country will not assist him in his work . . . Now, Father, these are some of my ideas. I appreciate your frank statement to me and I have to be equally frank with you. I have no animus whatever against Church Extension or yourself. Quite the contrary. I'm a plain spoken, rough Westerner— who couldn't be different if I tried." The Gannon opposition ended with his signature at the bottom of the last page.

I turned to the case of the old warrior in St. Louis, helped by confidence received from the Gannon treaty. But the same tactics would not work with Dr. Phelan.

"You'll never convert him," I was advised. "He has to be licked, and you can't lick him. You are right, but you permitted him to take a stand. You should have consulted him early. Once he is

in the ring he'll win or take the count. You don't dare write as
he will write. You can't afford to do it. Drop him."

I did not drop him, but found a mutual friend as a go-between.
The old lion did not roar as loud as expected, and promised to
pay me a visit in Chicago. I cannot do better than reproduce what
I wrote about that visit in 1922: "I knew he was coming, but happened to be in another part of the office building when he approached the door of the Society's suite. A moment later I came
around the corner of the corridor and saw him standing before
our door with his eyes fixed on the lettering on the transom. The
name of the Society was painted below on the door, but on the
transom glass were the words 'Fire Escape.' The Doctor did not
know me by sight, but knew that I must be one of the priests of the
Society. 'Look at that sign,' he said. 'How can a man know whose
office this is?' I pointed to the Society's name on the door.

" 'I didn't look there,' he answered. 'That other sign is too con-
spicuous: it deceives people.' Then a twinkle came into his eye.
'Maybe not, maybe not,' he went on. 'Come to think, it's quite an
appropriate sign for a Church society to have. 'Fire Escape,' eh?
I wonder if this Kelley isn't a bit of a humorist?' I assured him that
I really was, and we shook hands right under the fire escape sign.

"Dr. Phelan was one of the most genial and companionable of
men to meet, and one of the most bitter of men in print. He was
a Catholic editor of the old school—one of the McMaster type—
who believed he had a right to say what he pleased and criticize
whom he pleased. Bishop Hennessy used to refer to the *Watchman*
office as the 'American Congregation of Bishops and Regulars.'
Indeed both Bishops and Regulars had their flayings from Dr.
Phelan. Being the last of his kind, he bore the sins of the others
who had passed on and left the doughty old warrior the legacy
of their traditions. He carried the style of the pugnacious past into
a much more peaceful present, so there was no peace for him, or
anyone who offended him. He said what he wanted to say, and said
it all. His criticisms were to be feared, but much more his apologies, which were like the back kicks of a vigorous mule. He wrote
with power as well as freedom, but he presumed too much on the
understanding of his readers. So things that he understood, and
theologians understood, were not always taken at their true value.

One of his faults as a writer was that he scorned to explain what was plain to him, because he thought that it ought, therefore, to be plain to others. He did not quite see the progress that had been made since his day, and never could understand that some of it lay in the direction of a quieter life and a more submissive spirit. He loved the Church with the love of a soldier son who thought it best for her sake even to bully his brothers into doing the things that in his judgment were best for her. He left many wounds on the souls of others, by which he is remembered, but he did not keep hatreds in his heart. He was himself the humorist he suspected he had found in me. When told that he was very sick, in danger of death even, and asked if he would not have a priest come to hear his confession and give him the Last Sacraments, he responded humorously, in spite of his sufferings: 'Certainly, certainly. Safety First.'

"There! I went off on a sidetrack to talk about my dear old enemy. I am not sorry. Dr. Phelan has been too soon forgotten, for, though his pen was often dipped in vitriol, he fought the good fight before many of us young editors of today were born. He was the mentor of our fathers, and the delight of their Sunday afternoons. He helped keep the Faith in the desolate spiritual wilderness of the prairies. He put courage into many a scattered Irish family of the West when there was no soggarth or chapel to do it. They understood him, for they were fighters too. I do not think he was the less welcome in Heaven because he reached the gate with a bloody nose and a black eye."

On the way to California I stopped off to see Bishop Scanlan of Salt Lake City. I can close my eyes and see him still, but his type exists no longer. It is a trite old saying that men are moulded by their environment. Bishop Scanlan was the living reproduction of the mountains, plains, and skies of his field of long missionary labor. There was about him not a sign that he had ever for a single minute permitted himself to forget the problem that was his. It had worsted him but he had not given up. He knew that he could not win, but he knew, too, that he could still fight, and as he fought he accepted the conviction that in battle he was in his natural element. His back was accustomed to bending, though he held it straight when he walked. His brows were tilted downward as if to shade his eyes from a desert sun. The eyes themselves looked as if they had appraised many men and found them wanting. He walked, even in the house, with the heavy tread of the mountain man. He spoke few but direct and plain words. His voice was not attuned to the niceties of diplomacy. A chin beard and shaven upper lip would—but in appearance only—put him amongst the stern and hard pioneers of Utah who had made his field seem so hopeless. He listened to what I had to say in silence, with his deep-set eyes fixed on my face. I offered to help his missions if he would tell me their needs. If such an offer had been made to him decades before I am sure it would have brought a smile of pleasure to his face. But it came too late. "We don't want money," he said, "It would only do us harm. Give it to others—." He did not need to finish the sentence. As plainly as if he had uttered it I heard the rest, "where there is hope."

I left Salt Lake City that night, not wishing to change the old man's mind even if I could. He was what hard toil and long service in a hard land had made him. The rest of the world was unknown territory to him. Here he had taken up his burden and here he would lay it down. He had heard a Sermon on the Mount and would stay to practice what it taught as best he could. The grip of his hand when I left him told me that. I was quite surprised when, to his "Good-by, sir," he added, "And I thank you kindly."

But Bishop Scanlan has had successors who did not find Utah quite hopeless.

Toward the end of his long and useful life Archbishop Ireland came to Chicago to pay us a visit and see for himself. It was more than he should have done. The inexorable disease that killed him had struck. He stayed all day, reading our records, receiving answers to searching questions, and tramping all over the place. When I was about to leave him at his hotel he asked me to remain for dinner. Once or twice the old fire seemed about to flame up, but it died down quickly. I was seeing a man who had caught a close glimpse of another world and was losing his interest in this one. His visit was to satisfy his mind about us. When he returned home he wrote a letter of commendation for the society and its work.

To the North and to the West the sky was clearing. There never had been any storm clouds to the South. I turned my face to the East.

There the problem was most serious. All Catholic leadership had hitherto come out of the East. Such national works as the Church had were centered there: the Catholic University in Washington; the head office of the Society for the Propagation of the Faith in New York; the Apostolic Mission House on the University grounds; the Missionary Association of the Holy Childhood in Pittsburgh; our principal and oldest seminary, St. Mary's, in Baltimore; the largest charitable institutions in New York City and Buffalo. Even the most promising of our social societies, the Knights of Columbus, was spreading out from headquarters in New Haven. Institutions of higher education were more scattered, but the largest were in the East. Loyola University of Chicago was then only a college; St. Louis not much more. Notre Dame was struggling to find itself as a university. Detroit was a one-building combination high school and college while New York had Fordham. Boston College was flourishing. Georgetown was a treasured child of the District of Columbia.

The United States had had two cardinals in succession, one in New York and the other in Baltimore. Few had even dreamed at that time of a Western cardinal. The East had supplied archbishops and bishops for the West. Quigley of Chicago was from Buffalo, Foley of Detroit from Baltimore, Horstmann of Cleveland from Philadelphia, Christie of Oregon by birth a Vermont Yankee, O'Dea of Seattle a Bostonian, Keane of Dubuque from Washington, and Messmer of Milwaukee from Newark. Baltimore, too, had sent a Bishop to Indianapolis and an archbishop to Santa Fe, Boston gave a bishop to Mobile, Springfield one to Los Angeles and one to Sioux City. Only one Eastern diocese had a ruler from the West— Philadelphia. All the others were governed by bishops selected either from the ranks of the local clergy or from neighboring Eastern dioceses. The advice of Horace Greeley, "Go West, young man," appeared to have been heeded best in the Church.

There was no complaint about all this from the West. The percentage of native-born Western priests was not large, and the East was giving priests and people as well as bishops for Western parishes. Michigan had drawn for population heavily on northern New

York and Canada. Ohio owed many a parish to New England and New York. Easterners had the pioneering spirit. They scattered. Immigrants did not all stop in the Eastern industrial centers but followed the Yankee and the Irishman to the great plains. Priests came after them from Ireland, Germany, Poland, and Bohemia. The help that put many a Western diocese on its own was Eastern. Western bishops were by no means shy about traveling East on begging tours. And the East was generous. When, for example, the diocese of Wichita was established the new bishop came from St. Louis in a private car supplied by Senator Richard Kerens, but when car and company left he found that the total annual income he could expect, for all his episcopal works as well as for his living expenses, amounted to only four hundred dollars. And Wichita was then enjoying a boom which, like most booms and all balloons, soon blew up. In desperation the bishop went East to beg, and the generous East saved him. Governor Smith said, "You can't kill Santa Claus." No Catholic Westerner ever wanted even to take the smile off the nice Santa face that shone on him from the direction of the rising sun.

Was all that good for the Church in the West? In the beginning, yes! In 1905, yes and no. There were still many missionary dioceses. There are some now. Catholic centers had grown up in the Central and Western States. Chicago needed no help, nor Detroit, nor Milwaukee, nor Cleveland, nor St. Paul, nor San Francisco; to mention only a few. St. Louis and Cincinnati had been important almost as soon as Boston, and before Buffalo. It was time these centers looked after their poor neighbors. Too much Eastern generosity for these neighbors would prevent the placing of good share of responsibility where it really belonged. The Central States needed a saving burden. The West needed native-born priests. There were dioceses, like Helena and Tucson, without a single native-born pastor. I question if half of the clergy were native-born even in the Central States. Europe had to supply. It was high time for the West to become conscious of its responsibilities. It needed seminaries. It needed schools and colleges of its own. It needed to understand its own needs. It had to feel that it could do something big, give birth to something of national import. Thus the West could pay its debt with interest. It was the society that uncovered the lode. It was the society that invented the machinery. It was the society that showed how the metal could be extracted. There is no Catholic American missionary work today existing, East or West, that does not owe a large part of its inspiration, as well as nearly all of its education, to "Extension," which put the West on the Catholic map of the United States with Chicago as its heart.

It was no easy work. Many of Chicago's clergy were against us. New York and other parts of the East were against us. Even the Apostolic Delegate turned against us at the most critical hour of trial. But there was not one drop of malice in the opposition. All had been expected. All had been foreseen. And all came quite naturally out of the condition of the Church in America at that time.

Archbishop Falconio, later Cardinal, though he had warmly welcomed the Society when it was established, reversed his position when we began operating a chapel car. He had been a Franciscan missionary in Newfoundland and had ideas of his own about the way missionary work should be done. They did not include what he considered luxurious travel for missionaries; and a chapel car, he was quite sure, meant luxurious travel. "When I was a missionary," he snapped, "I went out with my pack on my back, slept in huts, and ate salt herring and dried cod. This Dr. Kelley wants to send missionaries out in a private Pullman with parlor, bedroom, and bath." What His Excellency forgot was that a chapel car, unlike the lone missionary "with his pack on his back," could stay for weeks and months, carry a temporary pastor into churchless towns fully equipped with his books and all the "literature" he needed for distribution during a course of lectures which the old-style missionary could not stay long enough to give. He forgot likewise that the first chapel car—like its successors—cost us nothing, not even railroad fares; that the railroads welcomed it, especially on the new branch lines they were building and along which churchless towns and settlements were springing up. We had no thought of denying credit to the old missionary. Chapel cars could never replace him. But it was the old American missionary himself, when he saw the results, who was the most enthusiastic supporter of the chapel-car idea.

Gladly did we hear from Rome. It was our opportunity and we knew it. Rumors of extravagance had crossed the ocean. Archbishop Quigley almost lost his quiet smile. He was fully conversant with every detail of our finances, and had approved of our methods. He liked the chapel-car idea, not only because of its missionary, but also because of its publicity, value. He sent a detailed report to Rome which brought back the first letter of encouragement. But trouble still kept piling up. Then the quiet smile on the archbishop's face disappeared. He went East. When he returned one sentence summed up all he had to say, "There'll be no more trouble coming from that quarter." And no more trouble came.

Little by little the East became friendly. Cardinal Farley of New York, who had thought with Archbishop Falconio, was a long time coming over but he came at last. We entered the East with our message, where it was well received. The Second Missionary Congress was invited by the Cardinal Archbishop of Boston to come to his See city, and the invitation was accepted. From the West and South the bishops poured into Boston. Even a chapel car came on for the great event. It is no tardy act of justice to say here that Cardinal O'Connell broke the Eastern ice for us, since I said it before and have repeated it many times since by voice and pen. It was the Boston Congress that introduced the society to its Eastern father as a grown-up Western son who had left home very young. I shall never forget the opening session of that Congress when, before a packed auditorium, the Cardinal half-turned to Archbishop Quigley who had a chair beside him and said with slow and meaning emphasis on every word, "Chicago and Boston understand each other." The two Archbishops met for the first time at that Congress. There was then nothing of the personal in the significant words. It was as if the Cardinal said, "The East Understands the West."

⋙ 14 ⋘

NORTHERN LIGHTS

I N 1908 Canada's "Extension" was already a going concern. The Rev. Alfred Edward Burke, president of the Canadian Society, was one of the most interesting and at the same time baffling of clerical characters. I had known him in my boyhood on The Island as the secretary of the "Prince Bishop." Father Burke did not, however, remain long in that position, and no one had to tell anyone the reason why. The Bishop had a Scotch conviction that it was his business to run his diocese. The easy way to explain that to a secretary who felt that his office imposed a load of responsibility for the Bishop on his young shoulders was to give him another job. Alfred Edward Burke became in consequence pastor of the little village of Alberton quite a distance from the cathedral. He was still in Alberton when a Canadian Society was talked of, and was more than interested. Had I not been an altar boy in the cathedral while he was on its staff? He felt, therefore, a responsibility for me. I welcomed his attention, not only because he was one of my beloved "characters," but because I knew that he was a highly talented man and a writer who had considerable influence everywhere in the Dominion.

Father Burke could stick. Indeed, when an idea fastened itself on him, or rather when he fastened himself on an idea, his talent for sticking to it was nothing short of genius. True, he had not always been right; but neither had he been as stubborn as the old Presbyterian lady in *Father Malachy's Miracle* whose thought about Catholics was thus perfectly expressed: "Even if the're richt th're wrang." I began and continued a long correspondence which had for its objective the planting of another good idea in the head of the pastor at Alberton. Father Burke set out to sell it to the bishops

143

of Canada. It was not the first idea he had tried to sell. His nickname on the island was "Tunnel Burke," because he had, with his friend Governor Howlan, tried to sell the Dominion on the idea of digging a tunnel under the Strait of Northumberland, thus connecting the island with the mainland. He did not sell the tunnel idea to the government, but the attempt to do so made a very decided improvement in communications inevitable. When that happened "Tunnel Burke" lost his nickname, and his good services were forgotten. But those who knew him were quite well aware of the fact that another new idea of some kind would soon attract him. All I really had to do was to drop mine right on the surface of the pool of Alberton. He struck—hard. I knew I had a "big one," but not that he was going to be so difficult to handle as later he proved to be.

Before me I have a nearly complete file of my correspondence with Burke. No one could say after reading it that the man looked upon frankness as a fault. Such letters are the joys of the historian who has also a taste for cryptogram. After long years of rereading there are still secrets buried in those letters that only God knows. "When I wrote that line," remarked Robert Browning, "only God and Robert Browning knew what it meant. Now no one knows but God." Burke's general meaning was not in question. One could guess that fairly well from the strong and vigorous script. It was the writing. There was no way of distinguishing many of the words from one another. But even in his letters he was an unending source of joy to me; all the more, perhaps, because he seemed to be a joy to so few others. Real "characters" seldom are. Most people disliked what they called Burke's "pomposity." It was not assumed but quite natural. He did think that he was a superior man and he was. He did have assurance but there was talent behind it. Superior men in Canada quite readily admitted him into the circle of superior men.

The task Burke took upon himself was no easy one. I think he enjoyed it for that very reason. The Church in Canada, like the country itself, had two languages and a racial line of division; a line which, while it once resembled a barbwire fence, has since lost at least some of its sharp points. When a difference of language prevents an interchange of thought, misunderstanding results. That was the obstacle in the way of Burke's admitted zeal and talent. He himself spoke both English and French, but that fact counted little. It was the goods that mattered; not only what they were but who made them and why they were offered for sale. When Burke tried to sell them in Quebec the label "Made in Ontario" was looked for. When they were offered in Ontario the label "Made in Quebec" aroused suspicion. But on both sides "Made in the U. S. A." was a just cause for suspecting that they might shrink badly in the first washing. Burke decided that selling the "Extension" idea was a harder job than persuading a government to build a tunnel, but more important. He did not propose to be licked twice. The Lord, I ventured to suggest to him one dark day, had had no particular interest in that tunnel or He would not have put the island so far away from the mainland and run so deep and damp a ditch between, but there could be no doubt about His interest in saving souls. Burke did not tell me that I had no business trying to interpret the mind of the Lord. I suspect that he had come to approve of such a stand on the part of Divine Providence.

It was my desire to have the headquarters of the Canadian work located in Montreal and the archbishop of that city its chancellor. There were good reasons for that, since the greater part of the missions to be aided were served by French priests; and Montreal was the largest city, as well as the business and financial center of Canada. Monsignor Sbaretti, the Apostolic Delegate to Canada, suggested Ottawa. Neither Ottawa nor Montreal wanted the honor. Burke was face to face with his first obstacle. He was altogether too English, in spite of name and blood, to be entirely acceptable to either archbishop. He had never been classed as friendly to French-Canadian aspirations, so he was received with all the politeness due to his standing while to both archbishops he was a Greek bearing gifts. The proposal of Father Burke was "a matter for serious study not to be settled in a single conversation." He soon knew that, so far as the archbishops were concerned, it could not be settled in twenty conversations. No, I am wrong. It really was settled in one, and Burke lost his first move. Not that he had failed to play well, for diplomatically he mentioned to Ottawa that Montreal also had been thought of. That seemed to help for the moment. Ottawa thought itself every bit as good as Montreal. The matter was again taken up for consideration, but the language question once more pushed itself forward and ground was lost in spite of the Apostolic Delegate's assistance. Archbishop Duhamel was just as suspicious as Archbishop Bruchesi. Burke could not understand why I was neither surprised nor shocked. In truth, the matter had turned out just as I had expected. From outside, the seriousness of the language obstacle could be seen more clearly than from the inside.

A short excursion into history may help others to understand.

The French in Canada, from the taking of Quebec by Wolfe, had been on the defensive. Abandoned by France and left to the mercies of a conqueror, they had withdrawn within themselves to survive as best they could. True, England made concessions as to their laws, their language, and their religion. But that was all. England quite naturally favored her own. Money, jobs, and offices were always entrusted to English newcomers. The French did not complain overmuch, but they welded the band of racial unity closer around the little group that England did not favor and France had deserted. They would be self-sufficient even in their poverty. Deliberately they chose an objective and a way of their own. The English objective was financial and political power. The French objective was the making of a race. Steadily the French worked at that. Nothing discouraged them. Around them they built three protecting walls: language, laws, and religion. They felt that these would hold at least until they became numerous enough to fear no longer. They had learned a lesson from the cavalier Montcalm, who came from behind his defensive works to give Wolfe battle on equal terms on the plains of Abraham, and had no intention of repeating Montcalm's chivalric mistake. The French were only poor farmers and woodsmen but they had ideals, and proposed to keep them at all costs.

They had not been without temptations to come from behind their walls. The United States tempted them when the American colonies broke away from the mother country. Bishop Carroll came from Baltimore to lend aid to the tempters. As an American patriot, it was quite right that he should do that, but he did not see that the French-Canadians had all they wanted of freedom at

that stage in the process of making a race out of a handful of deserted peasants. Carroll could not persuade Briand, the Bishop
of Quebec, though the latter was even then defending his wall
of religion against the English. An army followed the diplomats
with as little success. Arnold went back beaten, and Montgomery
fell and died before the fortifications of the city of Quebec. When
Bishop Plessis came to the episcopal throne in 1806 he had governors to fight, but his predecessors had saved Canada for the
Empire. The French had kept their plighted word and had remained loyal. There was all the more reason for leaving them in
peace to work out their own destiny, and the English did it, though
unwillingly. That last word fully explains the attitude of the
French-Canadian to many things. It represents the spirit which has
retarded full understanding. The French know that the English
have been slow to appreciate their viewpoint, to recognize the
value of ideals other than the Anglo-Saxon.

I did not then find it at all surprising, and certainly far from
shocking, that Burke was met at first with suspicion. The French-
Canadian was not yet ready to come out on the plains, for while
his work of making a race was really done, he did not as yet know
that it was safely done. He was still suspicious, still wary, still mindful of old perfidies; yes, and still mindful of offers of friendship
which were well meant but which, if accepted, would have been
to his disadvantage. Of course he was bound to make small mistakes, but small mistakes are quite often guards against a supreme
mistake. I have then no word of criticism for the archbishops who
lost the Canadian society to their dioceses. As things turned out
later it was better that they acted as they did, for the Canadian
society, adopting the policy of its American sister, which from the
beginning paid no attention to language or nationality in the face
of need, became one strand in a cord of union between the French
and English speaking Catholics of the Dominion. Only a few
months before his death a few years ago the second chancellor of
the Canadian society, the late Archbishop McNeill, expressed to
me his desire to add prominent French-Canadians to the Board of
Governors. "We have proved our good will, our fairness, and our
genuinely Catholic spirit by our acts," he said. "The next step ought
to be to ask our French-speaking brethren to enter with us into this

fine work of faith and charity." His successor, Archbishop Mc-
Guigan—born on the island—does not agree. He believes that the
two races should develop side by side in mutual respect and har-
mony; each making its own contribution in its own way to the
Dominion. I think he is right.

Something happened, on March 17th, 1908, that made the way
for Father Burke a bit easier. On the 300th anniversary of the
foundation of the University of Laval in Quebec the rector and
faculty conferred the Doctorate of Sacred Theology on both of us.
It was the delicate and gracious French way of saying a great deal
without words. The society was founded in Canada. The story
of the founding, once told, need not be rewritten, but I shall let
that long "out of print" book of mine repeat a little of it here:
"I had been telling Father Burke, through correspondence and in
personal meetings, a great deal about the society, and had been
urging him to consider the advisability of taking charge of a
Canadian Branch. He gave the same answer always: 'Find me an
archbishop and a leading layman and I shall make a start.' A combination of circumstances brought us to Quebec for the tercen-
tenary of the old University of Laval. Both Father Burke and
myself were to be 'tapped' by the faculty and made Doctors. When
the great affair was over we found ourselves on a boat going up the
River Saguenay, still discussing the desired archbishop and prominent layman. An amused listener to the discussion was Monsignor
Sinnott, secretary of the Apostolic Delegate to Canada. Monsignor Sinnott remarked: 'It is not necessary to go off the boat to find
your archbishop and your prominent layman. The Archbishop of
Toronto is on board, and Sir Charles Fitzpatrick, the Chief Justice
of Canada, as well.' Burke was face to face with his opportunity,
so he started out to find Archbishop McEvay and Sir Charles. He
found them, talked over the situation, and came back to make
terms with me."

The Canadian society was founded in Toronto with Archbishop
McEvay as its chancellor and the new Doctor as its president. Up
to the present (1939) it has had three chancellors, one acting-
president, and three actual presidents. The acting-president was
the late Bishop Power of Newfoundland. The second president
became Archbishop of Halifax. The present executive head is

Monsignor J. J. Blair, who came to Toronto from Winnipeg to take over its work.

It was the Great War that deprived the Canadian society of its first president. There were even pacifists who could see one good at least which came out of that war, for it called Dr. Burke away from Canada. He had expanded into national prominence with a weekly paper to which he gave most of his time. Soon it absorbed nearly all his time and the society became just "something else." Canada had too many questions of absorbing interest for a man who had never had a local horizon. He knew everybody and everybody knew him. His opinions were like dogmas of faith. No wonder Catholic Canada split over him. Half of his world swore by him and the other half at him. Nothing really could have retired him but a war, and, luckily, it was big enough to be attractive. So, brass cap on head, Lieutenant-Colonel Alfred E. Burke, Protonotary Apostolic and Doctor of Theology, went overseas, and soon in London became almost as well known as he had been in Toronto. But, ever a partisan, when the Canadian government changed its Commander overseas, Lieutenant-Colonel Burke was found at his side and, with the general, came home—but not to peace. He could not settle down. A visit to Mexico opened up what he thought would prove a new field of usefulness. He was mistaken, as many another good man who went there had been mistaken. He worked and sacrificed, endangered his clerical standing, and stuck to his "friends." He was almost killed by one of them, but he still stuck. It would take more than threats and brass knuckles to shake him when he thought he was right. As a matter of fact he was only half-right. Rome, partially at least in kindness, at last told him to go home and forget it. Being a good priest, he obeyed. Perhaps it was his obedience that merited for him a peaceful death near the Martyrs' Church of St. Stephano Rotundo in Rome. He was of the stuff of martyrs, though he often lacked the judgment that makes martyrdom glorious. He sleeps in peace in the Rome he loved. An old island friend, Father Reardon of Minneapolis, closed his tired eyes. It saddened me to think of his lonely passing. He could never be happy without a great something to fight for, and he had gone too high for skirmishes. He was too old and too many times wounded for a command, too intense to see any side of a question but the one he had made a part of himself. Longer life for such a man would have meant only extended frustration. He wanted to go faster even than the Church which was the star to which he had fixed his wagon, but the star kept peacefully on its track and would not be hurried.

For two outstanding good works in Canada Dr. Burke should at least share the credit: one the founding of St. Augustine's Seminary and the other the establishment of the Greek Catholic diocese. I am a living witness for him in both causes. The plan which brought about the establishment of the seminary, though not in the way Burke had expected, was suggested by him. I was on the ground and in the conference when it was outlined, discussed, and adopted. The objective was reached, but by another road than the one Burke did not realize he was tearing up. He was the first to see the need of a Greek diocese for the Ruthenians in Canada, and never dropped the idea till it was in other minds and more powerful hands. It was Burke who sounded the alarm over the proselytizing of the Ruthenian settlers and directed the first onslaught against the proselytizers. I ought to know, for at his request I wrote the appeal which, published by him, set the Catholics of Canada on guard.

Dr. Burke was a brilliant light against Northern skies, but he shone in a winter night when most people were at home around their fires, doors closed and curtains down. Only a few travelers through the cold saw him for what he was: a fighter with something of the prophet in him, an unlikable personality to many, yet one who could be and was very gentle and kind; a man who never had any true goal but right, though quite likely in the excitement of play to run the wrong way with the ball. Too intense he was. That seems to me the summing up of the character of a man who gave me trouble in plenty, but who never gave me trouble enough to make me want to cast him out of my heart, or to forget my admiration for his many sterling qualities.

One other man, at least, thought of Dr. Burke as I have tried to picture him, and for that man he would willingly have died. The man was Fergus Patrick McEvay, Archbishop of Toronto, a rock of good sense, sane judgment, honest piety, and sparkling humor. In no physical way did this genial tyrant—in a good sense I mean—

resemble the one who I think is most like him in spirit, Archbishop Glennon of St. Louis. Happier than his Toronto brother in turn of phrase, yet in Archbishop Glennon much that was Archbishop McEvay still lives, laughs, and rules. No one on earth but Archbishop McEvay could make Dr. Burke change his mind. He could do it with a quip. The Archbishop simply laughed Burke over to his side, and of all the things that Burke loved it was that pleasant process he loved most. I saw the Archbishop on what was soon to be his deathbed. He hid the rosary in his hands as I came in. His face was like that of a skeleton. Death had made his mark on every tightly drawn and sharp line of it. He knew. Burke came in and the old man's eyes brightened at once. The kindly but meaning shafts of his humor began to fly. Once outside the sickroom door, Burke broke down. "When he is gone I, too, will be dead," he mourned. The Kingdom of Heaven must have suffered the violence of a hearty roar of welcome when these two men threw themselves into whatever substitute for arms spirits possess; I mean when the Archbishop met the Doctor just one foot—if there is a spiritual foot—on the bright side of the gate.

Close to both men was Sir Charles Fitzpatrick, then Chief Justice of the Supreme Court of Canada, later Governor of Quebec, and a Privy Councillor of the British King. Had not Canada given up accepting titles of nobility for her citizens, Sir Charles would likely long ago have been Lord Fitzpatrick. But then the thought comes to me that, even had Canada not acted that way, Sir Charles really would not care to be Lord Fitzpatrick. He, too, had a will of his own, governed by a most delicate sense of right and justice. A born judge, Sir Charles was the most typical of all the Canadians I knew. Both languages were mother tongues to him. He saw the right and the wrong of both sides. A deeply religious man, he possessed the key to the understanding of the French heart. I suspected him of concealing the mystic under judicial ermine, of having a pocket for a prayer book in his legal gown, of preferring the quiet of the sanctuary to the noise of saluting guards. He—but Sir Charles still lives, and anticipated eulogies are neither fair nor, perhaps, in good taste.

No scene remains in the background of my memory more delightfully than the one which, at Archbishop McEvay's house in

Toronto, followed the announcement that the Canadian society had received its first large donation. Dr. Burke had given a few days in the city to soliciting interest and subscriptions. One night he came back with five thousand dollars given, for some unexplained reason, in bank notes instead of by check. He narrated the story of the day's adventures, which proved that the laity were willing to support the new society. Up to that moment the Archbishop had been doubtful. But when the roll of money was laid on the desk before him he snatched at it with a shout and threw it into the air. The paper band around the money broke and the floor was littered with bank notes. The company began bombarding each other with them till the air was green with the precious paper, the Archbishop shouting as he did his share of the bombarding: "We win. We win. Here's the cash that proves it."

Patience. There is yet another story to tell before I come to Rome.

◆§ 15 §◆

ON WHEELS

IF I were asked to name the influence which was to the greatest degree responsible for the quick growth of the "Extension" idea I should have to leave both my co-workers and myself out of the picture. Hard work and hard pleading eventually would have won for us, but the growth would have been slow. It was not slow. The dream had struck the imagination of thousands even if some thought it too good to be true. A "church on wheels" put the idea on wheels. To drag a church and rectory behind a locomotive into a village appealed to the imagination.

"What time are you going to church tomorrow morning, Mary?" asked an old "fallen-away" of his pious daughter one Saturday night after both had visited the first chapel car.

"I am going to the seven o'clock Mass, Father," she answered, adding hopefully, "you were not thinking of coming with me, were you?"

"Yes, Mary," said the old man, "I'm thinking of going with you. It's twenty-five years since I darkened a church door, and I never expected to darken one again. But when a whole parish is dragged up under a man's nose it's high time for him to pay attention."

When the first chapel car was put on the steel rails there were many who never had missed darkening church doors quite regularly on Sundays who nevertheless looked at it wonderingly and with not a little pride of possession.

"The old Church is moving, eh?"

"Quite so. Moving on wheels now."

Folks got a thrill out of that; they were so used to seeing her go slowly and carefully as befitted her age and her traditions. They

153

did not wonder at all when she built a cathedral, a school, a college, even a university. There was traditional warrant for all of these. Europe was bejeweled with her masterpieces of architecture, as literature was illuminated by her scholars. But this modern thing? This Pullman idea? This call on steam and steel to preach Christ Crucified? It was a shock and yet—a shock that made folks glad that they had lived to experience it. It had two effects; effects diametrically opposed to one another. An archbishop expressed the wish to see the chapel car burned up. But it pleased a Pope so greatly that he made its donor, Ambrose Petry, a Knight Commander of the Order of St. Gregory the Great. It was when the poets took it up that we knew the "St. Anthony" was doing its work on imaginations and that tropic growth surely would follow. One of the poets, Father McKernon, was the "St. Anthony's" first chaplain. Thus he sang to his moving parish:

> "God speed thee, harbinger of Peace: spread far the tidings sweet,
> The Mustard Seed fling to the winds whose wings are not more fleet.
> Hail! flying messenger of God; haste to the scattered sheep
> Who yet upon the spreading plains seek still their Faith to keep."

There really was nothing new about the chapel cars. Pius IX as ruler over the Papal States had one on his special train and, if I mistake not, it is still in existence as a relic of his long reign. The old Czarist government of Russia took the idea from him and placed several such cars on the Trans-Siberian Railroad. An Anglican bishop of Minnesota saw one of the Russian cars and put the idea on wheels in his diocese. The American Baptist Publication Society had seven or eight chapel cars, one of which gave me the inspiration to write a few lines about it as an editorial filler. Mr. Petry read the few lines. He did the rest by paying for the car which Richmond Dean, then general manager of the Pullman Company, planned and made out of a retired Wagner sleeper.

Peter Kuntz of Dayton, Ohio, a lumber merchant, seemed the last man on earth who would bother himself about such a thing as an imagination, being a practical and hardheaded man of business. But the "St. Anthony" caught him and he "went Petry one better." He gave us two steel chapel cars magnificently equipped, the "St. Peter" and the "St. Paul." I thought them well named since a successor of St. Peter had been our greatest encouragement, and

On Wheels

St. Paul's own recital of his missionary voyagings indicated that he would not have disdained any means of transportation to bring him into "fields white for the harvest."

White the fields were. The cars advertised their presence in the little towns and villages of the West as soon as they were shunted to the station sidings. The children were always the first to discover them and to spread the exciting word that "down at the depot" there was something new under the sun for that little community. The cars were veritable magnets drawing scattered flocks from forest and farm. But everywhere the best friends of the chapel cars were the railway men. A church on wheels and rails seemed to expand the horizon of the average man who lived so many hours of his life on wheels and rails.

"What's that car you got there, porter? Never seen one of that line before, nor heard of the line neither. What's she for?" It was a Kansas brakeman asking information from one Horace, chapel car porter.

"White man," said Horace, "dis year cahr don' belong to no railroad company. She's a church—Catholik Church wif everything in her from organ to preachah."

"What you givin' me? Churches don't go travelin'."

"Dis one does. Come on in an ah'll prove it. Man, you kin go to confession in dis year church cahr right now. Ain't dat service?"

The brakeman let Horace prove it; that is all except the confession part. But there were railroad men who took advantage even of the confessional. Catholics or Protestants, the railroad men were friends of the chapel cars and would do anything to help, such as the good service of spreading the news ahead that the car was coming. In a way it was their car and their parish center.

When we had three cars I appointed Mr. Hennessey superintendent of the work, but George would not agree to spread himself. He stuck to one car and let the Chicago office do the superintending, and it was better so. George was a Catholic Rodheaver who sang his sermons. Both organist and choir, he later developed into a lecturer and after-dinner speaker. He had the inherited wit and humor of good old Uncle Mick of The Island, his father. He served the society for eighteen years before he went into business in Portland, Oregon, following in his father's footsteps as an undertaker. When George reluctantly left us, the Archbishop of Oregon asked the Holy Father to confer a decoration on him as a mark of esteem for his long and self-sacrificing labors. Even the Sovereign Pontiff was not devoid of humor. To make a Knight Commander of the Holy Sepulchre out of an undertaker was to grant the petition of the Archbishop in the most appropriate way, and not without a suspicion of the humor. When Sir George passed away it seemed as if all Portland mourned.

From chapel cars to motor chapels was no great step and the motor chapels came; one pioneered in anticipation of the trailer. In fact we had the first real church trailer. But the roads of its day were bad, and in consequence the first motor chapel was not a great success. It was hard to keep a schedule in the rainy season. A motor chapel had all too frequently to be dug out of the mud of Texas roads or helped over bridges not built for such heavy equipment. Even the trailer found the going difficult. We were too far ahead of the times when we sent out the motor chapels. But England took up the idea and put it to work on her good roads. It is again at work in America, and now that the demand has come for trailer chapels we have concrete roads for them. But the railroad chapel cars are no longer as useful as once they were. Good roads and automobiles have drawn parish churches closer to scattered flocks. Even the little mission chapels felt the change when people began to take Sunday trips to church in town. Henry Ford was no missionary by choice, but he became one nevertheless. His little Model T types solved the church-attendance problem of a host of farmers who lived far away from the centers of population.

The railroad chapel cars proved to be more than traveling churches and parishes. They were messengers of good will. As the railroad men seemed to take them as part of their line's equipment and therefore as fellow workers, so whole populations of little towns and villages, no matter what their religious complexions, acquired a personal interest in them. It was often a problem to keep the chickens left by the people for the larder. Chicken-runs beside railroad sidings were not easily provided and chickens are tempting to the fraternity of the road. I wonder if even the gentle David Grayson could have overcome temptation when a thundering freight train smothered the cackles of a chicken being torn away from his home alongside the railroad right-of-way. And David was an honest nature lover. More chapel car chickens went into mulligan stews than into the pots of our tiny kitchens. But there were tramps who tried to make up for their light-fingered brethren by "squaring up" on their own long-neglected religious duties. They too felt the gentle force of having "a parish dragged up under your nose" after long years of never getting closer to one than a priest's kitchen door.

Mormon towns in Idaho often welcomed the chapel cars but never filled them. The Mormons always wanted the chaplains to come into their meeting houses and talk to them. Even the Mormon bishops were more than friendly. In one such town the "St. Peter's" congregation consisted, in the morning, of only Mr. Michael Casey, section foreman, but in the evening the chaplain spoke to a crowded audience of Mormons with their own choir doing the singing. The chaplains could say what they liked in their lectures to the Mormons who had no objection whatever to hearing the Catholic Church give an account of herself. But we made no Mormon converts.

This open-minded attitude of Mormons, in contrast to the closed-minded attitude of so many other people used to puzzle us in Chicago when we read the chaplains' reports, until one day when I pulled an incident of travel in Michigan out of my memory. It happened on a train during my lecturing days.

A young man sitting in the seat opposite to me in a coach kept glancing over as if he wished me to notice him and invite him to sit with me. But I was deep in a book and did not care for other company. When my eyes became too tired to read by the poor light of the kerosene lamps on the ceiling of the ancient coach and I put the book away, the young fellow came over without an invitation and sat opposite me.

"Are you a Catholic or an Episcopalian clergyman?" he asked, after offering a timid apology for the liberty he was taking.

"Catholic."

"May I ask a favor of you?"

"It is granted before you ask if it requires only talk. I am tired reading, but you'll have to do your share of the talking."

"No, please." He put up his hand. "I want you to do it all. It is a long answer to a short question that I want, and one in entire accord with your profession."

"Very well. Fire ahead."

"Will you be so good as to outline for me the arguments used in your theological schools to prove the authority of your Church?"

"You mean the infallibility?"

"If you wish, but would not that be included in the authority?"

"It would if you mean the teaching authority."

"That is exactly what I mean."

"I am getting off at the next station in about twenty minutes," I answered—I thought the information pleased him—"so I won't have very much time, but I can outline the arguments from reason and revelation. Naturally you would not expect me to quote the historical arguments from the Fathers."

"I am not particularly interested in the tradition," he said, "or in the Fathers, but I am deeply interested in the other points and should like to have them in the forms used in your seminaries."

The young man puzzled me and the thought crossed my mind that he might be a former seminarian, but I dismissed it, knowing in such a case he would not need to ask for the arguments. I began with the human necessity for guidance and marshaled, as well as I could remember, the facts that once had helped me out of a theological examination. He nodded approval as each point was made. I was still more astonished for I had expected opposition.

"You have ten minutes more," he said, "let me have the arguments from Scripture."

By this time my curiosity was fully aroused. "You are a surprise to me," I said. "What is your religion?"

"Let us not waste time on that."

I then gave him the arguments from Holy Writ. When I came to the promise of Christ to send the Holy Ghost to remain as Teacher in the Church to the end of time he was most emphatic in his nod of approval. The brakeman called my station. I put on my overcoat and hat and picked up my valise. He put out his hand to say good-by.

"I did not want to tell you my religion before," he said, "because I was anxious to check up on my own studies and I knew I could not convert you to my faith. I am a missionary of the

Church of the Latter Day Saints. You know it as the Mormon. All the arguments you have given are familiar to me, as they are to all Mormon students. We believe in the teaching authority of our church but we also believe that there was a revelation after that of Christ. You might have taken every point you made from a lecture by a Mormon professor."

"I think you mean," I remarked, "that the Mormon professor took his arguments from Catholic theology."

He laughed heartily, "Good-by," he said. "I hope we do not meet again, or at least I hope if we do it will be an occasion which will leave us no time for a fight."

Years later I sat alongside one of the Mormon apostles at a Boy Scout dinner. He began questioning me on the life of Father De Smet, and told me that he was determined to see that a statue to the great missionary should be erected by the Mormons, facing the fertile valley he had described to Brigham Young and in which Salt Lake City was built.

"I suppose you think," he said, "that I am a bit of a nuisance to be asking you so many questions."

"Not at all," I answered. "I once met a young Mormon missionary who asked more."

"Tell me about him. I am interested."

I narrated the story.

"He was a good Morman missionary," he assured me, "that is in all but one respect. He did not try to convert you. But then I must excuse him for he did not have time." He dropped De Smet to tell me about Bishop Scanlan and how much the Mormons liked him.

What became of the chapel cars? The pioneer "St. Anthony" is in use as a permanent chapel on the street of a little railroad town in the State of Washington. The "St. Peter" is in the possession of the Bishop of Raleigh, North Carolina. The "St. Paul" now belongs to the Bishop of Great Falls, Montana. All are still at work.

To the first chapel car goes the blame or credit of putting me on the wheels of the press and making an editor out of a country pastor. I had realized early that the movement would soon need an official organ and that an editor had to be found for it. But there was no editor to answer the need because there was no money to pay his salary. True, Father Graham, the first secretary of the society, wrote well, far better than I ever hoped to do, but he was one to paint the lily, never satisfied even with his best. Stern necessity forced me to take up the pen. A little quarterly was started to fight the good fight. The short editorial note that inspired Mr. Petry to give the "St. Anthony" was nothing but a filler demanded of me by the printer at a last moment before locking up. I was launched as a press captain without ever having served a day under the masthead. When the magazine grew into a monthly I found Mr. Baldus in Cincinnati, drove a hard bargain and brought him to Chicago. But "make-up" and selection took all his time and the "idiotorials"—as he dubbed them—were left to me. A step into the field of essays and short stories was a short one. Books followed and I was on the wheels of the printing press with a vengeance.

I was not long in discovering that the life of a country pastor is not good training for authorship, especially for the writing of editorials. Frankly, I did not know enough about the many and varied things an editor has to know. The books in my small library were as old as the everlasting hills, and my income was not large enough to add to them. There was no public library in Lapeer then, and even if there had been one its collection of light reading would have been no great help. I had a bookish neighbor, Mrs. Williams, but her tastes ran to literature and history. Nevertheless, her cozy library was at my disposal. It helped a little, since I appreciated the open fire and the chats with herself and her grave and serious lawyer husband, later a judge. Probably Father Graham did most for me by stirring up fights over current interests. He knew a lot, that bookish man. Had he not cultivated overmuch his diamond cutting and polishing he would have made an editor indeed. A year of this was ended by the move to Chicago where books came in plenty. Gradually I got the feel of the pen and liked it. More and more, Fathers Ledvina and O'Brien took over the details of the society's management. I became "the old man" at an early age, as well as a self-made journalist.

That was not all. The magazine grew larger as its list of subscribers increased. From a few thousand we soon jumped to seventy thousand; then to a hundred and seventy thousand; then to two hundred and seventy thousand. When I left the editorial desk we had three hundred and thirty thousand subscribers. In the early days I had to be business, circulation, and advertising manager all in one —a sort of peddler-editor. But subscriptions produced a regular income. Little by little we acquired a staff, and the enlarged magazine had the greatest circulation of any religious publication of its kind in the world. Accident had done an excellent job.

My first book was part of the accident. It was called *Letters to Jack*. The first letter in it was actually a letter to a definite Jack, called for as a correction to a boy starting out in life with more noise than production. That letter gave pragmatic sanction to a series of other letters, and the book went into nine or ten editions. Its success drove me deeper into authorship, all the more willingly because I had a sure publisher. What literary editor would dare reject the offerings of his "boss"? Poor Baldus! He was often hard put to find a diplomatic way to tell the boss that some of his offerings, by literary standards, were mediocre if not worse. He was satisfied with the editorials but, I suspected, at least apprehensive about the books. Still, I went on producing them between appeals for money and editorials, ground out almost as swiftly as Brisbane's. But mine was no daily grind—thank heaven.

With the magazine's growth the receipts of the society swelled into goodly proportions. We specialized in chapels for small missions, did a little school building, took up the work of educating young men for the home missions, and made special appeals for special cases. The Society soon had a hand in the building of more than half the annual crop of new churches in the United States. We expanded our work into Porto Rico and the Philippine Islands. Once when I was introduced to an English bishop by name he burst forth. "Are you Kelley, the Great American Beggar?"

I answered that I was the Kelley who did a lot of begging but had as yet no distinguishing title in the profession.

"Then," he said, "I'll give it to you. Come over and tell us how you do it."

I went over to start the work across the Atlantic at an English Catholic Congress. But my speech is still undelivered for a reason already mentioned. The liner "Empress of Britain" struck the collier "Helvetia" amidships near the island of Anticosti and sent her to the bottom. The liner herself was not lost but, badly crippled and with two compartments water-filled, she had to limp back to port. I made straight for New York and caught the "Kaiser Wilhelm der Grosse," the slim ocean racer of the day, but failed to reach the Congress in time to rid myself of the speech. I still have it. There are few miseries worse than an undelivered speech. Had I arrived in time England too might now have an Extension Society.

The idea of breaking the home missions banner out in England led me to look up two similar works on the Continent: the *Oeuvre de St. François de Sales* in France, and the *St. Bonifacius* Verein in Germany. I had the opportunity of studying methods of both and opening friendly relations with them. So the trip across the ocean was not entirely in vain. I came back with something new to drive the wheels of the printing presses that were making a triumph out of an idea more to be credited to St. Paul than to any other man after St. Paul's Master.

At last—Rome.

❧§ 16 §❧

ROME

MEMORIES of Rome as a rule run upward, from the pious to the holy; even to the sublime. Mine went through the sequence, but the most vivid of them was that of a holy Pope—there is great talk about his canonization—standing before his desk listening to an American bishop telling him an Irish story in Italian and breaking into a hearty laugh over it. The bishop was Dr. Kennedy of the North American College and the Pope was Pius X. The occasion was my first visit to Rome and my first call at the Vatican. The memories of many later visits, added to the first, form a mosaic. At what visits they were born I do not always know. I shall have to jot them down that way.

My early visits to the Eternal City were purely on business. The first was to secure a sort of general approval for the Extension Society. The second was to petition for a Papal Brief expressing stronger approval in a more solemn and definite way. Most of the other visits were to present reports and keep the Holy See aware of the fact that its approvals had produced good results and that the society was alive and doing well.

Sooner or later every Catholic movement arrives in Rome, but rarely by invitation. The policy of the Holy See toward new movements in different parts of the world is to leave them in the hands of the bishops during the early years of organization and development. This does not mean that the Vatican totally ignores them or knows nothing about them or takes no interest in them. Rome may be taking great interest while showing no sign. It is never her way to remain ignorant of any movement anywhere on earth that gives the faintest promise of good results. Rome knew all about Church Extension in America before I made my first visit. But the pleasure of telling the story was not denied me, for Rome knows human nature and is the worlds greatest listener. One wonders why a busy Cardinal will sit patiently for hours while a visitor from the other end of the earth talks himself dry, His Eminence saying nothing. But there's a reason. "Am I not taking too much of Your Eminence's time?" I asked, during such a one-sided interview with Cardinal Sbarretti. "You have your work to do."

He smiled genially and answered, "Not at all. This is part of my work."

There is the secret of Roman patience. The cardinals in Rome are the ears of the Church, trained to listen and learn. No one with anything of importance to say can claim that he went to Rome and was denied a hearing. A witty Texas bishop said, "If you want justice go to Rome. But before you go be sure that it is justice you want." When I went to Rome for the first time I was seeking only a hearing. That was what I got—brimful and running over.

There was no *direttissimo* then on the railroad from Naples to Rome, for Mussolini was at that time only an uneasy youth somewhere up North; perhaps wondering what would come out of that restless and brilliant mind of his. About then he must have been thinking of things far different from those which since, have made Italy over by a national receivership. It was not much of a train that first brought me to Rome. There were no trains in Italy that could be considered luxurious at the time. That visit must have been in 1907.

Entering Rome by the old route the advance thrill should have come at Monte Cassino, whose ghostly cloisters, surpassingly beautiful, still hear the prayers of living sons of St. Benedict. Monte Cassino is the first beautiful outpost of historic Rome. But I was hungry at Monte Cassino. Without more than a passing thought for the glory of monasticism that looked down from the mountain, I rushed into the station restaurant to find nourishment. It was there, but only to be had by me through the universal language of pointing. I was glad enough that I could speak that language. It got me two sausages, a green leaf full of the most delicious of soft cream cheese, half a loaf of bread which, oh joy! was mostly all crust, and my first taste of Chianti. Over that meal I poured the sauce of hunger. Even now I confess without shame that, while others justly have nobler memories of Monte Cassino, mine is mostly of cream cheese and sausage. I shall make it up to Monte Cassino some day—perhaps.

It is the dome of St. Peter's silhouetted against the blue sky that warns the traveler that he is coming into Rome. I saw it as the train rolled over the Campagna, passing herds and shepherds looking as if they had been there for centuries, ruined tombs and the broken aqueducts of the old Imperial City. Back rolled memory to see again a boy stretched out on the grass of a college campus one Sunday in June, book in hand but looking less at its pages than at a procession of prophets and kings, inspired poets, and harpers, all marching over the roads of the centuries toward one city, and from that city a procession of apostles leaving blood-red footprints on other roads reaching out toward the ends of the earth.

My first few days in Rome, may they be anathema, told me that all was not peace there. I had not come to the Rome of Innocent or Sixtus, but to the Rome of Garibaldi, of Mazzini, of Crispi— anti-clerical Rome. It was hard to believe. Wherever the eye turned it fell upon some monument of the historic Papacy which anti-clerical Rome was trying to ignore or forget. One Nathan was its Mayor. Could the Romans not at least have honored tradition by calling him prefect? But what a sorry prefect he would have appeared; the man who put trolley cars down narrow streets that had witnessed imperial triumphs, echoed the tramp of crusaders and heard the whole world sing hosannas! Right in the heart of Rome rose a white and gold monument that would have been a glory to New York but could be nothing but a disfigurement to the Rome of the ages. Nathan would have had Rome made over on the pattern of Zenith.

The spirit of the Rome of the time was as disturbing as its street cars. The statue of an apostate monk had been erected in the Campo dei Fiori right in front of the old architectural masterpiece of the Cancelleria. It is no honor to the Rome of today that the statue is still there. The home of Philip Neri, her apostle, was a dirty government office of some kind. The Roman College had become a duplicate of an ordinary city high school. There was talk of running streets through palaces and churches that the worth of all the steel foundries on earth could not replace. A student asked me how I liked the Rome I saw. I answered that I was just enough of a historian to lament it and just enough of a poet to weep over it. If Mussolini had done no more for Rome than give it back a part of its soul he would deserve a statue on the Capitolian Hill.

It was a storm-tossed Italian mind I read as I went here and there in Rome. In the Quirinal Palace was a worried King who had inherited a crown and an excommunication. He was enjoying neither. On the Vatican hill was a Pope who had by election inherited a tiara and a problem. He was too humble to enjoy the one and too patient to feel oppressed by the other. The people were trying to forget the days when they had lived without a crushing burden of taxes, and to extract a little hope out of thinking that they had what they wanted, even though it was costing them more than they could afford to pay. Rome's "meal-ticket" was still the Pope, while Nathan was dreaming of factories, which, thank God, he never got. Deep in the Roman soul was the desire to keep the blue of its sky unveiled. Outwardly Rome was being made over. Those who knew its people were well aware of the truth, that Rome could never be made over; for the true Rome is its traditions. The true Roman is a poet. But at that time he was making a sad failure of an attempt to set blasphemies to the music of Palestrina.

The people I met in Rome realized no more than I that they were living only a few short years before the coming of sweeping changes, but if they did not realize it they seemed to be filled with an uneasy feeling about it. Italy was beginning, all unknown to its people, to see the end of the expensive "liberalism" upon which it had founded a kingdom. The Romans still rejoiced over the taking of the city by the revolution. They still celebrated the anniversary of its fall. There was that white and gold monument of Victor Emmanuel on the Piazza Venetia. But the offense of the white against the black had all the vigor and flash of a battle to sustain a doubtful cause. Too often I heard the old qualified admission, "We were better off when we were worse off." Liberalism was unconvincing in spite of its arguments. Italy had not been ready for the change. The atmosphere of its capital was heavy and menacing. The stranger from a land of clear political skies could feel it better than those who had been living in it.

Rome

My business, however, was with the Rome of Peter, and I had little time to think of the Rome of Caesar. In truth there was no Caesar. All Italy was governed by a secret council in touch with secret councils beyond its borders. The nominal rulers were not made by the voters. It was a relief to turn away from them and cross the Bridge of the Angels into the old Leonine City, pass up one of the narrow Borgos—now joined in the wide avenue called "Conciliation"—which afforded only a glimpse of St. Peter's, and enter Bernini's Colonnade. From the square the windows behind which Pius X lived were plainly in view.

That Pius was the first Pope I saw. On every visit later during his reign I would see him again and speak with him more intimately than at my first presentation. I had, of course, laughed at the superstition of the Trevi Fountain promising a return to Rome for all who fling *soldi* into its basin. But Trevi can cite me as a witness in its favor, for I have always thrown in the coin and have always come back. May the Trevi make good again!

Pius X must have found it hard to be Pope; he was so humble and there was so much of the country pastor about him. His wisdom was built on the foundation of all good philosophy, spiritual and temporal common sense. The Romans now hold him to have been a saint and they are probably right. Saint he may have been, but a saint who saw no obstacle to holiness in the possession of a fund of humor. Though I saw him in full pontificals and surrounded by his court, it is not that picture of him which is clearest in my memory, but the picture of his laugh over the Irish story told by Bishop Kennedy in Italian. On the way back to the American College I asked the Bishop what had produced the mirth. "Oh," he said, "I was telling him that story you told me last night. He loves good stories."

Very close to Pius X, to his heart as well as to his administration, was one of the most impressive figures in the gallery of my memories, the then Papal Secretary of State, Raphael Cardinal Merry del Val, a strikingly handsome man who carried his perfect courtesy everywhere he went as gracefully as he carried his tall youthful figure. Even the passing years did not seem greatly to affect that perennially young Cardinal. When I saw him in 1929, only a few weeks before his death, he had lost none of his youthful charm, though then in his sixties. Officially the Cardinal was a Spaniard, but had been born and educated in England and seemed Spanish only in his charming courtesy. One part of him was Irish. He was, I feel sure, the most accomplished linguist in Rome, speaking Italian, Spanish, English, French, and German perfectly. "So perfectly, my dear friend," said one of his secretaries to me, "that he can make five different nationalities sure that he belongs to them." His knowledge of Latin gave him six tongues. He was an accomplished diplomat as well as a scholar. To satisfy his yearning for apostolic work he established and supported a club for poor boys in Rome. He was easy to meet but not easy to know, for his circle of friends was not large. Those who were within it, however, gave him the tribute of genuine affection. My own relations with him were, of course, purely official. I did, nevertheless, have some opportunities of catching glimpses of the man under the red robe. They confirmed the impression made on me by the prince. I came to think of him as an essential part of my Rome. He never knew that. I did not know it myself till 1934 when I returned to Rome and did not find him there.

I keep near me the copy of a little card found on the Cardinal's desk after his death on which is reproduced a few lines in his own handwriting. I like to look at it and be reminded of the one thing necessary for rich and poor, prince and pauper; but above all for those called to the practice of the dangerous art of ruling. I can pay no higher tribute to the Secretary of State of Pius than to reproduce it here in print and thus enlarge its appeal:

> "I have promised with His grace not to *begin* any action without remembering that He is *witness* of it—that He *performs* it together with me and *gives me the* means to do it—never to *conclude* any without the same thought, offering it to Him as *belonging* to Him, and in the course of the action, whenever the same thought shall occur, to stop for a moment and renew the desire of pleasing Him."

Only the accident of noble birth prevented Cardinal Merry del Val from being a humble pastor in England. Every time I talked with him I felt his desire to be in intimate touch with souls. I was sure that he would have preferred to preach to people rather than write to kings, to give spiritual conferences rather than engage in diplomatic conversations. The card tells me that I was not mistaken. He was the first great and powerful Roman friend of the

Extension Society. Perhaps, for that reason, I may, with some
show of right, call him mine. He never asked, nor would he permit,
any return for the many favors he so quietly bestowed, but to the
end of his days he was glad to hear that these favors had not been
given in vain. Others might have the credit on earth. All he seemed
to want for himself was a little of the spiritual merit. As I grow
older I feel deeper and deeper the joy of having known a few, alas
how few, such men.

Had it not been for Cardinal Merry del Val I must have returned
home from my second visit with nothing but a hearing. He saw
to it that there was more. I knew none of the ways into the Congregations used by the Holy See for the government of the Church.
But it was so easy to explain in English to the Cardinal that I told
him the whole story on my first visit. It appealed to him. He took
a personal interest in it. When complications arose it was the
Cardinal who instructed me in the science of untying hard diplomatic knots. When the whole question of a Papal Brief seemed
to be buried in the *dossiers* of a Congregation with no action in
sight, it was the Cardinal who told me how to dig it out of the
grave and who named the one to breathe life into it again.

Close to the Cardinal were two interesting men; one is now
known as Cardinal Canali. The other, Monsignor Tampieri, is dead.
The Secretary of State gave me Tampieri as a guide through what
looked to me like a labyrinth of negotiations.

"This American," said the Cardinal to the prelate, "is like all
Americans, in a hurry. Push him on as fast as you can. He says he
will not leave Europe till he has a Brief of approval. He is going to
appeal to the Holy Father himself for it, since that is now the only
way. You may profit by learning English from him."

Monsignor Tampieri did profit in that way; while I profited by
winning a friendship which lasted beyond his retirement and to
the day of his regretted death.

Roman Congregations are set in their way of doing business carefully and in accord with age-old traditions. Those in charge of their
work are men of unfailing courtesy, which does not mean they can
be pushed out of their accustomed gait. Rome makes haste slowly.
One soon learns in dealing with them that they represent an institution which does not die. There is no better exemplification of the

indefectibility of the Church than is found in the patient working of a Roman Congregation. Once a case is in its hands it is destined to be studied carefully by the Consultors who report upon it. "I have studied that question," is one of the sayings most frequently heard when one meets Consultors of the various Roman Congregations. Only when all the study is done and all the opinions are in does the case go before the Cardinals.

The business of my second visit in 1909 had become entangled through a petition similar to our own from our sister society in Canada. The two should have been presented and passed on together, but by an error they were submitted to different Congregations. The only way to get quick action was to have the Holy Father himself remove the Canadian petition from where it lay awaiting action and place it with ours under the competency of the Congregation of Extraordinary Affairs of which the Cardinal Secretary of State was head. But would the Holy Father do that?

I think that the strain of humor in the Pope helped. To find an American entangled in Roman red tape appealed to the humor in Pius X. At least he laughed heartily over it when, in an audience one rainy night, I showed the knots to him. But the laugh did not surprise me. Had I not seen how thoroughly he enjoyed that Irish story? When I saw the Holy Father's smile beginning to form I knew that I had won. It was better than a mere victory, for the Pope showed the greatest interest in the society's work and plans, especially in the very thing that had been most severely criticized at home in America as an innovation—the chapel car. He was enthralled especially by the pictures of the motor car. Tapping one of them with his finger, he said, "That is what we might well be thinking of to reach the scattered people out on the Campagna." The mind of the tenth Pius was very practical. So he took the practical step to untie the red tape that had me bound. The day after my audience the two petitions were in Cardinal Merry del Val's hands and nothing was left to do but write the Brief of approval which the Pope himself helped to outline.

The itch to write has always been one of my personal afflictions— and joys, but never did I have it quite as pronouncedly as when I learned from the Cardinal that orders had been given for the preparation of the Brief. I wanted to write it because I knew what I wanted it to say, and I had the audacity to tell the Cardinal so. There was a twinkle in his eye when he told me that he feared I might find it difficult to put off the editorial style and take on Roman solemnity. But he told me who had the task in hand, and how to hurry him up, warning me, however, not to expect American quick results. The information brought me to a new door in the Vatican and the good offices of the young Secretary of Briefs, Monsignor Frederico Tedischini, now too a Cardinal.

What an interesting career Monsignor Tedischini has had since the day I persuaded him to stay up late to expedite that Brief's movement and the day upon which he received the red hat! Most of the years between were spent in Spain as Nuncio and Dean of the Diplomatic Corps. He saw the monarchy pass, the republic come. He followed with seeing and understanding eyes the events that led to the disaster and the civil war. His recall to Rome from Spain was many times postponed because he could not be spared. When it did come, just before the worst happened, it perhaps saved him from a violent death. I have an inscribed photograph of him as I had known him in Rome, showing the charming young prelate that he was. A few days ago I saw his portrait as a Cardinal. Twenty-eight years and Spain had done their work, but I felt sure that it was Spain that had cut the deepest lines of care upon his face.

An American who had to stay in Rome on exacting and worrisome business, but fortunate enough to be *persona grata* to Bishop Kennedy, could not fail to make himself a sort of nuisance at the North American College; seeing a bit of home behind its great doorway. But the North American College on the outside does not look a bit like home. It is located on one of the narrowest streets of the old city and if there is anything imposing about the building one cannot see it from the street. Exteriorly the college never meant for me more than an archway gate in a high stone wall. When the door is passed a few steps lead into a cloistered courtyard garden. Such a garden would not be a surprising find in Florida, but there it would be neither old nor American; perhaps only the latest bad dream of a promoter. But that cloistered courtyard garden is no architectural bad dream where it stands, for it is Roman in Rome and old as well. It is really a bit of home to an

American visitor, not because of its appearance but because the cloisters echo the sounds of his own tongue. Among them some two hundred students from the United States pass from four to six years. Daily they go to the Roman universities with thousands of others gathered from the ends of the earth. From their number will come many of the future bishops and clergy of the United States. This college is a nursery of bishops. Two out of four American cardinals are of its alumni at the present time. One of them, the Archbishop of Boston, was rector of the college when he was consecrated. His successor, Bishop Kennedy, became an archbishop without leaving the rectorship.

Bishop Thomas Kennedy knew his Rome well, knew its people well and knew well what he wanted of his students. For them he had two constant cares: to make them show results, to which end he kept before their eyes the success of the Irish College in examinations, and to prove to all and sundry that they were outstanding in conduct and piety. There had been one small difficulty on that last point: American patience failed to develop to the same extent as American piety. It had happened that cassock-clad students passing through the streets on the way to lectures had more than once been insulted by the then plentiful supply of anti-clericals—the old "town and gown" trouble of the Middle Ages. Neither the Americans nor the Irish had been trained to take insults quietly. Their supply of the virtue of meekness was low. Bishop Kennedy's attitude on the matter was typical of his origin. He spoke to the students in regretful tones and to his episcopal visitors without any great showing of sorrow over the prowess in defense of his "Yankees." Neither the students nor the visitors were deceived. Some of the former received orders on different occasions to pack their trunks and go home, but none of them did. It might have been a cause for a real expulsion had they acted on a supposed one. If Bishop Kennedy thought he knew his students, his students were quite sure they knew Bishop Kennedy.

The college had a summer villa at Castel Gandolfo, purchased by Cardinal O'Connell up in the cool hills during his term as rector. There the students spend the months of the long vacation together, and there I was more than once a guest. Some study was done at the villa but there was much baseball. Cardinal Merry del Val loved to come there to play tennis during his own summer holidays. But the great event of summer life at Villa Sta. Catarina took place when new students arrived from America. What happened in the little theater in the gardens no outsider ever knew, and even rectors were outsiders for that one evening. No invitations went out for the "show." I sat with Bishop Kennedy's successor, Monsignor O'Hern, one night while the festivities were going on in the hall; but we were outside. I hinted and hinted again that I wanted to go where shouts of laughter were pouring out in a flood. But the Rector quietly ignored my misery. I never wanted anything quite so badly for two solid hours as to get into that hall. But neither then nor after did I have the opportunity.

There was one occasion when Bishop Kennedy almost expelled me, though I was no student of his. I had met a Canon of the Lateran Basilica, Monsignor Tiberghien, later an Archbishop, who became greatly interested in Church Extension. He was different from other Roman ecclesiastics in the fact that he was French and rich. One morning he handed me an envelope containing a thousand dollars which he said was *"pour votre belle oeuvre—*for your beautiful work." I was going to the Villa that day with the Rector. When I reported to him at the college I asked: "What would you say if I told you that I had just received a gift for the society of a thousand dollars?"

"I should say," he answered, "that you had met some rich American at Hotel Excelsior and held him up."

"But if it came from a Roman prelate, what then?"

"Roman prelates have no thousands to give you."

I showed him five one thousand franc notes, then the equivalent of a thousand dollars, and told him who had given them to me.

"So you are plying your trade here? Pack your trunk and go home," he commanded, "or I'll have the Holy Father set the dogs on you."

I did not pack my trunk and go home. I knew about his expulsions and went to the Villa as planned. Later I got another gift of like amount from the same man, who insisted on being my host every time the Trevi Fountain made good and I returned to the Eternal City to give it more *soldi*.

When, back in Chicago, I met Archbishop Quigley I had the

parchment Brief to show him. He read it carefully, folded it back into its case, and said: "It will do splendidly. Now you are safe from the critics. With that document you can do some real work and nobody can touch us. . . . Tell me whom you met over there."

One of those I met was a certain Monsignor Pacelli, Undersecretary of State for Ordinary Affairs; tall and thin, graceful in carriage, and with a face that might be that of a saint. He received me in a room high up under the roof of the Vatican, from the windows of which I could look down over St. Peter's. He sat quietly as if he had not a thing to do in the world but put me at my ease. He looked even then like a Cardinal and asked questions as Roman Cardinals ask them; that is, he would seem to throw out a short hint and rely upon it for a long answer. I little thought as I sat there pouring out what was in my heart about missions that I was talking to the man who would succeed the Pope of the Missions. I never saw Monsignor Pacelli again in Rome. I even missed him when he was visiting the United States in 1936, though he wanted to come to Oklahoma. Frank Phillips, who has a great ranch stocked with all the wild life of America, invited him to come down from St. Louis and spend a few days there with the buffalo and the Indians, and the Osages wanted to make His Eminence an honorary chief of the tribe. He tried to fit the visit into the packed days of his tour, but it simply would not fit. His reply to the invitation was held back a week in the hope that "something would happen" to clear the way; but nothing did, so reluctantly the Cardinal was forced to decline the eagle feathers and an unusual experience. On his return to Rome, in an interview given to the press, he expressed regrets that he had missed becoming a chief of the oldest Americans. Monsignor Pacelli's cordial "Come again" when I left his room so many years ago will, I hope, be accepted soon for an audience with Pius XII.

⊸§ 17 §⊸

MORE ROMAN MEMORIES

M Y FRIEND Monsignor Tiberghien once entertained me in an apartment near the Four Fountains next to the Quirinal Palace. Later I stayed with him in an apartment facing the Trajan Forum. There was one window of the first apartment which looked straight across a narrow street or alley into a window of the Royal Palace. I often looked out from the window on my side in the hope of catching a passing glimpse of His Majesty of Italy, remembering the proverb that "a cat can look at a king." Only a cat, however, could know if the King was there. I never saw him till one afternoon when the top of his military plume appeared on the street. Nothing else of him was visible since he was surrounded by the tall officers of his magnificently uniformed guard. The King is a small man.

To Monsignor Tiberghien's apartments came many delightful people who were not kings; none more interesting than my host. He made me forget my jealousy of the cat.

In all my life I have never met a more gracious host and altogether more charitable man than Jules Tiberghien, Canon of the Lateran Basilica. He had no official position in the Roman Curia but, in the reign of Benedict XV, had a very important unofficial one. He was a secret distributor of Papal alms for the poor of Rome. Few indeed knew him for that. At the Vatican he was merely an old friend of the Holy Father who now and then was called to quiet evening audiences. Had not the Holy Father, when simply Monsignor Della Chiesa, been a frequent guest in the apartment near the Quirinal? I was one of the few who saw the autographed missive sent from the Vatican, immediately after the election of Benedict, to "Our old and dear friend, now our beloved son, Mon-

175

signor Jules Tiberghien." Two fine keepsakes from the War Pope
to his friend were amongst the Canon's treasures, and one of them,
a silver-bound casket, was given to me after the Pope's death and
soon before the passing of his friend. In turn I gave it where it will
be guarded and treasured. It would have been a source of some wonder had the Pope's attendants, during the evening audiences of
Monsignor Tiberghien, known what his cassock pockets contained
when he was ushered out. Once I saw what was in them. Next day
Monsignor made his rounds of the poor. I suspected that when he
did, the Holy Father's money had doubled in a night.

Monsignor Tiberghien was, I said, French and rich. To meet
him at home no one would think him rich, but one would certainly know that he was French. He had the French carefulness
when it came to unnecessary spendings, but he had also the French
weakness for works of art. He possessed some fine pictures. These
and his favorite oeuvres were his failings or, if you will, his virtues.
Chief amongst the "works" were missions. His gifts to them traveled all over the world, and he himself had traveled just as far
though not so often. His idea of a vacation was to get away and see
missions in operation.

Mr. Gregory, a talented young First Secretary of the British
Legation to the Vatican, came often to see Monsignor Tiberghien.
He is British Minister to some place or other now. In conversation
one day, Mr. Gregory did for me a problem in what might be called
ecclesiastical mathematics. He added up certain persons and sub-
tracted certain existing conditions, divided the result by good judgment, and produced an archbishop. I waxed merry over it. Of course
I knew that he was wrong but quite forgot that I had never been
much good at any kind of mathematics. It turned out that Mr.
Gregory was right. The archbishop thus produced in advance was
the present Cardinal Archbishop of Chicago.

To the same delightful home often came Captain, now Admiral,
Yamamoto of the Japanese Embassy to the Quirinal, the first Jap-
anese Catholic I had ever met. He was a close friend of Monsignor
Tiberghien and a member of the leading Catholic family of Japan.
I met him later in Paris and was led by him into one of the never-
to-be-forgotten events of my life when he gave a dinner for me at
Henri's. But of that later.

I knew one British Minister to the Vatican, but years after meeting the clever Mr. Gregory. He was the Count de Salis, an Irishman who had the rather odd distinction of being one of the greatest living authorities on the Balkans. His legation occupied apartments in the Borgese Palace, in the very heart of old Rome. Every inch an Irish gentleman, he was one of those chosen few in diplomacy who could turn a physical weakness into a mental asset. He was hard of hearing. He let you know that by keeping one hand cupped about an ear when you started conversation with him. The Count certainly was a little hard of hearing, but not too hard. He was most afflicted when he wanted to do all the talking himself. I met him in Rome on my last visit. I understood that he had retired and had come back only for a rest. But Rome draws back those who fall under her spell and there he was, still the doctor who had a finger on the pulse of the East and a saddened eye on the pale face of Europe.

The scholastic side of ecclesiastical Rome is full of interest. Its life centers chiefly around the lecture halls of four universities: the Gregorian, the Minerva, the Propaganda, and the Appollinare. Their students troop twice daily out of an innumerable number of colleges and houses of study. To watch these students come out from lectures and start back via the Pincio park to their colleges is to be transported to the Paris, the Bologna, or the Salamanca of the Middle Ages. Each college or religious house has its distinctive habit. The flash of a blue cincture going by discloses Latin America; one of red, with blue buttons and white collar, our own part of the same America. A red blaze proclaims the German. Combinations of colors, shown as a rule in the woolen belt, spell out the names of all nations to the initiated. The habits of Franciscans, Dominicans, Carmelites, and other orders are the uniforms of their students. Rome is full of such uniforms, seen chiefly before and after lectures. At other times they remain hidden in quiet houses of study seldom entered by visitors.

There are places of special interest in many of these houses. The North American College already referred to had an impressively beautiful chapel which few tourists ever get to see. The building itself was once a convent and housed at least one canonized saint. Its halls seem made for ghosts, so old are they; but Yankee lads do not bother about ghosts. The Beda College is filled with English converts, most of whom had been clergymen before they "went over to Rome." One interesting exception to the convert rule was Sir John O'Connell, a distinguished member of the Dublin bar, over seventy years of age and a baronet. He is now a priest in London. But officially there are no lords in the Beda, though perhaps there were students with a claim to titles. The English College itself, to be distinguished from the Beda, is the oldest in Rome and is known as the Venerable. It supplied martyrs generously to England during the days of the Elizabethan persecution. Its chief glory is that, of its first forty graduates, thirty-nine were martyred, beginning with young Ralph Sherwood. Not one left the Venerable for home without the moral certainty that he would buy the palm of martyrdom with his blood.

Though myself far from being English, yet, of all the colleges, I loved best to visit the Venerable; it was so much like treading on holy ground. There is a charm about its family life that is very attractive, and it is always hard for me to escape a committee from the student body inviting me to break bread with them, which means a talk right after supper about anything that gives them a peep across the sea. The whole student body, about a hundred, dispose themselves around their recreation room, run true to English form with lighted pipes, and settle down to listen, laugh, or applaud like congenial members of a London club. I never fail to pay a cozy visit to the Venerable when I visit Rome.

Surprises await anyone who drifts into the life of ecclesiastical Rome. One is always unexpectedly finding fellow Americans in strange places about it. In a recent visit I had one of these surprises when I visited the rector of the Gregorian University. I expected to compromise on French as to language, but he was a New Yorker. In the General of the Oblates I met an old friend from San Antonio, Texas. The General of one branch of the Carmelites was another old friend, but from Chicago. The Assistant General of the Augustinians is a Philadelphian. There is always an American assistant to the General of the Jesuits.

To the Superior General of the Sisters of the Holy Child goes the responsibility for my greatest Roman surprise in the spirit and in the flesh. A reception to their newly appointed Cardinal Protector was being arranged and the good nun invited me (that was in 1929) to deliver an address on Cardinal Gasquet, the former Protector who had died some months before. Assurances that I did not know enough to cover the life and works of a great scholar as well as a great churchman acceptably were quietly swept away with the promise to send me books and more books. Then the camouflage of modesty had to be pulled off: I confessed that I was afraid to face the audience I thought this intellectual lady would call together. She reassured me on the point, "Only a little gathering of friends at an afternoon tea—nothing really formal—quite unnecessary to prepare a long and learned discourse, quite!—only one Cardinal, your friend Cerretti—nothing at all to worry about." She had her way. Those talented people who have a "way with them" force one to walk it. I came to the "simple afternoon tea." The good Superior had not deceived me about that tea. But after the quiet function was over the guests were directed through the garden to a hall. Here were many more than the "few friends." Every Embassy to the Vatican Court seemed to be represented. From the platform I picked out the handsome French Ambassador, the Marquis of Fontenay, as a start for surprises to come. But my eyes stopped dead when I saw, seated in the front row and right before me, one of the great ponderables in the flesh, a large man with an odd drooping blond mustache. This little affair, "nothing at all to worry about," had grown. Nothing was more responsible for the growth in my eyes than the presence of G. K. Chesterton. Knowing well that to read persistently and thoughtfully another's writings is to sit at that man's feet as a pupil, I felt like a schoolboy awaiting a call to recite to the master. But it was no recitation in this case. I had committed no oration to memory, but had come to this "little gathering of friends" with only a few notes for guidance. I had been in tight places before but none felt quite as binding as this one.

When I arose to speak I kept my eyes away from the formidable critic in front, but I could do nothing about my ears. Before I had worked off my opening pleasantry they were saluted with a hearty good-natured and very sincerely given tribute of a chuckle. The first serious remark brought out a decided "Hear! Hear!" from the same source. Was it possible that I was interesting Chesterton?

It sounded so! He became my whole audience, and the best audience I ever had. Nothing needed to be diagrammed for this keen and good-humored big man. He could see the spot on the map as soon as the pointer reached for it. The last word of a bit of humor was lost in his delightful mirth. Never again would I fear to speak before Chesterton. But never since have I had the opportunity. Nor shall I have it, for G. K. is dead, God rest him.

Another surprise came out of that afternoon tea. In referring to the late Cardinal's ancestry I mentioned what I thought he owed to the French blood in him. No sooner had I returned to my seat beside Cardinal Cerretti than a bishop with a long, thin, Chinese-looking beard came over with extended hand. Most impressively he said: *"Je vous remercie, Monseigneur."* I was so struck by what seemed to me a display of quiet emotion that my face must have implied a question, for he hastened to add: *"pour ce que Monseigneur a dit de la France."* Ha! there it was, the all-embracing patriotism of the Frenchman. There is nothing like it on earth. I was not a bit surprised next day to receive an invitation to a reception at the French Embassy. I went, to show my appreciation, but I was poor company, for I had never been at a diplomatic reception before and really did not know how to carry on. I never went to another. To me they are more dangerous than lecturing before Chesterton on a subject I knew little about.

During my early visits to Rome there lived in the old Palazzo Taverna—but in its very humblest apartment—an Irish priest of my own remote family stock, who edited an English weekly called *Rome*. His job was a trying one, for the Vatican, which might if it only willed be the greatest news source on earth, is, as a matter of fact, great in its silences. Monsignor O'Kelly had to gather up facts for his paper as best he could, use them with discretion, and await the reaction. The highest encomium that could be given him as the responsible editor of *Rome* was that he actually kept it alive. It died with him, and both funerals brought out wreaths and regrets. His apartment, cluttered all over with books and "copy," was one of my favorite hangouts. I went so far in my liking for Monsignor O'Kelly as to visit him in a mountain retreat in summer near Genezzano, and, still in his company, take a donkey cart over the hills to Subiaco. The donkey was so small that our excursion, in pity for the little fellow, soon became a walking one. When we reached the top of the last mountain we were in no shape to enjoy the wonder of the *Sacro Speco* of St. Benedict. But that's another story. I was talking about the editor. A news item which seemed well loaded with explosive had appeared in his paper. It contained extracts from a pastoral letter of the then Archbishop of Udine on the Roman question—a thing not to be fooled with. Yet this Italian Archbishop had not only discussed it but had more than hinted that it was not so difficult of solution as appeared on the surface. He even suggested one. Had the Archbishop of Udine written under "inspiration"? I asked Monsignor O'Kelly for his opinion.

"You are going to see the Cardinal Secretary of State tomorrow, are you not?" he questioned.

"I have an audience booked."

"Why not ask *him*?"

"Because he naturally would think it none of my business."

"If it is none of your business it is none of mine, and yet the Secretary of State knew that I was giving publicity to that Udine pastoral. Better ask him."

I did. To my astonishment Cardinal Merry del Val launched into a long explanation of the whole Roman question, indicating all possible solutions. He never once mentioned the Udine pastoral by name. He did not say whether it had been inspired or not. But before I left his apartments I had a good grasp of the question as the Holy See looked at it. A few days later a Judge of the Rota, Monsignor Prior, dropped in to leave a copy of his book on the question with me. Monsignor O'Kelly smiled when he called and saw me reading it. "I see the Cardinal talked. There are times when they do, you know," was his only comment.

I began to understand the value of the experience of nearly two thousand years. That conversation, seemingly so short and casual, grew unexpectedly, years later, into the high spot of my life. Look for it soon.

Of the number of times I have been in Rome the count is lost, but when I left the Eternal City after my first visit I must have forgotten to take half of my heart back with me. Rome is the one foreign city in the world which never seems foreign to me, for I have always, on each recurring entrance, the feeling that I am coming home. Since the first, my return visits have been fairly regular; every three years before I became a bishop; every five years since, with some added for good measure. The first was the best, and the last was the saddest because it made me wonder if I should ever see Rome again. I had thought to hunt up that lost half of my heart and carry it back but—I could not. It is over there yet and there I shall let it stay.

I have seen and conversed with three Popes: Pius X, Benedict XV, and Pius XI. All were different, but there was a special something in each one that I liked. In Pius X it was his gentle and holy simplicity. In Benedict XV it was his personal generosity and manifest will to justice. In Pius XI it is his unconquerable youth, bravery, and intellectual vigor.

"Are you not tired after the work of the week, Holy Father?" I asked him when he received me the day following the closing of the Holy Door at the end of the last jubilee year.

"I could begin it all over again tomorrow," he answered.

"You must be glad it's over, Holy Father," said a visitor to him after the preceding jubilee. "What with receptions for pilgrims from all over the world Your Holiness must be tired to death and glad to have a little time to yourself."

"I shall be dying of lonesomeness," the Pope answered.

The years are weighing on Pius XI but he seems not to feel them. The seventies were not even noticed. He is the youngest old man I have ever known. Once I spoke to him about a priest who had given the savings of a whole life to his work.

"He has the great secret," said the Pope, and he there and then told me a story out of his own life that proved it.

I was born in the year of the Fall of Rome, the year that asked the Roman question, and I have heard the question answered. But it is not of that I am thinking. An era ended with Pius IX. It was a sunset. The night was Leo's, but it was a night like that pictured on his heraldic arms, with a brilliant star casting a no less brilliant ray of hope down on a symbolic tree which lifted a straight trunk over the darkened earth, *Lumen de Coelo*. Malachy made no mistake there. His prophecy was literally fulfilled. Followed three reigns in one, for there was unity in them. The tenth Pius "made straight the paths" by spiritual preparation—his far-spreading devotion to the Christ daily reborn by Holy Communion in the souls of men. The fifteenth Benedict, facing the world's greatest war, designated by his generosity the place of that Christ in hearts. The eleventh Pius finished the era with the question's answer, and set the Church again in her place as the teacher, ready to receive around her *cathedra* the truant children of a world redeemed. Not alone on Vatican Hill have I seen the change. All Rome—all Italy for that matter—was metamorphosed before my eyes.

Yet I do not know ecclesiastical Rome. Twenty visits or more are only twenty visits or more. Rome cannot be known by visits. Rome has to be lived, since every spot in it is history. I did know many of its dignitaries and officials—a little. I chatted with them, laughed with them, ate with them, discussed with them; that was all. For no one can pass an invisible line which centuries of experience in government have drawn between the social and the official side of their lives. They are kind, courteous, considerate. But they are never imprudent in speech or act. To talk with them on subjects apart from their work is to uncover unexpected intellectual treasures, which are shown without the slightest reserve or the least sign of pride of possession. Cardinal Merry del Val, as I said, could turn to any one of five or six languages and speak each equally well. Cardinal Marini had oriental languages at the tip of his tongue and much more than languages. Cardinal Laurenti, the humblest of men, could not talk at all without seeming to count off philosophical and theological points on his fingers. His hands always came to their work as they were wont to do in his professional chair, instinctively. Cardinal Lauri was one of Rome's greatest teachers. Indeed the Curia is always drawing on the universities.

I have done my pleasant lingering with Roman memories filling twenty-five years. I presume my pardon and now, feeling sure that it is granted, let other memories go back to their cells untouched. I let them go all the more willingly because my *soldi* are in the Trevi Fountain. Of course I do not believe in the superstition, but there is the will to return to be considered.

18

MEXICO

IN 1910 Mexico was to me little more than a colored space on the map of the American continent. Later it took on some editorial importance. In December, 1912, I had enough interest in its problems to ask retiring President Taft what he intended to do before leaving office about the problems Mexico was raising. He registered amusement. "I shall leave Mexico, my dear Father," he said, "as a legacy of love to my respected successor." I still hear the Taft note of ironical relief. He knew what a long line of chief executives before him had only partially realized—most of them too late—that Mexico was an upturned diplomatic tack in the American Presidential chair. There was a rumor during the Taft administration that the President's famous meeting with General Diaz, dictator of Mexico, had not been arranged as a mere exchange of neighborly courtesies, but as an opportunity to tell the General that his reign should soon be nearing its end. The whisper never became a voice. All that the public learned about the meeting was the ceremonial part. Taft never mentioned it and Diaz possessed the Indian gift of stolid silence. If the rumor had any foundation in fact, Mr. Taft's successors, not to speak of the bankers, must many times since have thought hard and bitter things about the advice he followed. The only peace we ever have had in Mexican affairs was during the administration of the old dictator.

Mexico fairly burst upon me not long after Mr. Taft had left the White House to take possession of his lectureship at Yale. A revolution had succeeded in 1911, and Madero became President in November of the same year. In him the country had at least a constitutional President. He proved to be the last of his kind as he may have been the first. 1914 found the American Navy in possession of Vera Cruz. 1915 saw Carranza ostensibly in power, after a revolution committed to excesses of murder and looting, with open and bloody persecution of religion. The Taft legacy of love to his respected successor became a legacy of trouble. It almost cost that successor his second term, for the Mexican question entered more deeply into the election of 1916 than the politicians realized.

When the religious persecution had shown itself in its full ugliness, a Texas priest, then Provincial of the Oblate Fathers who had missions in Mexico, made a special trip to Chicago to ask the help of the Extension Society for the religious refugees pouring over the border into his state. The tales Father Constantineau told were harrowing: exiled bishops, tortured and starving priests, nuns driven out of their convents and mistreated, schools looted, churches robbed; and these only chapter headings. The details were to the last degree horrible and revolting. "I came to you," said Father Constantineau, "because your society alone seems to be in a position to handle the situation."

He won me.

At the time of my Texas friend's visit the society had reached the stage of admitted success; that is to say its critics were no longer either numerous or noisy. Bishop Donohue's dream, expressed at the Chicago Missionary Congress, of dotting the West and South with chapels for the neglected or scattered of the flock was fast becoming a reality. We had generous friends and the means of reaching them quickly through a monthly magazine which commanded attention. It would not be hard to plan a method of raising funds both for the care of the exiles and the telling far and wide of the tragic Mexican story. The one obstacle to be overcome was that I had no authority to draw money for that out of the society's treasury, and money was a first necessity. Prudence also whispered that I had no right to add a new objective to the society's charter. This same prudence suggested my bringing Father Constantineau to Archbishop Quigley and asking him to tell his story all over again.

Archbishop Quigley, now a man about fifty-five years of age, had a marked aversion to the thought of being "influenced." There was in his dark, keen eyes just a hint of suspicion, which was in fact not suspicion at all but the very prudence which was whispering to me that I should go slow. During the conversation I said little or nothing. The Archbishop gave a laconic decision prefaced only by one question addressed to me, "Have you the money to draw upon?" I answered that I had.

"Then take it down to Texas, and if necessary to Mexico, and use it. I'll stand by you till you get more. Go yourself and do what is to be done."

I knew what that decision meant. I had been given a charter with no qualifying clause in it except the counsel to use common sense in acting on it. There were times later on when I thought the time limit of that charter had expired. I was mistaken. He who signed it by one curt sentence is dead. I have long ago left behind me the resources by which it was made effective. But I cannot shake off my interest in Mexico.

As a nation our people are appallingly ignorant of any history other than their own; hence our many mistakes in passing judgment on Mexican troubles. We inherited, too, a great deal of English indifference for outside problems, as well as the English habit of looking only at the bulge in other people's pockets. Neither the English nor ourselves try to learn foreign languages, but we are worse than the English on that point. They at least have their trained diplomatic performing seals whose tricks bring trade returns. We play and pay high for our fun without knowing the game. And even in diplomacy we are burdened with hearts. But on our Mexican neighbor we have usually turned the jaundiced eye of age-old and unreasoning religious prejudice. My first shock, when I began to study the history of Mexico, was not in discovering the faults of Mexicans but in seeing our own. History tells the unprejudiced student of Mexico that we have been chiefly responsible for a century-old process of meddling which inevitably led to our neighbor's ruin.

The old Aztec name for Mexico was Anahuac, but the strange name is no more a puzzle than the nation itself has been to us for the last hundred years. Few Americans at present pretend to understand her people, and these few are more than likely to be disillusioned sooner or later. The romantic school of "historians" has had, for a long time, at least so far as books in the English language are concerned, a free hand in dealing with colorful Mexico. What these books lacked was the truth. Mexico was not, for example, a nation held down for three centuries by the force of an occupying Spanish army. There never was a great number of Spanish soldiers in occupation. The Mexican people did not in 1810 rise in rebellion to cast off the yoke of Spain and establish a free republic. The first revolution was in favor of the legitimate Spanish King whose name was carried on the banner of the leader. Only the realization that Spain was too weak to defend her greatest and richest colony made the later and successful revolution under Iturbide acceptable to the people. He was the Washington of Mexican independence. Neither was Spanish Mexico, according to the standards of that time, an illiterate nation. Humboldt noted the fact that she was better off culturally than our own. These are only a few of the points upon which English-speaking peoples have been sadly misinformed. Mexico has been a puzzle to us because we have known so little of the truth about her history. We extended our inherited prejudices about Spain to everything Spanish, and Mexico was Spanish enough to be included in them; as, indeed, was all Latin America. These prejudices, and the proud resentment with which they were and still are being answered, have been, all unknown to both statesmen and traders, our greatest obstacle to an understanding with other American peoples. More harm has been done to our commercial expansion in Latin America by the misleading and bigoted reports sent home by missionaries than by all our commercial rivals put together. If we are out to win the friendship and trade of Latin America we must first remove from our minds the obstacle of ignorance about these countries. Ignorance is an addition to commercial sample cases that has been costly to the seller.

One of the first problems coming out of the Carranza-Villa persecution was how to supply a clergy for the future, since the Mexican seminaries had been closed and confiscated. Their former students had often been impressed into the revolutionary army. The exiled bishops begged the society to open a seminary in the United States. In March, 1915, it was done. Before a month was over we had one hundred bedraggled theologians from across the border knocking at its door. I should have been glad had there been more, for every priest educated in the new seminary—we had taken over a building in Castroville, Texas, for it—could not fail to go back as a missionary of good will.

When the opening of the seminary at Castroville was announced I stated that we had only money enough to run it for three months, but it remained open and at work for three years. The money came in. About one hundred priests went from its classrooms back across the border. If I remember rightly only fourteen were left unordained at the end of three years. These took their last year of theology elsewhere. Digging into records I found two small but interesting booklets, one dated March 1, 1925 and the other June 1st of the same year, of the *Boletin de los Exalumnos del Seminario Nacional Mexicano de San Felipe Neri.* Our graduates had formed a little association at home, though death, even martyrdom, had taken toll of them. The first rector at Castroville was the Bishop of Tulancingo, who later became Archbishop of Linares (Monterey). Six bishops lived at one time in the seminary. The last rector was Dr. Manuel Reynoso, and the faculty was made up of former professors from Mexico. There is now at least one bishop among the alumni. I remember that during my one interview with President Wilson he asked, "Is it true that you intend to open a theological seminary for the Mexican clergy in the United States?" I answered that the institution was already open and running.

"That is good news," he said. "You could not do anything better under present circumstances than to have the future clergy of Mexico know Americans better."

It was a joy to work for the exiles, but there were shocks. One in particular I shall always remember. The exiled bishops and priests in San Antonio had been clothed and cared for, when I heard stories of want in Vera Cruz and started for Galveston to see if I could get a boat for that port. There I met Chaplain Joyce of the United States Army who told me that he had done all that could be done in Mexico, first at his own expense and then on borrowed money. I arranged to return the borrowed money to him. He informed me that most of the Vera Cruz exiles had been sent to Havana, but that some of them could be found in New Orleans, a good many in Galveston. A group of the exiles met me in the cathedral rectory there and I sat down to listen to their stories. One was a medical man of Irish-Spanish descent named Muldoon who spoke little English and was concerned less about himself than about "two little red-readed Irish boys left in Tabasco." The most distinguished member of the group was Frederick Gamboa, who had been Secretary of State in Mexico and the writer of devastating diplomatic notes to Secretary Bryan. As a maker of devastating notes of that kind Gamboa was a marvel. He has since had a distinguished literary career. When I heard their stories my first thought was to show these exiles that at the root of their troubles were the old persecuting Laws of Reform of 1857; pointing out how impossible it would be for such things to happen in the United States, the Constitution of which, in the main, assigned the state to its proper sphere and protected the rights of conscience. "Your whole trouble," I said to them, "comes from Juarez and the Laws of Reform. If you are going to do anything to help yourselves, lift the banner of liberty of conscience. If you do not, matters will go from bad to worse until at last no liberty at all will be left in Mexico."

To my astonishment several members of the group disagreed with me and defended both Juarez and the persecuting laws. I remember how one, a lawyer who had proclaimed himself a fervent Catholic, told me that what was good for the United States would never work in Mexico.

"I admit," he said, "that everything we have came from the Church; religion, education, social service, prosperity. But Mexico wanted a complete government by the laity. To get it we had to have laws which, I admit, were unjust to the people and oppressed the Church. To pay for the revolution we had to seize the property of the Church. It is quite true to say, as you do, that thereby we lost much. We are Catholics and we want the spiritual ministrations of the Church. We do not want her persecuted. But to be absolutely sure that the clergy, who are our best educated group, cannot enter public life we must have laws which may be invoked at any time as a club to beat them down."

He certainly was frankness personified.

"Do you not realize," I argued, "that if you want a democracy you cannot build it on persecuting laws, the very existence of which proclaims that your liberty is only a sham?"

"I believe," he said, "in the ideas of Porfirio Diaz which called for the laws to be kept in existence but not to be enforced. We had no persecution under Diaz."

"Without admitting that there was no persecution under Diaz, suppose that instead of Diaz you had had a Villa?"

"I am suffering," he said, "because we have had a Villa; nevertheless I firmly believe that the Laws of Reform should be retained."

Argument was useless. The man admitted that his position was unreasonable, but he stuck to his point. When the meeting was over and I was alone with an American friend, I expressed surprise that the group of exiles had not repudiated the sentiments of the lawyer. "If they had been Americans," I said, "they would have been on my side at once."

"Don't be too sure of that," he answered. "You may learn before you get through with this Mexican business that your own government is in covert sympathy with worse sentiments than those expressed at that meeting."

He was right, as I discovered later to my horror.

I went to New Orleans and persuaded Archbishop Blenk, who spoke Spanish well, to come with me to Cuba. We did what we could to relieve the sad situation of the exiles there. Word came before we left that former President Theodore Roosevelt was anxious to secure accurate information on the Mexican situation from us. We gathered a number of affidavits in Havana and took a Ward Line steamer back to New York. At the dock, awaiting our arrival, was Mr. Roosevelt's secretary, Mr. McGrath, who drove us to Oyster Bay direct from the ship. There we were shown at once into a large room hung with hunting trophies. My eyes were glad to wander over the great expanse of that room. It was my ideal of what a living room should be. The former President came in wearing a heavy tweed suit with knickerbocker trousers, golf stockings, and rough shoes. Once before I had felt "Teddy's" handshake and had seen his expansive smile. It was at a Spanish War Veterans' banquet in Detroit. I had given the invocation and was seated at the speaker's table. When the President arose to leave after his speech, seeing how anxious my neighbors were to shake hands with him, I stepped back and left the line to them. But Mr. Roosevelt had seen the move. After shaking hands with the man in front of me, he asked him to step aside a moment, and I saw the full glory of the Roosevelt smile. "Good night to you, Father," he said, "I wanted to tell you that I hope we may meet again." The friend of the strenuous life could be most gracious.

Mr. Roosevelt led the Archbishop and myself to a smaller room, sat down at his desk and went right to business. "What did you bring me?" he asked.

I handed him the affidavits one by one. He read them carefully, looked at the signatures and the attestations. "These are all right," he concluded, "but I heard that convents have been broken into and nuns ravished. Have you anything to prove that such things happened?"

I slipped a paper from the bottom and said, "I was going to keep that back for reasons which you can guess."

"Of course, I understand quite well," he replied, "but I don't believe in keeping back any of the truth. The whole thing is damnable, and I intend to let the American public know it. You had better let me have that paper also."

He wrote a syndicated article on the Mexican situation based on the documents the Archbishop and I gave him.

It was not very hard to raise the money for relief. Catholics contributed gladly to an appeal backed by the facts. The appeal led to the White House, and one day I found myself face to face with President Woodrow Wilson. I came in full confidence that a man who had written as he had on the American Constitution would understand at once. I began by telling him that I did not advocate intervention in Mexico, but that I did hope he would not permit the American Government actually to favor persecution and murder. He listened for perhaps five minutes and then interrupted. I cannot repeat the exact words he used but I do remember the substance of them, "I have no doubt but that the terrible things you mention have happened during the Mexican revolution. But terrible things happened also during the French revolution, perhaps more terrible things than have happened in Mexico. Nevertheless, out of that French revolution came the liberal ideas which have since dominated in so many countries, including our own. I hope that out of the bloodletting in Mexico some such good yet may come."

The rest of the talk did not matter. It lasted for perhaps forty minutes. Before it ended Mr. Wilson had asked me to pay a visit to Mr. Bryan and go over the question with him, but I knew that it would do no good. An echo of Mr. Wilson's words to me was heard later in his speech at Indianapolis when he stated that the Mexicans could shed all the blood they wished in an attempt to gain their liberties, and that he would see to it that they were protected in so doing. Bitterly I reflected that one of the liberties they would not get happened to be included in the "inalienable rights."

I went to see Mr. Bryan. When I presented myself I was told that the Secretary of State would not see me. I mentioned that I was there in answer to a suggestion of the President, but was informed that the President had sent for Mr. Bryan who was about to cross over to the White House. I replied that, as I had no other business in Washington, I could wait until Mr. Bryan returned, but was told that it would be quite useless to wait as the Secretary did not want to see me. I picked up my hat to go, but when I turned around Mr. Bryan himself was standing at the entrance to his private office. The thought crossed my mind that he had heard everything. He beckoned, I thought a bit ungraciously, and said, "Come in here."

When I entered he pointed to a chair and sat down at his desk, wheeling around so as to face me and acting like a man braced for an unpleasant interview. He had my card in his hand. "What was it you wanted of me?" he snapped.

I answered that I understood the President had told him the nature of my business. He made no reply to that except a grunt of disapproval. I had heard how irritated everything about Mexico made him. A report had come to me that an American resident of Mexico who had called on him heard him say, "Who is he anyhow? Another fellow who has had a cow killed in Mexico?" I began to speak along the lines that I had used with the President. Mr. Bryan did not listen for one minute but abruptly asked what were my politics. I told him that I was a little low on my stock of politics but that what I had were Republican. That avowal did not help much. I saw very soon that my friendship for Mr. Taft was bothering Mr. Bryan. I suggested that I had not come to talk about my politics or my friendships but to talk about Mexico in the hope that the United States would do nothing to favor religious persecution in that country. Mr. Bryan did not now seem in any hurry to go to the White House. He calmed down, but it was evident that he had absorbed the usual false notions about Mexico. The propagandists had reached him. I dipped into history. Mr. Bryan calmed down some more.

"Your secretary," I remarked casually, "told me that the President was waiting for you. Don't let me take his time and yours. If you wish, I can come back."

He ignored the remark, but stood up and said, "The Catholic schools in Mexico are anti-American."

I asked him for the source of the information. He walked over to a corner where there was a little old-fashioned iron safe, opened it, and pulled out a primary textbook of Mexican history.

"There," he said, "is the history that is taught in the Catholic schools of Mexico. Look at this paragraph. Do you know Spanish?" I answered that I knew enough to get the sense of the paragraph.

"Well," he went on, "it has been translated for me and I know what's in it. Read it."

The paragraph blamed the United States for all of Mexico's troubles.

I closed the book and said: "Mr. Bryan, I should like to suggest that you go through the records in your office of our relations with Mexico since about the year 1810, and then try to put yourself in the place of a Mexican. You will be forced to admit that the book tells the exact truth. But I am not now particularly interested in that matter. You said that this book is the one used in the Catholic schools of Mexico. You probably know that a Catholic book carries what is called the *Imprimatur* of a bishop. It is usually on a flyleaf opposite the title page. I have not looked at that part of the book but only at the page you opened for me. Will you," I handed the book back, "see if there is an *Imprimatur*?"

He turned all the pages up to the first chapter and said, "I don't see any."

"I thought you would not," I replied. "As a matter of fact the book is one used in the government schools."

I parted from Mr. Bryan two or three minutes later. He was hunting for his hat when I left, but he shook hands this time. Evidently he had forgotten that I was a friend of Taft—at least for the time being.

Outside the door of the State Department I dropped a cherished illusion about the binding force of liberty of conscience in our ideal of democratic government. I knew that both Mr. Wilson and Mr. Bryan were committed to aid the revolutionists no matter what they did, but I knew also that I had made both of them uneasy when I had kept insisting upon the rights of conscience. I felt pretty sure that some official notice would be taken at least of one side of the question. I had not then learned that Samuel Gompers had come into the situation against us, but I did know that the Mexican propagandists were working hard and that they had reached both the President and the Secretary of State.

Attention actually was paid to what I had said. A letter came to me signed by Mr. Bryan. An intimate friend of the President told me that Mr. Wilson himself had written it in his own bedroom in the White House and sent it over to the Department of State next day to be put on official paper and signed by Mr. Bryan. In it there was a promise to call the Mexican government's attention to American ideals. I did not go back to Washington and hunt around for my dropped illusion. By this time it had probably melted away where it fell. I realized that it is one thing to have a principle and another thing to hold on to it under all circumstances. Liberty of conscience as set forth in the Bill of Rights was not for export.

I have had friends who idolized Woodrow Wilson. That was quite natural. Anyone who can wave a magic wand over words and make them line up and march in rhythmic swing is sure to find admirers and even idolaters, no matter what may be the objective of the maneuver. I like the magic myself and admire the cleverness. But I reserve adoration for truth. Right principles are sacred things which have universal application. One cannot half-love them. They demand all. Hence my admiration for the literary genius and learning of Woodrow Wilson never grew wings enabling me to follow him to the heights of his world-wide ambitions.

19

MEXICANS

BEFORE me I have what appears to be a snapshot of a most disreputable looking peon; unkempt, unshaven, clad in rags. It is the picture of an Archbishop who later became an Apostolic Delegate—Ruiz y Flores of Morelia. He had crossed the desert into exile. I find another picture, this time of a man who looks like a banker. He is not an archbishop, however, but a priest. Some friends had dressed him up, thinking that thus disguised he might have a better chance to escape the slaughterers. A third snapshot shows a tall, dignified man sporting a well-trimmed mustache, the Abbot-Bishop then in charge of the Shrine of Guadalupe. Before his picture was snapped I had asked him to put on his pectoral cross. He pulled it out of concealment under his vest. There is also a posed photograph of a group of exiles taken in San Antonio: archbishops, bishops, professors, pastors. Most of them are now dead, for I am looking back to 1914.

Why so many churchmen fled from Mexico is easily explained. They stayed as long as they could and some too long. When they fled it was to save their people from a new revolutionary method of stealing by a process simple and clever. When the revolutionists entered an episcopal city it became the custom to arrest the bishop and the most important of the pastors. Ransoms were then demanded for their release but, since neither bishops nor priests had any money with which to pay, they were put in charge of soldiers and sent out to collect from door to door. The Archbishop dressed as a peon had his ransom fixed at 100,000 pesos, and after being given the third degree in the revolutionary way, was turned over to the soldiers for the begging expedition. He raised as much of the ransom as he could and was then permitted to leave; but word was sent ahead and when he arrived at the next town he was again arrested and the method of extortion repeated. Archbishop Ruiz had tramped over the desert to avoid the towns. When he arrived at the border he was a sight for the angels.

Amongst the exiled Mexican bishops who did not live in the seminary were three outstanding men who came later to Chicago and lived there. One of them was at the time Archbishop of Linares, Francisco Plancarte, mildest of men and deepest of scholars. His specialty was Mexican prehistory. He had made excavations and discoveries of his own, had mastered to a considerable extent the picture writings of the ancient inhabitants and had thus become an expert in deciphering them. In Chicago he was a constant visitor to the fine collection of Mexicana in the Newberry Library and aided in their classification. He lived in De Paul University and there, in his little monastic bedroom, wrote two large volumes, *Prehistoria de Mexico*. These were put into print in Mexico City and a very limited edition run off to save the work from the fate that had overtaken one of his unpublished studies as well as his library and collection of antiquities. I never saw Archbishop Plancarte without his beaming smile, for no adversity was strong enough to ruffle him. He had the happiness of returning to his diocese, but died not long after.

Archbishop Plancarte's close friend was Archbishop Leopoldo Ruiz y Flores. Whether he caught it from the older man or whether he had it by nature I do not know, but in disposition he was of the Plancarte type, though he had suffered more from ill-treatment and imprisonment. Archbishop Ruiz was impervious to excitement, never failing in politeness, and eternally charitable in speech. I never heard him utter an unkind word even about his enemies. He had delightful little ways of expressing himself. One day he came to my office with the others to act as their spokesman. "We have come," he said, "to find our handkerchief."

For the moment I was puzzled. "Did you by any chance leave your handkerchief here?" I asked.

"We always leave our handkerchief here," he assured me. I was puzzled enough to be silent and let him explain. "You see," he added, "a handkerchief is used to cry into, so when we have tears to shed we come down to find you because you are our handkerchief."

Then he made his request in the name of the others. How could the human handkerchief refuse?

When the Calles government agreed to stop the worst of the persecution it asked that a native Mexican be appointed Apostolic Delegate. The Holy See selected Archbishop Ruiz. But soon he was exiled again, and for the third time. He lived in San Antonio, Texas, until a short time ago but, having resigned as delegate, he is now back in his diocese.

The companion of the archbishops at De Paul University was an Indian priest named Francisco Banegas, who, like Archbishop Plancarte, was a student of Mexican history. He, too, devoted the time of his exile to research and writing. Two volumes of the work done in Chicago were published later, but most of it is still in manuscript. Banegas found a helper in a non-Catholic layman who had lived in Mexico but lost his property by confiscation. With time on his hands this man sought out the episcopal exiles and devoted himself to them, assisting in their work of research. Eber Cole Byam thus became a sort of walking encyclopedia on Mexican history. When I was writing my own book on Mexico three years ago he came to assist me in its documentation. Out of twenty-one chapters he documented all but three. I had to give a whole section of the book over to him. Too feeble to do anything but study and write, Mr. Byam had occupied himself with research for more than twenty years. When the new persecution broke out under Calles he was living in Queretaro with his friend Dr. Banegas, who had been made Bishop of that See. Hearing that I needed him, Byam packed up at once and came to Oklahoma. "I have very bad news for Your Excellency," he said when I met him at the door.

"Bad news? Can there be more bad news?"

"This bad news," he said, "is that last week I was received into the Catholic Church."

"I wasted at least three years trying to make a Catholic out of you," I answered. "Don't tell me that a Mexican succeeded where I failed."

"I fear so," he said. "Even in the house of Bishop Banegas I remained a heretic, but when the new persecution broke out it was too much for me. I had to get on the side of the martyrs."

Mr. Byam died in Oklahoma in 1937.

For many reasons the most interesting man amongst the exiles was the late Archbishop of Guadalajara, Francisco Orozco y Jiminez. No one could put a higher value on the dignity of his office than he. The trappings of his rank sat on him with such grace that in them he appeared born to the purple. A palace fitted him and the miter became him. One could think of him as a great prelate-statesman in the court of a medieval monarch. But under the ermine of the great cape there could have been a hair shirt. The Archbishop could shower love on a child, and while he lived with me few were his visitors but the children of my parish. They flocked to him. When I entered my home after a day's work downtown it was more than likely my ears would be saluted with shouts from the reception room where the Archbishop was having a children's party. He never seemed to mind fingers that were sticky, perhaps because he himself had supplied the candy that made them so. One child would be strutting around the room wearing the pectoral cross, another trying to fit the big amethyst ring on two fingers. The episcopal skullcap would be adorning the curly head of some little miss who had come along with the rest to see her best friend. The sisters teaching in my school were glad the Archbishop did not come to visit it too often because each visit meant a riot. The truth was that the princely prelate loved his own. There was all the innocence of childhood in him.

Archbishop Orozco's exile was bitter to him, for he was a man of action. Born in Zamora, he studied at the Latin American College in Rome. In 1887 he was ordained a priest and went back to Zamora where he became vice-rector of a preparatory college, then a professor, then full rector with the chair of philosophy. As soon after his ordination as 1902 he was made Bishop of Chiapas. Personally he had inherited a considerable family fortune which he immediately began to spend, keeping up an old tradition amongst the bishops of Mexico by lavishing it on public improvements, even to the building of an electric light plant for his town. Ten years after his appointment to Chiapas he was made Archbishop of

Guadalajara. In 1914 he was driven out of Mexico. For years he lived with me.

The Mexican government was more afraid of Archbishop Orozco than of any other man. In spite of his gentleness they knew his power. "Why don't you leave the Archbishop of Guadalajara alone?" Ambassador Morrow asked President Calles, "He is one of the gentlest and kindest men I have ever met; the last man in the world to hurt anyone."

"You do not know him at all," Calles answered, "I tell you that he is not an archbishop but a general."

One afternoon, returning home from the city, I passed the door of the Archbishop's room. He invited me to enter. When I did so he walked over to a table and from it took a prelate's lace surplice, called a rochet. I recognized it as the only one he possessed, but he held it out to me. "My friend," he said, "I want you to have this."

I began to examine my conscience, fearing that I must have admired the garment in his hearing and, therefore, had, in Mexican eyes, a claim upon it. "No! No! Your Grace," I said, "I have three or four and am far from needing another."

He shook his head and pushed it into my hands, saying, "I shall not need it any more."

"If you insist on my having it as a souvenir of your visit," I protested, "let me bring you one of mine and we will exchange. Then we both shall have souvenirs."

This time he shook his head vigorously. "No, I cannot take it with me. I put you under a pledge of secrecy. I am returning to Mexico."

Knowing that the Mexican government was ready to apprehend him on sight, I protested: "You are governing your diocese quite well by correspondence from here. Even if you succeed in reaching home you will have to remain in hiding with the constant danger of being taken and shot."

I could see the tears in his eyes. "Let it be death," he said quietly.

He was frankness itself when I asked him what had caused him to come to such a decision. "I have heard that it is being said by some people that the Mexican bishops are not brave; that they deserted their people to save themselves; that if such persecution had come to Irish bishops they would have acted differently and died at their posts. I am not questioning the courage of Irish bishops, for I know enough of their history to concede that they did die bravely in Ireland. But you, my friend, you know that the Mexican bishops were not allowed to do that. Some of us were expelled by force and some had to leave to save our people from being robbed. Now to show of what stuff the Mexican hierarchy is made, one of us at least must be a victim. I am the one surest to meet a firing squad. If it be God's will, I am going to meet it."

I protested, but to no avail. He made me promise I would not tell the other exiled bishops. He himself intended to tell them only that he was going to San Antonio and say nothing about extending the trip. After a week in San Antonio he would go to the border, assume a disguise of some kind, and get into Mexico. Once across the border he could take a train and get off at the nearest small station to the mountains of Jalisco. There he felt he would be safe for awhile among his faithful Indians.

The Archbishop carried out his plans to perfection and reached the mountains. Once in his diocese he went into action and thus wrote history hard to duplicate. He actually succeeded in bringing his clergy together for retreats in groups of from eight to twelve. The Indians had a method of signaling the approach of the soldiers, so that he was always warned in advance if they were coming out to look for him. When they did, he changed to another hiding place and there gathered a new group of priests around him for the spiritual retreats. He made a confirmation tour, always "on the run," and lived in hovels and caves. I had given him a little portable typewriter. On his last sheet of paper, when he felt that the end was near, he issued a decree making me an Honorary Canon of his cathedral and dispatched it by an Indian runner to the nearest post office. That document, typewritten by himself and sealed only with a rubber stamp, is a most cherished possession.

But there was an end to it all. One day the Archbishop went to one of the large parishes, Los Lagos de Moreno. There he sang a Pontifical Mass on the feast of the church and administered confirmation. But at evening he was arrested and sent to Tampico in a freight car filled with soldiers. On the way he was able to have a telegram dispatched to me which read, "My father is very sick and

I fear for his recovery." It was code. Knowing that the Archbishop was arrested and in danger I hurried to Washington and interested some foreign diplomats who sent instructions to their consuls at Tampico to do everything possible to help him. At one time three of the consuls occupied by turn the cell next to the Archbishop's, from which they could see if he were led out to execution. But that step was too bold for the officials to take in view of the fact that, during the trip across to Tampico, a lawyer friend had gotten the Archbishop to sign a demand for amparo, which meant an appeal from the military to the civil courts. The military did not like it and tried to have the Archbishop withdraw his appeal so that they alone might deal with the case, threatening to kill him if he did not do as they commanded. One captain, with the strange name, for a Mexican, of Robinson, drew his revolver, shouting, "What's the use of bothering any more? One shot will settle the matter." The Archbishop was inflexible. Then the persecutors had a false proclamation for a revolution printed with his name on it, and showed it to him. He protested that he had never signed such a proclamation. They assured him that they would use it as evidence to justify his execution and thus shame him before his American friends unless he gave up his appeal for amparo. The consuls advised him to withdraw the petition. He did so, and was put on a train, brought to the border, and again expelled, coming back to me feeling that he had vindicated the courage of the Mexican bishops.

When a comparative peace permitted the Mexican exiles to return home I went to Guadalajara to visit my friend. He was the same man in his palace that I had known in exile, the same man who had gone down to Mexico to face a firing squad. There was some sort of ceremony or entertainment for me every day. One evening when we were going to a reception, and had to pass through narrow streets crowded with people, I noticed that the Archbishop was keeping the lights on inside the car. As we had to proceed very slowly through crowds on very narrow streets I became nervous, for an enemy could have shot through the windows. Diplomatically, I suggested that the lights might burn out the battery of the car. He smiled and said that I was quite right. But he did not switch off the lights. He wanted everybody to see him and thus understand that he was far from being afraid.

Of course the Archbishop was exiled again, this time by Calles. It was after I became Bishop of Oklahoma. He was past seventy then and showing signs of breaking. No wonder! It had been determined that he should be shot, but since the government feared the people it was arranged that a soldier, cleaning a gun near a door through which he had to pass, was to be the "accident." A man in authority, who respected the Archbishop for what he was, heard of the plot and sent an officer to arrest him. The officer took him from his house, still dressed in his cassock and without baggage. On the way through the city the Archbishop said, "If I am going to be killed, would you not be kind enough to stop at a house where I know there is a priest so that I may make my last confession?" The only answer was a shake of the head. The automobile stopped at the airport where a plane was waiting. The officers flew the prisoner to the Arizona border and left him there. But before leaving they knelt down to ask his blessing. They then told him why they had taken him and why they could not talk before. Still clad in his clerical house dress, the Archbishop made his way to a rectory. Later he went to Los Angeles.

I was not surprised to hear a short time after that he intended to return again to Mexico. I left for Los Angeles at once to persuade the broken man to stay where he might die in peace. On arrival I drove directly to the house in which I knew he was staying. At the door his host met me. "You are too late," he said. "He is gone. I wish you had arrived yesterday."

Somehow the Archbishop got back to Mexico and again went to the mountains. He felt the end coming and then boldly set out for Guadalajara. When it was known that he was dying, the government gave assurance that he would not be molested. The man who had lived so long under the threat of execution was at the end given the grace of a peaceful passing in his own city. But hatred was not through. When the people wanted the funeral rites held in the cathedral the local officials demanded 30,000 pesos for the privilege of permitting the requiem, as well as a tax on every bell tolled for him. Authorities in Mexico City shamed them into withdrawing the preposterous demands. The cathedral was crowded and 50,000 people turned out to follow the body of their saintly prelate to the grave or to pray for him as it passed through the streets.

Francisco Orozco y Jiminez was of the stuff of martyrs, gentle as a child, bold as an eagle. In France they still call the great Bossuet the Eagle of Meaux. Francisco Orozco y Jiminez may, in happier days to come, well be known as the Eagle of Guadalajara, not because he was a great orator, like Bossuet, but because he was a great brave soul.

A hundred times at least I have been asked how the rampant anti-clericalism of Mexico can be explained. In a seemingly Catholic country it simply does not make sense. Those who ask the question, however, are usually Americans or Englishmen who live under democratic forms of government which at least respect the will of the people. In Mexico the will of the people counts for nothing. Voting is only a bit of sport for a Sunday afternoon. No one expects it to be taken seriously—and it never is. The business of the *politico* is not to do the people's will but to force his own upon them. He does that by the simple process, after the farce of voting, of keeping the army on his side. That accomplished, it is in his power to enrich himself and his friends. Only one power can break him, that of the Church persisting in teaching the moral law. The *politico* and the moral law cannot live together. Therefore the guardian of the moral law must go.

There is something to be said, however, for the perennial Mexican "patriot." He has just enough education to plant in him a dislike for work. To dig he is not able; to beg he is ashamed. Business, public utilities, mining, manufacturing, merchandising are all for the most part in the hands of foreigners. What is left for the half-educated dandy who must have money for the kind of life he wants to lead? Only politics! But politics mean revolution. He buys a gun and a uniform. If he attains his objective he needs more money, and resorts to confiscation. The Church is the easiest victim. She is not likely to fight back. The foreign investor is now having his turn, for the Church has nothing left.

The rest of the answer takes us back into the history of Mexico. There was, under Spanish rule, a concordat between Church and State which gave to the Crown a right called the *Patronato*. In our own political world also there is a thing called patronage. We have it in party government and use it. But with us patronage concerns only state and federal offices. In Mexico under Spain the *Patronato* gave to the Crown the right to nominate to ecclesiastical benefices. As a rule Spain used the *Patronato* wisely and for the good of religion, but not always; especially toward the end of her three centuries of colonial domination. Independent Mexico wanted the *Patronato*, but those who asked for it were the last into whose hands the Church dared entrust it. In their hands it would have made slaves of the people, and entrenched tyranny could not possibly be put down except by a miracle. The Church refused the *Patronato* to the succession of thieves and murderers who insisted on being Mexico's rulers. Had the Church yielded she would have gained the peace of slavery, and her people the vices of slavery. Her clergy would have become nothing better than a group of time-serving politicians quarreling ror place and power. The people, scandalized by a scandalous clergy, would have drifted back into the slough of paganism and death. The Church had learned much because she had suffered much. Refusing to grant the *Patronato* she made an enemy of every grasping *politico*. With it he need neither dig nor beg. Without it he became a persecutor. The true reason for anti-clericalism is the same everywhere—lust for power and greed for gold. ——

Why do Americans stand by such scoundrels? It must be confessed we have done so from the beginning of the so-called Mexican Republic. First, because our people do not know the truth. Second, because they are easily propagandized. Third, because anti-clericalism, directed mainly at the Catholic Church, appeals to inherited bigotry. And last, because they are subtly influenced in their thinking by a secret revolutionary body in Europe which exists for the purpose of overturning such existing governments as it cannot control, as well as the influence of religion everywhere. Even in Turkey this organization has worked successfully. The people sometimes believe that they are governing themselves and in minor things sometimes they are. But in the great things which depend for their triumph on underlying principles of right and justice the people do not govern. They are as helpless as was an American President in the gilded halls of Versailles.

Three centuries of their history bring no shame to the Mexican people, for they wrote a record of extraordinary progress, away from the savagery of cannibalism and human sacrifices, away from wars to secure victims for the altars of barbarity, to peace and enlightenment. The Mexican people rose to notable accomplishments in religion, philosophy, architecture, painting, ceramics, science, and literature; everything that marks the upward climb of a race. Pupils they were, but pupils with talents beyond the ordinary and a divine hunger to make use of them. Theirs were the first schools in the Americas; theirs the first artists; theirs the first philosophers; theirs the first saints. They dotted the land with architectural triumphs which to this day have not been equaled in the Americas; changed arid plains from dust to verdure by feats of engineering not yet surpassed in the most modern aqueducts; cared for their sick in perfect hospitals; and built for themselves cities of beauty. And all was done under tutelage.

Sometimes it is slavery that kills nations, as it killed the Roman Empire. To Mexico—a veritable empire in its mineral wealth, its fertile fields, and a people who could learn to do great things with hands and mind—decadence did not come from slavery. It was "liberty" that produced it—"liberty" won before it could be ordered by test and preserved by the lessons of experience.

Not even God could give intellect and free will to man and make sure that evil should never come out of the gifts. Not even the highest ideals of the mind and the noblest sentiments of the heart can perfectly guard a people from itself. In the mass are always lumps not fully kneaded which defy the power of the leaven. In a people not well prepared for liberty the human lumps are plentiful enough to make the bread of civilization a failure. There were too many such lumps in Mexico—the "patriots" who ruined the nation.

To tell the story of that ruin in all the just and righteous indignation it merits is not possible. A high degree of indignation makes one dumb. The hand is halted and the tongue is stilled before an ugly picture of greed, lust, ignorance, and deception. In all the list of Mexican "liberators" scarcely one is found who does not merit reprobation, scarcely a character that does not call for scorn, scarcely a speech that was not a lie, scarcely a law that was not proclaimed for selfish interests. The sins against Mexico are as black as night and as red as blood. They are being perpetrated against a people who have proved the good in themselves, shown their ability, exhibited their gifts, and recorded their triumphs.

When Carranza became President of Mexico he appealed to its Congress and Senate to grant liberty of conscience to a people hungering for it. The answer to the appeal was his murder.

~§ 20 §~

LOSS AND GAIN

ARCHBISHOP QUIGLEY died in Rochester, New York, in the home of his brother, on July 10th, 1915. His body was brought to Chicago and laid away in a mausoleum he himself had built as a last resting place for the archbishops of Chicago. I had visited it with him while it was under construction. "That will be my shelf," he said, as he pointed to a recess high up in the wall.

"Your Grace is quite cheerful about it," I remarked.

"Why not?" was his only answer.

Well, why not, when the work is done as best one knows how to do it? Why not, when it was assigned but never sought? Why not, when unselfish devotion on this earth makes a rift in the clouds that veil eternity and shows it to be a glory of the Kingdom of God?

There was a time when signs and omens were held in high repute even in the halls of kings. Today they are for the most part banished to the dimmed lights and faked mysteriousness of the rooms of crystal gazers. But if they still counted for anything in the highest circles, they would have made a mark in Chicago when the successor of Archbishop Quigley took over his office and dignity.

When George William Mundelein was named to the Archepiscopal See of Chicago there were few who knew more about him than the fact that he was Auxiliary to the Bishop of Brooklyn. In spite of the diligent reporters of the Chicago press, who gathered up every bit of information they could get for their "stories," the new Archbishop was still just a new archbishop when he was enthroned in his cathedral on February 9th, 1916. What more could have been expected at the time? He had served as a pastor, as a chancellor, as an auxiliary bishop, but these were no uncommon

207

steps on the way higher up, even if the last was softened to the tread by a bit of green carpet. The new archbishop had been a builder. There was a Gothic gem to his credit in Brooklyn. But he had made few public appearances even as a bishop. He had never been his own master and he had kept his place. Really there was nothing for Chicago to get excited about. The archdiocese would do the right thing—and did it—for the new chief pastor had been sent by Peter and would be welcomed as any other sent by Peter would be welcomed. On the morning of February 9th, 1916, only Chicago knew the name Mundelein, but next morning the whole world knew it.

What the whole world did not at once realize was the ominous meaning behind what had put the name Mundelein into headlines on the first page of every newspaper on earth that day and for weeks after. There had been little talk about anarchy or communism before February 10th, 1916. For a month after the 10th little else was talked about. An anarchist in Chicago had decided to advertise anarchy in the anarchical way. He found what he thought was his opportunity. Thirty or more bishops, the presidents of three universities, executives of some forty railroads, the resident judges of all municipal, county, and state courts, as well as the leaders of all the great corporations of the second city of America were to be gathered together in one place to partake of a banquet. He fed them arsenic.

There were some people who did not accept the story of an anarchist poisoner. But they could not explain the poisoner's laboratory or his letters to the police glorying in his act. All they could do in the face of facts was to shrug their shoulders and remark, "It does not make sense. Why should anyone have wanted to kill three hundred leaders in the life of the second city of the country?" Such a curt dismissal of evidence, weak as it was, would be much weaker today. The war that was "to make the world safe for democracy" was on then. Today it is the crop it raised that we are gathering. We did not know Marxism very well then. Now we have Russia to study, not to speak of Spain. Then we had only a few choice "parlor pinks." Now we have red college professors. It is what has since happened in the world that makes the "Poison Banquet" now appear to have been both a warning and a prophecy.

Dostoevski has been called the prophet of the Russian revolution. So, in the main, he turned out to be. But he was more than a prophet of that particular revolution. From the philosophy of revolution which he so carefully outlined, even though he hated it, he became the prophet of all modern revolutions. He dreamed the ugly pictures that we see. An attempt to kill three hundred people at one stroke in 1916 was at the time thought too horrible to be true. But today it is hard to get a shocked expression for wholesale "liquidations" running into millions. It was hard to believe at the time that the "Poison Banquet" had world-wide significance. It is not so hard to believe today. In a small but horrible way it forecast what has happened in a great and more horrible way in other countries and in our own time.

The banquet was really a civic welcome to the new archbishop. No more distinguished gathering of leaders had ever before come together in Chicago. About three hundred guests sat down to dinner in Cathedral Hall of the University Club. When the second course was being served more than half were showing signs of acute distress. With pale faces men were hurrying to the door. Some had to be assisted. Confusion reigned. Doctors followed the stricken guests outside. Dr. John B. Murphy, the great surgeon of the day, rushed a vial of the soup over to a laboratory with a hurried order to have it tested and a report returned at once. In the meantime he and the other doctors who had not as yet succumbed gave first aid. When the report came from the laboratory the wisdom of the emergency step was apparent. The soup had been poisoned.

I was seated at the left of the Archbishop. On his right was the Governor of Illinois, Edward F. Dunne. Neither of them showed signs of physical distress. The Archbishop asked me to make inquiry as to the cause of the trouble. I went out to find the manager of the club. Once outside the door of the hall I began to feel ill. I had rooms in the club and resolved to go to them and lie down for a few minutes, but I barely reached them before I had to be assisted. Both my rooms were full of distressed guests, many stretched on the floor. The first victim to fall, the city librarian, was groaning in my bed. I lost consciousness. When I opened my eyes two doctors were standing over me and I heard Dr. Murphy say, "He'll come out of it. Let us go down and see to the others."

I had an address to give at the banquet and, remembering that fact, staggered to my feet, made my way back to the hall and sat down in my place. "It's poison, Your Grace," I whispered to the Archbishop, "Are you affected?"

"Not at all," he answered. "Who did it?"

"No one knows, but I came up in the elevator with police, detectives, and reporters. I heard one of the latter say that the newspaper offices are wildly excited and are sending their whole reportorial force over here."

The Archbishop showed no sign of excitement. He was only anxious that the sick should receive proper attention. The toastmaster, Mr. Carry, opened the program as if nothing had happened but as it went on he showed that he too was ill. The Archbishop of Milwaukee, passing behind my chair, stopped to say that he was leaving to catch a train home and was not sick. Crossing the bridge to reach the station, the poison caught him. He reached Milwaukee but was put to bed at once. Not all the guests, however, were stricken. Those who did not care for soup and took none of it were saved. Those who left some of it in the plates suffered little. The metallic poison had dropped to the bottoms of the plates.

My call to speak came quickly. I had the typescript of that speech in my hand and remember beginning to read it. Memory fails to recall anything else about it, but those who were not too sick to listen said that it went well enough. I remember watching a playlet I had written for the occasion. It was given under the musical direction of Father Finn then at the head of the famous Paulist Choir. He went through with his task while being held up at the piano.

It was an ambitious plan the young anarchist, who was a cook in the club, had worked out. For months before, he had been studying chemistry by a correspondence course. Had he succeeded he would have left no judges in Chicago except those of the Federal courts, who had been unwittingly overlooked when the invitation list was being made up. Fortunate mistake for them! When the newspapers told the story next morning none of these judges desired an apology for the error.

The man who saved us from the worst was the chief steward of the club who, passing through the kitchens that morning, inspected the already prepared soup and did not like the color of it, though he did not suspect that it had been poisoned. What he thought was that the preparation had not been quite perfect. He ordered four out of five kettles thrown away and new soup made to fill them. The guests had gotten only one fifth of the dose intended for them. So no one died of the actual poisoning. There were small pea-like substances floating as flavors in each plate, and these too had been poisoned. The worst happened to the guests who had eaten them. Eleven out of twelve men at one table escaped because none of them had eaten these or had taken all the soup on their plates. When the banquet ended about ninety percent of the guests were in the hall because most of the sick had returned after treatment.

The next night about one o'clock I was awakened by the ringing of the telephone in my room and informed that the poisoner's homemade laboratory had been discovered. His arsenic bottle was empty and there were signs that mercury had been taken out of another bottle. For forty-eight hours, the time mercury takes to get its grip, those who knew about that laboratory watched the clock. There was no remedy for mercury poisoning. I for one sat waiting for the verdict as the hours dragged slowly by.

For weeks, even months, the alleged poisoner himself kept ragging the police by mail from Chicago and New York. He defied them to catch him and wrote them that he had been and would again be right under their noses. Two weeks after his disappearance I had a strange visitor; strange in the sense that the story he told to gain admission and stay for half an hour was flimsy enough. He explained that he was a medical doctor from Germany who wanted to settle in Chicago. My visitor kept smiling enigmatically at me as he talked. That enigmatic smile was the distinctive thing about him. When he left I went over to the club to describe my visitor to the manager, Mr. Doherty. He recognized the frozen smile. The visitor did not call on any of the German pastors to whom I referred him. Later a suicide was found hanging in an Indiana woods. The police whispered that the body was probably that of the poisoner. But others had a different opinion, one not at all complimentary to Chicago's Chief of Police. The "Poison Banquet," as it soon was called, produced one of the great unsolved crimes. The man responsible missed his objective but probably was smart enough not to make another mistake by getting caught. For myself, it was years before I tasted soup again at a public banquet. I still look on it with both eyes full of doubt when it is put before me, thinking of the man who called himself Jean Crones.

Archbishop Mundelein had never been in Chicago before he was welcomed by the crowds of people who packed every foot of space in and around the La Salle Street Station to catch a first glance at their new spiritual leader. I had made my annual retreat at St. Andrew's-on-the-Hudson while he was making his retreat for consecration as Auxiliary Bishop. That was in 1909. Dr. Burke of Canada was with me and the three of us met at table every day. In a retreat there is little time for chatting but when we were leaving Dr. Burke remarked, "There is a gentleman who will go far."

Certainly neither of us thought for a moment that it would be far West. But the Bishop was a good conversationalist as well as a good director of conversation. "It will interest you," he said, when I called on him in Brooklyn after his appointment to Chicago, "to know that when I received the official news I went to my room and dug up the little memorial brochure that you had written about Archbishop Quigley. I took it to bed with me to read before I went to sleep." He had a winning smile and used it. "I wanted to find out what kind of an archbishop the president of Extension thought I ought to be."

He was a diplomat. Like all Chicago, I naturally was curious and I hoped that his conversation would tell me something about himself. All it told me was that he intended to be the Archbishop of Chicago and to spend the rest of his life at the job of being a good one.

At the distressful banquet I caught a hint of that in one word he used. Right in front of the speaker's table, and running at right angles to it, the clergy who came with the Archbishop from Brooklyn were seated. Souvenirs had been provided in the form of hand-illuminated programs. They were really works of art. The book itself had been lithographed in outline so that the illumination could be filled in. One of the Brooklyn priests picked up his copy at once and looked through it. Turning toward the Archbishop, he held it up and said, "The last word."

"Yet!" added the Archbishop.

He said "yet" in such a way that no one who heard the word could possibly have missed his meaning. He was starting out with that word and intended to keep it before him for the remainder of his days, and he was young enough at the time to expect confidently that these days would be long in the land.

There was a wise old pastor in Chicago who had all the deference in the world for a superior but who could not bring himself actually to like the new Archbishop. I knew the old pastor well. One day when we were alone he said, "I just cannot like him as I liked the others, and I do not think I am prejudiced. I will nevertheless give him loyal service, for I know of nothing more dangerous to one's soul than to interfere in the slightest way with a man marked for success."

Archbishop Mundelein was a man so marked. Though I speak little of the living in this book I have no hesitation about saying that. He is Chicago history. Already he has the unique distinction of having a town, a bank, a seminary, a women's college and a hall of philosophy named after him. The seminary is the finest and most complete in the world. The other institutions which he added to the multitude already in Chicago were all inspired by him. "Without him was made nothing that was made" during the last two decades in the life of Catholic Chicago.

◆§ 21 §◆

WARTIME

DURING wartime the society kept forging ahead. Perhaps, besides the blessing of God, we had developed a technique. We never hesitated to spend money to get money, yet we did little personal solicitation. It was a matter of pride with us to be able to say that we never went to anyone to beg without an invitation. It was different with written appeals. Tears dropped from every one of them. They had to, for we had learned that the purse strings somehow always get tangled up with the tear ducts. It came to pass that when we should have gone backward we actually went forward.

Personally I was learning fast how an editor lives, works, and watches his step. His readers teach him these and lots of other odd capers. There is always a vigilant group of subscribers who know not each other in the body but act together as an editor's finishing school. Scarcely a day passes without a lecture from one of them. They are set on keeping the editor fully informed about their views on everything. There is now a magazine which prints nothing but letters to the editor. What a winning idea! Nothing could be more interesting than the vagaries and the vulgaries—with some of the common sense—of the human mind!

It was no easy task to keep readers satisfied during the war. No matter what one wrote there were those who were quite certain that it was wrong. To write one's mind was courageous but dangerous. An abbot of French birth, and a great supporter of the society, hit so hard on one side of my head that he knocked it over just in time to meet a slam from a German-born prelate who landed a right on the other. A wartime editor must know especially what not to write.

Wartime

Just before America entered the war the clever propaganda of Lord Northcliff was at its best—and worst. No editor could dodge it and few could trace it. I must have been a very difficult proposition, but at last someone came out in the open and almost asked me to name my price for advocating America's entrance into the conflict. The only reason he did not reach the money stage was because I did not let him get that far. Perhaps I lost my one and only chance to become rich that day. The opportunity came soon after to issue a declaration of independence. It was not neglected. "The Pigs of War" appeared but we were already in. Looking back over the hectic months after America entered the war I wonder how it came about that the editorial was received in such deathly silence. Those who liked it dared not say so. Those who did not must have been afraid it would be followed up with something worse. For a non-pacifist no one could hate a war beyond our borders more bitterly than I hated that one. It was not the fighting and the dying that were the chief causes of my hatred. It was the distant consequences that I thought I could foresee. Now I know that I actually did foresee them.

But about that editorial. It will not bear cutting. It was then and still is all or nothing. I make no apologies for reproducing it just as it was printed.

THE PIGS OF WAR

"A few days after his arrival at home, in Chicago, the American Minister to the Balkans addressed the Irish Fellowship Club in a most diplomatically careful speech, describing some of the horrors of that part of the war which he had seen, after having briefly sketched the causes that led to the first outbreak. His Excellency went back farther than most of us in studying these beginnings, and referred to the underlying reason of the bitterness between Serbia and Austria, which, he said, was simply a question of trade. Austria had been the principal, almost the sole market for the one product that Serbia offered for sale outside her own borders. Hungary began to compete for this trade. As the latter formed part of the Dual Monarchy, Austria, by tariff regulation, favored her. Serbia, anxious to reach other markets, then sought to secure the port of Durazzo, so as to give her an outlet on the Adriatic Sea. Austria objected. The Serbians believed that the greatest opponent to their nation's ambitions was the Archduke Franz Ferdinand; so Serbians assassinated him. The war was on.

"Some of this is, of course, ancient, if half-forgotten knowledge to any one who had interested himself in the war from its inception; but how few of us knew at the time, or know now, for that matter, what was that Serbian product which caused the first disagreement, and thus really brought on the conflict? The Minister mentioned it in a most casual way. It was PIGS.

"Ellis Parker Butler jumped into fame as a humorist with a near-classic and few-paged bit of fun called PIGS IS PIGS. Everybody who has read the story remembers how the little fellows, of the GUINEA variety, increased and multiplied on the hands of the conscientious Hibernian freight agent, until they passed from a trifling annoyance to a very real distress, from a very real distress to a serio-comic disaster, and from a serio-comic disaster to a great official railroad problem. In a bigger way Mr. Butler's story has repeated itself; only the repetition is serious, not funny. It is a tragedy, not a comedy. The pigs of Serbia were, in truth, pawns on the chessboard of war; but to their aid came Emperors and Anarchists, Kings and Socialists, Archdukes and Grand Dukes, Presidents and Bishops, Clerks, Peasants and Generals, Big Wigs and Big Money Bags—all following where the pigs of Serbia lead.

"When it is all over, will the question of Serbia's pigs be taken up for consideration? Perhaps not, for it may then have been quite forgotten. Of a certainty, all the original Serbian pigs are already dead. The men who raised them are either killed, exiled or prisoners. The women who tended them, poor creatures, are in too deep sorrow to think of their charges any longer. But the ghosts of Serbia's pigs are not laid. The curls on their shadowy tails are question marks that have been, and are, irritating a world to the ·point of sheer madness. So a Tragedy is in full swing on the stage of the Universe; and who now cares to remember the poor piggy of the Prologue? The question of the pigs of Serbia has been appealed to the World's Supreme Court of the Sword. It costs more than billions of pigs are worth to take a case there. So the varied sorrows are on us—all to pay the cost of the gory litigation over Serbia's pigs.

"Were Serbia's pigs worth it? Ask the scarecrow thing that waves its bloody rags and grins with its carrion-eaten mouth there—out there between the trenches. Even a stilled and rotting soldier's tongue can answer your question. Ask beside the sodden mud of the long line of battle graves, where human bodies are planted against the resurrection day of God, like corn in the furrows of a grim old farmer. From out these graves will voices arise to answer at least that one query. Ask the woman of the look that is produced only by a combination of bereavement, hunger and despair. She may be chary of words; but in her hopeless eyes you may read a reply. Ask the ruined cathedrals, and from their desolate choirs and silent organs will there steal a De Profundis that you may hear and understand. Ask of the overturned thrones, the shattered parliaments, the hovels that were palaces, the fields of corpses, the rivers of blood, the dead ships that lie on the ocean's bed, the bodies that float on the waves until flesh and sinew fall away and the bones one by one drop to be scattered wherever wind and wave bear them on the flood. All these are eloquent, with a fire no living orator dares attempt to imitate. They proclaim that Serbia's pigs were not worth the cost. What a disaster would it be for civilization ever to forget that, with so much that was beyond price, have we paid, are paying, and will still pay, the outrageous toll for them.

"New issues have pushed, and are still pushing back the problem of the pigs of Serbia. International questions of the honor of nations, the freedom of the seas, the rights of languages and of nationalities, demands for religious liberty, disputes over boundaries, questions of state, of dynasties, of credits, of national aspirations, all have come to the front; but, through these serious and momentous difficulties the pigs of Serbia still run riot. The porcine ghosts have broken into dumas, reichstags, parliaments and congresses. They have rushed unchecked into chambers of deputies and senates. They have soiled the marble floors of the palaces with their filth, and have trampled over the soft beds of the rulers; for the questions of state rights and human rights were forced on the consideration of the world by the question of the rights of pigs.

"It now appears that no nation, even of this far-away New World, dares refuse entrance into its counsels and aspirations to the pigs of Serbia. Alone amongst the great powers of the earth, girt about by protecting oceans, our nation stood at peace, asking only the chance to dry the tear of sorrow, and fill the mouths of the hungry; but it was not to be. The ghosts of the pigs of Serbia were good swimmers, and at long last they reached our shores. Their deep gruntings are in our ears. Their shrill squealings echo in our halls of legislation, our editorial sanctums, our schools, our colleges, even from our pulpits. Dreadful beasts! They are still unsatisfied, though they have eaten up one continent and have bitten deep into all the others. They demand our flesh, our blood, our treasure—and they will have it. For the pigs of Serbia have multiplied and have grown till they are the pigs of the Universe.

"When will they stop, these pigs of Serbia? When will they go back to their own swineherd kings? How can any one tell how long it will take to eat up Civilization? It took centuries to win what we have of it, but the pigs of Serbia can devour it all in a few short years; and there can not be many more years left in which to finish their gory meal. After that? The wallowing, perhaps vomitings of revolutions over a stricken world, plethora, sleep. Alas for human progress! At the end, it may be sleep—in the mud of desolation and ruin. Can our country save civilization by our sacrifices? It is the one hope. Let us pray with faith and act with charity—that the hope may be realized. We hate war. We love peace. But we have always done our duty. We will do it now—every single one of us.

"For every great war have nations coined honors for those who fought. For the heroism of every bloody event in history have the rulers struck medals, and founded orders, to perpetuate deeds of glory or adorn the breasts of the great. Each Military Order has its emblem; for one the eagle, for another the lion, for another the elephant, for another the lamb of the Golden Fleece. What shall be the world-accepted emblem to commemorate this, the greatest and bloodiest of world wars, with its deeds of heroism unparalleled, its records of generous and unselfish services? If you seek the emblem that best expresses its ignoble beginnings, its disregard up to this hour for individual life and rights, its grasping greed, its broken covenants, its ruthless repression, go you to the devastated fields of Serbia and pick out the skeleton head of one of Serbia's pigs."

When the war was at its worst two men were put on trial charged with writing and publishing that editorial in a radical paper. They answered by giving my name as the writer and first publisher. But they added that the foundation of fact had been laid by an American minister. There was no getting over that. The only thing to do was to do nothing. I wonder how many wars could be traced to more disgraceful beginnings than the pig market.

It was during this time that the movement for a union and consolidation of American home and foreign mission societies began to be agitated. It came to a head after the war and brought about the reorganization—almost the rebirth—of the great international Society for the Propagation of the Faith and the founding of the American Board of Catholic Missions. The initiative came from the Extension Society. A word about it may help to keep the historical record clear.

When the movement for consolidation and union was being

taken up in America the Congregation of the Propaganda in Rome was considering something of the kind for the Universal Church. The head of Propaganda at the time was Cardinal William Van Rossum, a native of Holland and a member of the religious order popularly known as Redemptorists. It is no criticism of the Cardinal to say of him that he possessed little of the Italian mentality. He had not reached his high position through the careful training of curial service. There was no "give" in his character. Conditions were supposed to fit themselves into his plans; he did not consider making his plans flexible enough to be fitted into conditions. Let it be admitted, however, that his plans were in the main excellent. He himself was a man of sanctity, and his heart was all missionary. But Italian tact, Italian caution, Italian tradition would have been helpful to him. Cardinal Van Rossum was no diplomat. He was a good man but stubborn. He did not understand how anyone, anywhere, could see the smallest flaw in what he thought flawless. The best of ideas seldom are like that. The flaw in the Cardinal's idea was its proposed universal application in every detail. A Roman ecclesiastic in the service of the Church might have permitted that flaw to creep into his planning, but he certainly would not have left it there.

It was fortunate for American missions that Cardinal Van Rossum was thinking along lines of consolidation and union, but it was unfortunate that His Eminence did not know more about Americans. Nevertheless, unhesitatingly I record the fact that it is chiefly to Cardinal Van Rossum that the credit should go for the most enlightened and progressive step made in centuries for the advancement of the Catholic missions of the world. And more: if in eternity the Cardinal reads that statement and knows that it comes from me he will be an astonished soul indeed. Once he shook his finger—only politeness made it the finger and not the fist—at me. Once I left his room with the determination that I would never again set foot in it. But I said that he was a saintly man; so I did come back into that very room by his invitation and there found the same hand extended in cordial greeting. "You must know, Monsignor," he said, "that infallibility does not adhere to the cardinalate."

Firing opened on the project for a united American Board from two quarters: Paris and Rome. The movement began to take shape about 1916 when the Cardinal asked me to promote it in America. It came to a head and a headache for me in 1919. It was years—perhaps five—later when it took on its final form and was adopted.

Once I passed a Paris battery against the plan and did not know that it was aiming at me. Misleading newspaper reports from America, some overly enthusiastic, started the batteries in France. America was supposed to desire the leadership of Catholic world missions, according to the news heard in the Paris offices of the Society for the Propagation of the Faith. The implication was that we intended to wrest leadership from France. No such thought had ever entered our minds. True, we were in favor of making Rome the world headquarters both for authority and distribution, which implied the removal of the Paris office to the Eternal City. That alone would have been sufficient to alarm Paris; but it was Cardinal Van Rossum's idea, not ours. We had agreed that it was logical, if the work of missions was to become in all things Catholic, that Peter's See should be its center. But there was no thought of enmity to France.

Paris used heavy artillery. The influence and trenchant pen of Monseigneur Baudrillart, rector of the Catholic University of Paris, was secured and a blast from him appeared in the *Echo de Paris* in February, 1921. I had met the rector on his visit to Chicago as a member of a French Commission sent by the government to thank American Catholics for the aid given France in the World War. Delegated by the Archbishop of Chicago to receive and entertain its members, I had heard Monseigneur Baudrillart speak at a luncheon for the visitors at the Chicago Club. Never had I heard a man more eloquent. The French language becomes music itself on the tongue of a great orator, and Baudrillart was a great orator. His discourse that day was the perfection of thought and diction, he himself a worthy keeper of the best traditions of the French pulpit. But in his attack on the proposals of the American Board there was little sweetness. To him our plan was nothing but the organization of an "immense monopolizing trust of all Catholic works, allowing nothing to subsist outside itself." He took it for granted that it was aimed at French "political and commercial interests" and dictated by the same interests in America. If the good prelate had only known the indifference of American business to missions! The rector feared that the success of the plan would bring all Catholic missions into American hands, which, he asserted, meant "Irish and German hands more or less Americanized." *La Croix* published a good part of the attack prefaced by its own editorial comments: "It is Monseigneur Baudrillart who speaks, and this is what he says: 'We ought to know that the press and certain great Catholic associations, even in countries of the Allies . . . are returning to the old day hostility. Why? The long delay in renewing our relations with Rome, certain denatured or exaggerated facts serve as pretexts for new campaigns, and that in every country of the world.' The eminent prelate, whose heart bleeds when France is less great, gives a precise fact: the campaign conducted—everywhere, but particularly in the United States—against the French distribution of the world-wide work of the Propagation of the Faith and the Holy Childhood. The consequences of this campaign? The obstacle, the only obstacle up to the present? The means to avoid it? We prefer to quote. It is from the *Echo de Paris*."

I heard and read all this in Rome and answered in a private statement prepared for certain officials. I did not want to make matters worse by answering it in the press. A few quotations may be of interest: "It is quite impossible, it seems, for people living in the intense nationalistic atmosphere of Europe, to understand that America is completely outside of, as well as indifferent to, many of the things that are considered of the highest importance over here. Europe is divided into many nations. These nations are themselves divided by different languages and interests. Intense nationalism is the rule and not the exception. Commercial rivalry has been tremendously developed. Colonial possessions are considered of great commercial and political importance. As a consequence of all this, it frequently happens that the first thought coming into the minds of many people in Europe, when a religious question is brought forward, is how it might affect their national interests. In America the situation is quite different. America is scarcely to be thought of as a nation in the European sense. It is a continent. The United States of America is too large, too rich and, I might say, too indifferent to world politics, even to consider using a religious movement to advance its world interests. A question about

Catholic missions is one to which the American Government pays little or no attention. American businessmen know practically nothing about them. Catholics themselves look upon the matter entirely on its merits as a work of religion. The assertions of the Rector of the Catholic Institute of Paris will then be a shock to American Catholics. They may make for ill-feeling. I am absolutely confident that it never entered into the mind of a single American bishop to think of the commercial or political interests of the United States when he voted to establish a Board of Missions. I myself would have considered my time wasted had I devoted it to aiding in the preparation of such a plan for any interest other than that of the Missions themselves. No other attitude would have been understood by our people. As a nation we do not care for colonies. Are we not trying to get rid of the Philippine Islands? Our experiences in Europe have not made us very enthusiastic for world dominion at the expense of the rights of small nations and—we regret it very much—sometimes at the expense of justice and right, as well as the interests of the Church. We want to develop the Church in the United States; but at the same time, and in order to do it well, we recognize the fact that there is only one good internationalism, the common bond of the Gospel of Christ. So we realize that we have an international obligation to assist Catholic Missions. We want to fulfil that obligation because Christ imposed it upon us, and not because our country has any worldly interest in the matter at all. The money we hope to give may be devoted to the missions of any nationality. If an International Board should be founded, we do not suggest more than one seat on it for ourselves. If we had had the ideas with which the good Rector credits us, our bishops would quietly have established their work on the basis of one of our existing societies already approved of, without troubling the Holy See with the business at all. This would have kept our money at home, would have enabled us to develop our own seminaries to perfection and to have sent out our own missionaries. If the American bishops were considering the commercial and political interests of their country, then their plan is very unwise, for they propose to collect for French missions as well as those of other nationalities. On the other hand it has the advantage of being very Catholic . . . The thought that the world in the future is to be filled, through American activity, with 'Irish and German missionaries, more or less Americanized' seems to distress the good Rector . . . Here again it is difficult for us to understand. Catholics in America do not worry about the nationality of missionaries, unless such missionaries become more national than Catholic. We have, for example, been spending our money very freely in the past, as he admits, to support the French. We are just as willing to support the Germans if they do the work of Christ. And as for Irish missionaries, it might interest him to recall the fact that France, as well as the rest of Europe, owes to the Irish 'Monks of the West' a very large part of the foundation upon which its present Christian glory is built. American Catholics do not quite see the danger there might be in 'Irish and Germans more or less Americanized' preaching the Gospel of Christ. We have a fixed idea that even the 'Irish and Germans more or less Americanized' were included in the command of Christ to preach the Gospel. Clinging to the idea that France should dominate the Catholic missions of the world is really exchanging a greater glory for a lesser one. It was never intended by Christ that any nation should dominate, to the exclusion of others, but rather that 'from those to whom it has been generously given much should be expected.' France has given the world an example of generosity and zeal. From France America has taken that example; and because we are at present happily situated financially, we are prepared to be good pupils. It was France that taught the world the lesson. It scarcely becomes a zealous master to take anything but pride in the work of his disciples."

With more light on the question, the French heart ceased its pounding and the firing stopped.

In Rome it was Cardinal Van Rossum who opposed the American plan. Yet it was really he who had been responsible for it. A year before the first meeting I had discussed it with him and he had approved and warmly commended it, requesting me to represent his views to the American bishops. I had reported to him on the progress made and from him had received thankful acknowledgment and new instructions. All this was known to the Bishops' Committee. They had read his letters. The surprise of finding him in opposition later was a shock. What had happened to cause such a change in a man whose honesty was beyond question? I never really knew for certain but could surmise that some of the fears expressed by the Rector had reached him. He may have become convinced, as any European might, that politics and commerce really had been dipping into the matter. The possible awakening of American ambitions to command the trade of the world was common talk in Europe. Would not American business consider the commercial value of the control of world-wide missionary organizations? But it was improbable that the Cardinal would think for a moment of commercial interests. What he really feared was that America would fall before the temptation to devote the greater part of her funds to missions at home. Did we not have our own Indians, our Mexicans, our Negroes? Did we not possess the Philippine Islands? I can see now many reasons for the Cardinal's change of heart but, knowing Americans and especially American bishops, I know also that none of them were valid.

The attack took the form of charging that I was the only one behind the plan; that it was not the American hierarchy but myself alone who wanted it. That charge had to be answered. Happily for me the Archbishop of New York, the late Cardinal Hayes, came to Rome when the trouble was at its worst. As a member of the Bishops' Committee on the question he could inform Cardinal Van Rossum of his mistake. That was what he did. The suspicion was then voiced that I had influenced the Archbishop to help me for reasons of personal friendship. I heard a secret: Archbishop Dougherty of Philadelphia was on his way to receive the red hat. I waited until he arrived, called, and told him the whole distressful story. Philadelphia and New York were too strong for the rumors. The testimony and interest of Cardinal Dougherty were invaluable. He talked not only with the authority of a member of the American Board but out of long experience as the devoted missionary bishop of two Philippine Islands dioceses. In both he had practically ended the Aglipayan schism. Besides, as he journeyed to and from his missions and America to get the help he needed for his work he had taken advantage of opportunities to learn a great deal about the whole field of the Far East. He was and still is the only bishop in America who actually governed four dioceses in succession. His friendship is still one of my most highly valued possessions. On the new Cardinal's advice I restated the case to the Holy Father, both prelates supporting, and we won him. But on a reconsideration of the whole plan later we lost the point of uniting the home and foreign missions work under one national body. Separate organizations were demanded for each. The unity denied the national work was, however, provided for in each separate diocese. The American Board of Catholic Missions became a work for home missions only, and that is what it is today.

When the historian, fifty or more years in the future, reads and studies documents still in my possession, but destined for archives somewhere after my death, he may be inclined to blame overmuch the eminent man who so persistently opposed the missionary plans of the American hierarchy. This short sketch was written to guard against that danger. Cardinal Van Rossum in everything was acting for the interests of the Church and her missions. That he was in the main mistaken, had nothing to do with his sincerity. Nor was he doing anything but what the question at issue called for. Without him all might have been too one sided. The Holy See, as usual, left the case, so far as study and discussion were concerned, to the department to which it belonged, which means that the Church waited for all the light that could be had. Friends of mine at the Vatican raised no voice to help me while the discussion was going on, though I knew I had their sympathy. It was simply not the thing to do. The cardinals I visited listened but expressed no opinions. The time had not come for that. I remember again the cardinal who said, "Listening is part of my regular work." The Church has time as long as time lasts. She speaks only when she knows. Listening is part of her regular work.

If human nature, even by the exercise of the most scrupulous care and the most prudent caution, could succeed in avoiding all errors, then the temporal administration of the Catholic Church would be visible perfection. But the Church does not claim and never has claimed any such perfection for her human side. Therefore in action she is slow, methodical, careful, inquiring, missing nothing even in questions which seem to men very trivial. But Rome knows that nothing which touches eternal values is trivial.

22

THE THIRD LONDON

THERE is a man of many controversies in London. He believes in them, loves them, adores them, never misses an opportunity to get into them. If the chance fails to appear for another when the one on hand is being disposed of he goes out with his lantern seeking till he has found it. Lecturers at Notre Dame University in Indiana have to be warned, for this man goes there every year and has taught his student audience the very British art of heckling. By profession he is an author. By taste he is a forum fighter. "Why do you think Lunn became a Catholic?" I asked a professor at Notre Dame.

"Lunn could not help himself," said the professor. "Ronald Knox showed him that he was wrong and he himself discovered that there is no peace possible for a zealous Catholic."

How true! I hate controversy as much as Arnold Lunn loves it. Sweet to him, it is bitter to me. But seldom was I out of the trenches of controversy after the Mexican revolution passed from the hands of the mild Madero into those of the Reds. The names of Lind, Cabrera, Ross, Castellot, Henriquez, Beal, *et al.*, are not names of men but of fights for me. And though hating fights I fear nevertheless that I kept provoking them. One publication of mine alone was challenge enough to call out opponents. I called it *The Book of Red and Yellow, a Story of Blood and a Yellow Streak*. I cannot help thinking how Arnold Lunn as a Protestant, an Englishman, and a youth, missed a great opportunity. Had he been a Catholic, an American, and a bit older during these days of bitter controversy, he would even have given up skiing, his worldly passion, to revel in the pure enjoyment of battles royal.

I never went into a controversy with a thought for a way out.

225

All of them just burst on me. I had no time to think of the end. But when I had been buried for years in the Mexican question I had what, for a time, I held to be a brilliant thought; nothing less than a plan to end all such controversies permanently. Already there were rumblings of a religious crisis in Guatemala. The Conference of Peace was having its first recess in Paris. All the members of it were leading liberals. Liberalism stood—I thought—for liberty of conscience. The Conference had proclaimed its intention of making a Covenant for a League of Nations. How simple! I would ask the Big Four to agree to an article in the Covenant barring membership in the League to nations refusing liberty of conscience to their peoples. The Big Four could not possibly, as liberals, reject the idea. I did not, however, know all my liberals. I knew the Mexican type, but I also knew those who called themselves Liberals in Canada. There was a world of difference between the two. Perhaps the liberals of Europe would favor the Canadian rather than the Mexican idea of liberalistic principles. There were the proclaimed liberal principles to give confidence. How could any reasoning man get away from his principles? But I did not know Europe's politicians; nor the fact that one weakness of liberalism is the liberal.

My mind was made up. I would go via London to Paris. If I could secure a hearing I knew what to say. "Gentlemen and Liberals: You are at work making a new world; a world, to quote from the eloquence of one of your number, 'made safe for democracy.' Democracy is the rule of the people; the majority protecting the rights of all. You are going to bring the nations together in a League not only for permanent peace among themselves but permanent justice for all the citizens of the earth. Gentlemen, the foundation of peace and justice according to your own principles is liberty of conscience. See to it that the unity you plan is firmly fixed on that rock, and—etc., etc., etc."

I called at the office of the Secretary of State in Washington before leaving. Mr. Lansing was in Paris but I met Mr. Frank Polk, his assistant. Would he be good enough to give me proper letters? Mr. Polk would be that good, but was not particularly enthusiastic about it. He knew that I had Mexico in mind and Mexico was in no American diplomat's mind at that time. President Wilson had bigger game to shoot. Mexico would have to wait. Mr. Polk would do what he could. But Mr. Polk couldn't do much more than furnish a nice but very general letter of introduction addressed to no one in particular. He was most anxious to have in return a promise that I would not carry the irritating Mexican question too near the edge of the bull ring.

The trip over on the "Baltic" was made pleasant for two reasons; Dr. Shannon, editor of the *New World* of Chicago, was traveling with me and he introduced James Gibbons Huneker of New York to me before the boat had gotten farther out than the Sandy Hook light. We let the famous critic do nearly all the talking. It made the voyage short and agreeable, for "Jim" Huneker had no living equal as a conversationalist and few as a literary and musical critic. To follow his conversations with a notebook would be to record the fair part of a liberal education; for education, like faith, comes by hearing—a truth textbook professors are prone to forget. But "Jim" was not strong in faith. Later, when I met him in New York the night before sailing a second time, he told me that he wanted me to read a book of his just coming off the press. "I'll send a copy to you on the boat," he promised. The promise was kept. With the book came a note asking me to be sure to write and tell him what I thought about it. "You can throw it overboard if you don't like it," he added. When I had read the book I knew that the author had asked too much. What to do? Tell the truth or say nothing? To say nothing after the gift and the note would be nothing short of boorish. To tell the truth? Worse still. I read the note again. If the morals of the book shocked me I might suggest a few betterments. They did shock me. But there was a suggestion about throwing it overboard. Over it went. From London I wrote to tell him the fate of the book. "I had only one qualm of conscience in doing it," I said, "I feared for the morals of the fishes." I think he forgave me, for, writing to his friend Jules Bois, he said he met Shannon and myself. "I like priests," he added, *"Mauvais sujet que je suis."* But he was not really such a bad subject. He was really worried about that nasty book, which was a good sign. "People think I am a bad Catholic," he said one day when we were alone. "I let them think so, but I steal into St. Xavier's all alone when Easter time comes around. Don't tell anybody about it."

At the end of the voyage I saw Huneker at the rail of the "Baltic" while we were being held up in the river Mersey by a fog. He was looking down at the dirty water. I joined him.

"It's a filthy river, isn't it?" I remarked.

But Jim was as gloomy as the fog. Straightening up to go below he left a reminder of his wit, "Filthy? Yes. The quality of the Mersey is not strained."

It was early on the morning of February 26th, 1919, when, after a night of chills, we arrived in what I have called the Third London. I had seen London before the war, my first; London during the war, my second; and now London after the war, my third. Three Londons, all the same in buildings and climate; all different in people. The first London laughed and played but was a bit supercilious. The second London sinned and prayed and was a bit anxious and hopeless. The third London was quiet enough after victory but had not "bucked up" to any very noticeable degree. In the third London a moral let-down, too, was plainly in evidence. The war had hit the soul of England hard, and people seemed to have changed overnight. Nowhere more than in England had a certain cold politeness to visitors always been in evidence before the war. It had now almost disappeared out of the life of ordinary business. The London prewar store clerk had been a silk-hatted and frock-coated approach to a blue-blooded baronet in his manners. It took only a little shopping to learn that he still had the silk hat and the frock coat but had lost the manners. At that I did not blame him, for a hard war record was often evident in a trembling hand, a lost arm or leg, or in twitching muscles.

Most of the first night of my London postwar visit was spent in the cold streets. Hotel after hotel refused rooms, often curtly and ungraciously. I had my nephew, Jack, with me that time as secretary. It was his first sight of London. But he started off bravely at midnight to find lodgings in the strange city, and at last came back with permission from the Euston Station Hotel for us to sit up till morning before the Lounge Room apology for a fire. Jack promptly curled up on the floor and fell asleep. I sat there shivering till sunrise, when I went to Westminster Cathedral to say Mass and beg a bed for a nap. A priest told me to go to St. Michael's Club and there I would be given a room. The club did not have one for a stranger. I showed my passport and my card, pointing to a line on the latter which assured the interested that I was a "Protonotary Apostolic to His Holiness." Bless you, had it been His Holiness in person who was begging a room in London that day he would not have been believed. "We have to be so careful," the matron assured me. A chaplain in Canadian uniform passed and the matron spoke to him by name. I knew that name and told him of my plight. With considerable difficulty the matron was persuaded to let me use a room for that morning only. "Monsignor certainly needs a sleep," the chaplain said. I must have shown the effects of my twenty-four hour vigil and the bitter cold accompanying it. I borrowed the bed "for three or four hours." But I could not sleep. My dignity had been assaulted in English postwar fashion. My nerves were dancing jigs. I was hungry. No use to try. I left the inhospitable club without even asking the matron if I owed her anything. If I did the debt is still due, and is likely to remain due till we meet in the Valley of Jehoshaphat. There I'll tell her again that it was a "Protonotary Apostolic to His Holiness" she rejected, and enjoy her confusion when I charitably and magnanimously withdraw the charges against her and her club.

As I lay on the bed which pity had leased to me "for three or four hours" I remembered that my friend Edward L. Doheny was in London "out Hampstead Way." He was occupying the London house of John McCormack the singer. I had promised to call on him and was glad enough now to keep that promise. Mr. Doheny was in London organizing a British-Mexican petroleum company and had a staff of his New York officials with him. Jack and I searched the McCormack house out and for reward received two square meals, the promise of a two-bed room for one night, and assurance from Mrs. Doheny that "Tay Pay will fix you up." Tay Pay was T. P. O'Connor, M.P. My Doheny friendship was signed and sealed that day to last till death. Even a Protonotary Apostolic to His Holiness could appreciate a handout.

Of course I knew who Tay Pay was. Everybody did. Mr. O'Connor had, it seemed, been in the House of Commons since his birth, the Nestor of that venerable institution. A call over a telephone that acted much like the matron of the club at last brought me an invitation to come down to the Houses of Parliament. There I saw Tay

Pay and gratefully put away some tea and cake. By this time I was taking no chances. I heard Joe Devlin of Belfast in action bedeviling the British Empire to the evident pleasure of the British. A scolding from Joe Devlin was always gratefully received by a House that could admire his oratory and appreciate his sallies of wit and humor. I was cheering up. Tay Pay found quarters for us at a hotel, one room. We could have it for a week, perhaps longer. Who could say?

There was no fire in the room—"against the law, sir!" There were not even matches—"but there is a shop around the corner, sir!" We had to have a fire, so I went back in the morning to see Tay Pay about it. I had indoor work to do before I got to Paris, and the pen would not stick to cold fingers. Tay Pay telephoned the manager. "Yes, the gentleman could have a fire if a doctor certified that he needed one—one scuttle of coal per day only." Tay Pay got the certificate, but I would have to get a candle and burn coal by the lump to make one scuttle last out a day. A valet said, "Most gentlemen keep it all for the evening, sir!" Which meant: You can walk about all day to keep warm, and go to bed when you are tired walking. It sounded logical under the circumstances, for it was my feet that were freezing. Heat under the collar would not reach down that far.

Jack came to the rescue. What a lot that boy had learned as a member of the Royal Air Force! He went foraging. "I found where they keep the scuttles, Uncle," he said. "We'll have a fire as long as they don't miss half a dozen a day. Better tip the floor crew as an encouragement to blindness. I served with Tommys, you know. They never see anything they don't want to see." Perhaps I owe the hotel for that coal, but I didn't think it prudent to ask, when I paid the bill.

I got to love Tay Pay and never failed to visit him whenever I came to London. He had a cozy apartment in Westminster and one could be sure, at least in the evening and on Sunday afternoons, of meeting interesting people around his open fireplace. Perhaps it was because I first came to him in helplessness that he persisted in calling me "me boy." Perhaps it was a general name for all his intimate friends. One could always get a fight at Tay Pay's, and no one resented honest contradiction. I met an Irish millionaire—but he lived in England—and an out-at-the-elbows artist one Sunday afternoon before the crowd came. Both were at home at Tay Pay's, and Afternoon-Coat-with-Striped-Trousers had no quarrel with Holes-in-the-Coat-and-Thin-Shoes. Tay Pay himself knew everybody and had a good word to say even for his political enemies. These he had acquired in Irish events after the war, for he was the last Nationalist in the British House of Commons. I heard him say, "No one who loves Ireland should ever utter a word against Sinn Fein before her enemies. I know what the Sinn Fein people are saying about me. No matter. Sinn Fein is now the only voice that Ireland has. Were it wrong a thousand times over I'd beg of my friends never to say or do anything to hurt or weaken it in the minds of Englishmen. The National Party has had its day. It did good things for Ireland which time will reveal. But it can't do any more. It's dead and gone. Let its virtues come to light when rancor passes. You can't trust the Irish in a homemade fight, but when the fight's over they're always different. No people ever speak more kindly of the dead than the Irish—God bless them."

I used to think that it was a misfortune for Tay Pay to be living in England, and at the wrong time. A few decades back in Dublin he would have been the life and soul of any gathering around Curran or Father Healy. I could picture him in the habit of the Monks of the Screw, giving back blow for blow and crack for crack. He was not religious in practice when first I met him but, with each recurring visit, I could see the gradual process of regaining his soul going on.

"I have bad and good news for you, Monsignor," said Cardinal Bourne to me when last I saw His Eminence. "You will be sad to know that Tay Pay is dying, but glad that he will die in the arms of Mother Church."

Tay Pay died like that and London loved him all the more for it. As for myself, I never once doubted that he would find his way back. He had not gone far away and he had in him so much of kindness and charity that he just had to return to the living font out of which they came and drink of it again. And there was so much logic in his trained intellect that I was quite sure he would find the road of the mind easy going once he started. But if he missed that one, the road of the heart was marked plainly enough in a man who loved his friends well and was too just to hate his enemies.

No wonder Tay Pay was fond of Doheny. They did not see eye to eye on Irish politics but they were much alike in other things. But I never think of Doheny at one of the Tay Pay teas. Someone might ask for whiskey. The only thing Irish that Doheny hated was the whiskey. In all its forms he despised alcohol. I doubt if he would have taken a drink to save his life. John McCormack used to call White Rock and ice a Doheny highball. Not even his closest friends would dare drink anything alcoholic in the presence or in the home of Edward Lawrence Doheny. But Doheny was like Tay Pay in his generosity and charity. In fact, I thought that much of Tay Pay's generosity was in partnership with Doheny. I am not sure, but I have reason to suspect that many a poor Irish boy has Tay Pay to thank for discovering him, and Doheny to thank for giving him a chance. In the worst of Doheny's troubles Tay Pay fell back on his knowledge of his friend to say, "It can't be true. Doheny is not that kind of man, and I know men, me boy."

When as a bishop I visited Tay Pay he started at once calling me "My Lord" in overseas style. He even got as far as "Your Lordship." But before I left he was "me boying" me again, and I felt that I had not entirely been cast out. London is not the same any more for me. Tay Pay, who was not a saint—and if a sinner only one by default—is dead. Cardinal Bourne, who was much of a saint and yet could love the sinner, is dead. I would be lonesome in London.

Shane Leslie's was another literary household to which I often brought my loneliness during two long stays in London. Sinn Fein had him under suspicion but, bless you, there was nothing the least bit suspicious about the Leslies. Shane was Irish, but his wife was American, a sister of Mrs. Bourke Cockran of New York, and a daughter of Mr. Ide, once our Governor-General of the Philippine Islands. Leslie's writings had great charm of style for me, and the man in life flashed colorful changes, both Irish and English, that were delightful to one who, like myself, had been trained in the more practical and matter-of-fact associations of American life. He liked being a bit odd. Someone told me in Paris that Shane had had a book condemned by the Bishop of Northampton, whom I knew to be his friend. I was alarmed, for wounding an author's pride in his literary offspring is a pretty serious thing. But I might have spared myself the alarm. When I arrived in England the first newspaper I read had in it Leslie's apology and the withdrawal of that book. He had made the mistake of thinking that what can be written in French for Frenchmen could as acceptably be written in English for Englishmen. The offending passages of the book were flashes of a mood induced by Gallic surroundings. But the author preferred his faith to advertising, hence the retraction. Shane was a convert to the Church. As someone said, "It's the devil and all to get the Irish out of one's system so as to be free to write the things that sell." I would not have put the statement in just that form; and who would want to get the Irish out of his system?

I stayed with the Leslies one evening till quite late, half after eleven, and remembered that the Cardinal's house, where I was a guest, was dark after ten. I should have to wake the porter up to get in. Shane wanted to see me home and ordered a taxi. When it came, another idea struck him. "I am going to stop at Father England's in Sinister Street, and go to confession," he announced, "I haven't been to confession for months."

"But surely," I ventured, "Father England is not hearing confessions at eleven-thirty P.M. He is in bed."

"He is never in bed," Shane assured me, "No matter when I call he is either downstairs with his poor or upstairs with his books. I'll go."

Go he did and his wife with him. I paced up and down the cold hall of the rectory while they told their tales to the priest-friend, and I had to stay after that for a chat. It was after one in the morning before I rang the porter's bell at the Cardinal's house. But I was not a bit repentant, for I had seen another flash of light from the many facets of the well-cut Leslie emerald.

Through the Leslies I met Archbishop Mannix of Melbourne, who at the time was a deftly self-inserted thorn in the flesh of the Lloyd George government. Had the Archbishop not been so serious of mien I should have suspected that it was the humor and not the inconvenience of his situation he was feeling during an exciting visit to London. By some slip of caution the Premier had ordered the Archbishop taken off a boat on his way to Ireland and his further progress to visit his family stopped. His Grace was gracious.

The Bishop Jots It Down

He settled down in London to await the Premier's next move. But what move could he make? The Archbishop was a British subject and could not, for exercising his citizenship right of free speech, well be made over into a British "object." The Premier hoped he would take it upon himself to slip quietly over to Ireland without permission and thus lift an embarrassment. The Archbishop would do nothing of the kind, so Lloyd George passed up his move and his Australian Grace won the game as far as amused public opinion was concerned. It is not really true that an Englishman cannot see a joke. The only sober face I saw when the matter was discussed was the one owned by the Archbishop. Even the Premier had a laugh at himself. The Archbishop was too dignified even to smile—outside. When he left for Australia he carried back his dignity and his opinions, unscathed.

By this time Shane had left the Irish Party and admitted that Sinn Fein was the soul of Ireland. He was one of the speakers in the great Trafalgar Square meeting held to champion Archbishop Mannix' rights as a citizen. The Archbishop lodged at Nazareth House in Hammersmith, and during his stay half of the Australian hierarchy had rallied round him in person, including Archbishop Clune of Perth who made the first contact between Lloyd George and Michael Collins.

There are other jottings to be made about the Third London, but I am in a hurry to get out of the cold and go to France where I have to see the Liberals. And besides I am coming back to London.

23

PARIS AND BATTLEFIELDS

IN THE Psychology of Knowing-When-One-Is-Licked there are
two schools: the first holds that it is not in reason to invite disaster; the second that the playing of a sporting chance is reward
enough in itself. Before I left New York on my way to Paris, I had
reason to believe that I should soon have to join one or the other
of these schools. Remembering what the Paris of 1919 was sure to
be like, and adding the fact that I had to turn out a monthly grist
of editorials, it looked as if my school must be the second. But I
was going to make the test. I went to Paris.

The eyes of the world were all on Paris in 1919. If it is in the heart
that hope centers, Paris was then the heart of the world. Frenchmen
would find nothing strange about that, since they believe that
Paris is always the heart of the world. Whatever other faiths they
may lose they cannot lose their faith in France. They may in action
deny their old motto, "Gesta Dei per Francos," because so many
no longer believe in a directing Providence, but they have not
given up the substance of it. They believe in the destiny of the
Franks, even though without God they cannot explain it. When
Frenchmen no longer believe that about France the country will
become a wilderness simply because no Frenchmen will be left to
believe in anything. A story is told of a discussion between Clemenceau and a fervent convert to the Church. It was on the Divinity
of Christ. The Tiger was confident he could break down the faith
of the man whom he greatly admired. But he failed. "We have at
least one faith in common," he said, as the subject was dropped,
"—faith in France." How French! But after the Great War, if the
outside world still smiled tolerantly—and with a modicum of admiration—at what it considered an excess of patriotism, it neverthe-

less accepted in another sense the conviction that, for a time at least, from Paris was due the coming of a new life and almost a new earth.

There were some solid reasons based on human experience to give strength to this almost catholic confidence. Nearly every great achievement of man, nearly every great literary masterpiece, nearly every change at a turning point in history, nearly every advance in civilization and culture, had followed a tragedy. The Conference of Peace was gathered in Paris to write an epilogue to a new and more terrible one. Such audacious things had been done in an excitement that caused man to lose his head, that the world was ready for audacious things done in the quiet of peace and thought. "What distinguishes us (as men)," said Pericles, "is an incomparable audacity which walks with us in the calm of reflection." Then there were the slogans of the war which we had taken so seriously: "A war to end war," "a war to make the world safe for democracy," "a war to save civilization," "a war of regeneration." More than half the world had come to believe in them, especially Americans, who believed in them sincerely, for we had been led into the war by one whose clever pen could pull an ideal out of the very Slough of Despond. Dangerous men the scribbling dreamers!

I am not saying that the idea of an article on liberty of conscience in the Covenant was laughed down in Paris. It had already been suggested and discussed. Indeed it was regarded as "quite sound, even desirable." Without, for one thing, making the case of intolerant Mexico an international one, and thereby imperiling the doctrine of the farsighted Mr. Monroe, such an article would outlaw the anti-God monster in that country without the direct intervention of the United States, which no one wanted. Any nation that knocked for admission at the door of the League could enter only on an agreement of good behavior. If Mexico did not give such assurance, all the more she would have to rely on the Colossus of the North and on him only. Either way the idea was sound enough. But Mr. Wilson by this time was tired of Mexico. He wanted her to quiet down until he had finished his world job and was sitting safely in the chair of power as head of the League. It was a great dream: to step from the Presidency of the greatest nation on earth to the presidency of all the nations. And it looked as if the dream might come true. What a small matter were the inalienable rights to threaten such a dream! He was for a liberty of conscience clause in the Covenant of the League but he did not press it against Lord Robert Cecil, Venizelos, Larnaude, and Vesnitch; which meant Great Britain, Greece, France, and Serbia.

Lamartine wrote a line of verse—one little line—that jumped out of the page at me one day: "*Les hommes trop près des hommes sont méchants*—Men too close to men are bad." A whole sermon, even a book, could be written with that line as a text. But where would Lamartine have men be? I am quite sure that he would have them close to God. There's the rub! We plan in the glow of inspiration; our idealism is at white heat before it is put to work, say at making something like a nation or a constitution. We beat it into the form seen in dreams. But we forget, with the crowd around watching the iron on the anvil, to put the thing back into the Divine fire. Then we get nothing that more than faintly resembles the dream: man's work without God, the clamor of the crowd, the poorly made result of shaping an ideal which cannot be shaped correctly without the aid of the fire. The inspiration of George Washington's Farewell Address might have been the inspiration also of Lamartine's line. Here we were! And here was the crowd around the anvil on which peace and the League were being forged. But the makers were close to men, and God was kept at a distance. Time would tell. Indeed, time has told.

The setting was glorious in Paris, for glorious was the stage on which this last triumph of Liberalism was to be played. A bloody pageant that had eclipsed for a while every other show on earth had closed in tragedy. It began with Charles, the first King of the Franks, setting up the Christian Empire of the West. Its second scene was another Charles hammering Abd-er-Rahman the Moslem down there between Tours and Poitiers and tearing the crescent out of the French sky. Scene after scene of impressive glory followed with conquering kings who were saints, sinners, fighters, builders, crusaders. Then the glory of Versailles before the fall of monarchy, and the tragic scene played to the roll of Santerre's drums right over there in the Place de la Concorde; when the head of a successor of Charlemagne dropped into the basket of the guillotine. Such a stage! Now it was cleared and reset for the great triumph.

A living emperor had dared to dream the dreams of dead emperors. He had fallen before a world's defense of liberalism and democracy. That world was now to be made over according to the pattern set by new dreamers. Despotism had played itself out. Start the orchestra with the Marseillaise before the curtain goes up. But could anyone but a fool, knowing history, hope that with the spoils before him and the knife in his hand man would think like a Washington or a Jefferson of inalienable things or sing like a Lamartine?

Someone had, however, ventured to think of the "inalienable rights." The article to safeguard them had been discussed by the Friends of the League in London. When it was read, Mr. Thomas, the English Labor leader, was in the chair. "Here is one article to which there will be no objection," he is reported to have said. And no objection was voiced that day. But the article never appeared again. Who killed it? That, of course, was not then to be told. But it was whispered to me that Venizelos of Greece was the chief executioner. The student of the ways of the East might be enlightened enough to tell why.

No use going into the heart of things yet. A "look-see" at the people around will be less trying.

I had scarcely settled down in an apartment on the Boulevard St. Germain before a grave Syrian gentleman called. His mission in Paris was to convince the Big Four that France should be given the mandate for his country. Why he came to me was a puzzle; who sent him a greater one. Gently I told him that I was nobody. Just as gently he ignored my humble assertion. "It would be a charity at least, as well as an act of loyalty to the Church," he ventured, "if Monseigneur would deign to help Syria to secure a protector like France."

I smiled over the suggestion that France was so very Catholic. He noticed that and quoted a French statesman, "Anti-clericalism is a benefit which must not be exported." To the colonies, of course, he meant. "We are not afraid of an anti-clerical France—in Syria," my visitor said. I was not so confident, but the affair, intensely interesting as it was, nevertheless was none of my business. The good man persisted, "Would Monseigneur talk with the chairman of the French Senate Committee on Foreign Affairs? He would like to meet Monseigneur." I saw no reason why I should not talk to the Minister about Syria—and after all there was a chance to get in a word about the Covenant.

Mr. Franklin Bouillon was a Radical-Socialist. What could I do with him? He was also an excellent propagandist for France. He said little about Syria—I think he knew that France had the mandate in her bag—and much less was he inclined to talk about the "inalienable rights." But he seemed, like the venerable Syrian statesman, to take my presence in Paris very seriously. Who did these gentlemen think I was? I did not find that out till later, when it was too late to have a good laugh over it.

A few weeks later I ran into Judge Julian Mack of Chicago at the Hotel Continental, and by him was introduced to Judge Marshall of New York and Dr. Adler of Philadelphia. I spent many pleasant evenings with the latter, a sincere, learned, and good man. The hotel had many Jewish guests from all over the world. What on earth were they doing in Paris? I learned later by confessing what I was doing there myself. The Jews were holding international conferences daily. They too were thinking of the "inalienable rights," but were centering their thoughts about them chiefly on Poland. They had the ear of the Council through President Wilson and much to do with the terms under which the Polish nation was rebuilt. They told me that they were interested in my proposed article on liberty of conscience. But I could get no particular help from them. Quite probably they had been informed quietly that the article had been dropped and that it would be unwise to try to pick it out of the Gutter of Discarded Things. They were wise men. Poland was important to them. And perhaps they had already been assured on the subject of Palestine. Anyhow, they got what they wanted. Sadly I thought of the words of Scripture about the lack of wisdom in the children of light. The Jews at least knew that what was worth having was worth going after.

On the Rue Malesherbes lived a most interesting, even lovable, man. That word lovable certainly fitted the kind and gentle Francisco de la Barra, "El Presidente Blanco" of Mexico. He had come to Paris an exile, in poverty, to begin life all over again. The personal struggle had been hard but when I met him it had already been won. He was recognized even then as an authority on international law. In his apartment I met many interesting people, not the diplomats but the "necessary men"—those who keep diplomats on the safe legal road. One was Dr. James Brown Scott, an American whose advice was never lightly disregarded. De la Barra was eager to help me. He was one Mexican statesman who really believed in the "inalienable rights." His pleasant library became a place of refuge, his delightful conversation a soothing influence when things looked hopeless. He seemed to know everybody and to be loved by everybody he knew.

"Will you ever return to Mexico?" I asked him one day.

"I do not think so," he answered, "I have now a new home and a new place for my work. My children have to be thought of. They are at school here where I can see to it that they get a good education."

"You would not wish to be President of Mexico again?"

"No, Monseigneur. I have no ambition but to be at peace and rear my family as well as I can."

One afternoon the former President of Mexico himself opened the apartment door to me. He was alone, the family away and the servants off for the day. We conversed for perhaps ten minutes before he had to answer the bell again. I heard a cry of glad surprise, "Ah! Carmelita!" It was the widow of General Diaz calling on the old family friend.

Señora Diaz was dressed in black but with taste as well as modesty. She conversed quietly. Her voice had in it a soft note unconsciously suggesting, but not proclaiming, a deal of sadness. When Mexico was mentioned she showed no bitterness, but it was evident how much she wanted to go home. There was talk about the old President, but nothing about his long reign, its successes or its failures. When she spoke of him it was about his patience in exile, sickness, and old age. Carmelita was no longer young herself but she was not really old. She walked straight and sat straight on her chair. I looked from her to "El Presidente Blanco." How gentle and charming these Mexican *hidalgos* could be. I thought of the pictures I had seen of the brute-faced bandits who had taken their places—and wondered. I should not have wondered. There is no reason to wonder over the follies of a mob anywhere. Was I not in the city that had dreamed the dream of freedom and then allowed it to fade away into the red mist of murder?

My host in Paris was Monsignor Aceves, chaplain of the Spanish Church, but himself a Mexican *hidalgo*. It was he who placed the beautiful apartment on Boulevard St. Germain at my disposal. I soon discovered that he was more than the chaplain of a foreign church in Paris. Behind the apartment which he gave over to me was a publishing house owned by him and from which he issued hundreds of good books in Spanish. That back-yard and half-hidden publishing house sent literary apostles all over Spain and Spanish America. Monsignor Aceves had a real work in hand and was doing it well.

The Knights of Columbus were on the eve of finishing their war mission of charity to the soldiers when I arrived in Paris. Their resident overseas commissioner was Edward L. Hearn. My first visit to his office in the very heart of Paris was to renew old acquaintance-ship. To me Mr. Hearn was a friend but to Jack he was a lifesaver, for Jack had discovered how much iniquity was wrapped up in the yellow and blue packets of French government cigarettes. He had taken very few of the American kind into France, and was driven by necessity to the *paquet jaune*. Quickly he switched to the blue-wrapped kind and then despair settled down upon him.

> One is yellow and one is blue.
> One is vile, and the other too.
> One is poison; the other will slay.
> One is cabbage; the other is hay.
> The war would have ended before it was through,
> Had the French filled bombs from the Paquet Bleu.

The tragic verse may defy scansion, but what the boy really wanted was an American cigarette. Thus did Mr. Hearn become Jack's life-saver, for he had many American cigarettes left over and few American soldiers left to smoke them. With one special brand Mr. Hearn was overstocked because nobody wanted it. It had been made at home and, he assured Jack, "contained forty percent of Turkish tobacco." But the whole shipment of that special brand had some-how been spoiled on the way over. Mr. Hearn did not smoke and in consequence wondered why the soldiers were so generous in giv-ing the special "KC" brand to German prisoners, as well as to such allies as they had reason to dislike. The soldiers knew. Jack was given a box of one thousand as a present. He smoked one and tried another on me. There were nine hundred and ninety-eight certain to be left. Jack disliked the *concierge* at our apartment. "I'll give the fellow those cigarettes," he said; "they'll poison him." But the man had been brought up on French cigarettes which were so much worse than the "KC" brand that they changed his disposition. After the gift he insisted on taking his hat off to Jack every time he saw him. A great friendship blossomed between the two and it was the cigarettes spoiled by bilge that made it. Later Jack met Mr. Hearn in Rome and between them was founded a new order of chivalry called the Knights of the Appian Way, the plot being laid on that ancient road. The order has only two members. Its constitution has but a single provision—my permanent exclusion. I had suggested for its decoration a star made out of bilge-water cigarettes with the motto *Per Mare ad Nauseam* suspended from the nose by a ribbon the color of nicotine.

Diplomacy in Europe differs from diplomacy in America in the matter of time consumed. With proper credentials for admission one could go to Washington on Monday, see the All Highest on Tuesday, and get yes or no for an answer on Wednesday. In Washington one begins as far up as the wings of influence will carry and goes downward only to consolidate gains. In Europe one begins with a porter and ends with a king. Woe to him who forgets a single functionary. Time is nothing in European diplomacy. You see an official today and wait a week to see the next. So I had time to be in Paris officially while actually traveling over the battlefields of France and Belgium. I had only to remember a date ten or fifteen days away.

The war was over but its gruesomeness was still on the battle-grounds. As we motored from Paris to Brussels, by way of Amiens and the North, meeting burial parties was not at all unusual. We traveled fast. My memory of the trip is still like the rapid showing of a movie film made up of cuttings. It began with rescued rolls of barbwire within a few miles of the gates of Paris, wire only a short time removed from the battlefields; then long dazzling white lines across green meadows which were the chalk bottoms of filled-up trenches; then Amiens and its glorious cathedral still guarded by sandbags against artillery fire; then Albert with its leaning statue of the Blessed Virgin looking down on its ruins; then villages marked by nothing but a signpost, even their stone houses scattered far and wide; then towns with clean streets through which we passed between piles of stones and bricks that once were stores, churches, and dwellings; then fields so full of shell holes, smashed tanks, and exploded shells that it seemed as if not even a fly could have lived through what horrors they had seen; then tight little pillboxes scarred but still standing; then the ruins of the Cloth Hall at Yypres; then the shot-pierced houses of Lille; then Antwerp and the sea. There were bullet holes even in the doors of my hotel rooms. We almost lost the signs of war only where some of its most interesting battles had been fought—in Malines, at the palace of Cardinal Mercier.

When we entered the courtyard of that palace the newly elected President of Brazil and his suite were leaving after an interview with His Belgian Eminence. Our party must have presented a strange contrast, in clothes dusty from the roads, to the spick, span, and silk-hatted South Americans. But we were received promptly by the Cardinal. He liked Americans and especially the Knights of Columbus commissioners, Hearn and Larkin, who had done so much for his people.

One can live in a palace and yet not live palacially. The Cardinal's rooms were poorly furnished, and in them we again picked up in the walls and doors the marks of bullet holes. The Cardinal, tall and ascetic, had little to say about his own part in the defense of Belgium's soul, but he lived up to his reputation as a man who wanted to know everything. He pounced upon me when Mr. Larkin told him of my interest in missions. He had a way of asking questions that called less for answers than for discourses, and had me wound up before I was ten minutes in front of the battery of his inquiring eyes. "American plans for missions?" he queried, "I have heard something about them. They seemed very American; therefore large, even grand. What are you going to do? Become the great missionary Church of the world? How fine! Tell me. Tell me all about it."

Before I knew it I was on my feet pouring out all I had in bad French. Then and there I discovered that, poor as was my diction, I could give a lecture in French. I had never tried that before. The Cardinal did not take his eyes off me for a second. Their lids even did not seem to move. His spare form was leaning forward, ears intent, lips smiling. It was like having an interested audience of hundreds, for the man before me was hundreds in one. I have spoken to thousands in halls, theaters, tents, even in the open air. I never spoke to a greater or a better audience than Cardinal Mercier, an audience of one.

When we were back in our car and out on the road to Brussels Mr. Larkin handed me an Irish compliment. "I had no idea you could speak French like that, Monsignor," he said. "When I hear Frenchmen talking I can scarcely understand them. But when you speak French I understand perfectly."

Mr. Larkin meant well. On the other hand—but I did not discuss the matter. What the Cardinal thought about my French I never learned. The Belgians are a polite people.

When the party was leaving the Cardinal's presence he held me back and asked the others to wait outside as he had something very special to say to me in private. I stayed alone with him for another fifteen minutes. That fifteen minutes, and what followed it like fate, will make a chapter all by itself. The date of it is worth recording: Saturday, May 10th, 1919.

It was a lower road we took back to Paris. We started, after I had said Mass in the Cathedral of SS. Michael and Gudula in Brussels, on Sunday morning, May 11th, passing out by Waterloo, going through the battlefields of Mons and Chalons, and arriving in the evening at St. Quentin. The upper road had been a Way of the Cross for French and English, Canadians and Australians. Another Way of the Cross was before us, the bitter way tramped by our own soldiers. At St. Quentin we lodged in a half-ruined makeshift for a hotel; my own room was open to the night with one wall of it shot off. A half block away was a barbwire enclosure full of German prisoners, from which the sound of shooting came to wake me during the night. When I asked a man next morning what it meant, he shook his head, "We have no protection here," he said, "no protection at all against possible danger from the great number of prisoners. The city has less than one fifth its former population. I suppose the few guards take no chances."

Soissons was next with its cathedral in ruins. Nothing here could be repaired. I picked up a book from the stone heap that was once the seminary. Nobody wanted it so I took it away as a dusty souvenir. It was a volume of the sermons of Lacordaire. We came to Rheims at noon and called on the Archbishop, Cardinal Luçon, who insisted on being our guide for a visit to the cathedral.

Frenchmen can put an appealing heart throb into any story. When I saw the destruction war had done to that Gothic masterpiece of Christian architecture my thought was less of sadness than of anger. The Cardinal reversed it for me. He held up a glass jar filled with what looked like leaden rain drops, explaining that the melting roof of the cathedral had showered them down during the burning. "We call them," he said, "*les larmes de la Cathedral*—the tears of the cathedral!" Only a Frenchman, standing in the desolation that had once been his place of glory, could say that. After dark we were in Ste. Menahould, where the Knights of Columbus still had a hostel open. Here were very few signs of war, for the Germans had taken the town early and had occupied it long. "Our Saint protected us from the worst," I was assured by the innkeeper.

That night I slept in a royal room. It had more than once sheltered kings of France. All that bothered me about it was the distressing fact that it lacked a bath. But kings were never, in their day, quite as exacting as a modern American covered with the dust of war-torn roads. A basin had to serve. In the morning an invitation came from the Mayor to pay a visit to his office. Mr. Hearn told me that I must take it as a sort of royal command. "Mayors over here," he assured me, "are some pumpkins. No, I did not say bumpkins. I am talking United States. And, by the way, bring your purse with you."

I needed that purse for the Mayor had designs on it. After showing me some shot-riddled portraits on the wall he began to tell me how Ste. Menahould had saved the town. Though possibly an anticlerical His Honor was also a politician. The citizens wanted a statue to the saint set up in her favorite community. "It would be a great honor if a distinguished American prelate had a part in such a patriotic and religious act, here in a town saved by a saint on the very road of the conquering enemy." The Mayor put it far more eloquently and persuasively than that. I did my clear duty as a guest of Ste. Menahould. The Mayor, I hope, succeeded in erecting the statue. If he failed it certainly was not the fault of Mr. Hearn, who saw to it that his friend Larkin—and others—did even as the "distinguished American prelate" had done.

On the way to the Argonne we met many squads of German prisoners. As the car was full of cigarettes I succeeded, behind the commissioner's back, in tossing several cartons to them. Their guards took no alarm at the scramble that followed, probably because there was a treaty between them on the question of dividing the spoils. But the commissioner was very severe in his warnings about giving cigarettes to recent enemies. Then he turned his head away and looked toward the horizon. He had made his protest and duty required no more. Besides, he had plenty of cigarettes. One German prisoner stepped out of a ruined barn on the road and lifted his hand to stop us. With many apologies he explained that he was a sort of trusty who had found the bodies of several American soldiers in the woods. "Would the gentlemen be good enough to stop at the American camp farther on and inform the commanding officer?" The gentlemen thanked him and carried the message.

The Argonne Forest had a wonder in reserve for us, and the commissioner knew the way to it. We passed a German cemetery with monuments that would have done credit to any burial place—permanent monuments of stone—and ran up a side road for perhaps five hundred yards. "Go into that forest," the commissioner directed, "go in alone, and when you come to anything that surprises you shout back at us."

I went in and found a sidewalk leading deeper into the woods. I shouted and the others came. "I wanted you to get the first thrill," said the commissioner, "there are plenty of others for the rest of us. Let us follow the sidewalk to them."

He was right. That forest had surprises in plenty. We came upon a military city perfectly camouflaged from air observation. Yet it contained cottages, warehouses, a hospital, and even a fallen movie theater. The best of the cottages had housed both the German Crown Prince and General Von Kluck. There were bathrooms and a cleverly arranged water supply. A sort of pergola marked the site of a beer garden. The hospital was built on the side of a depression leading down into a pretty valley. It had had three floors, with a perfect surgery. The water was carried into the valley through iron pipes which also served as handrails when going down hill. "The

Germans left souvenirs," remarked Commissioner Larkin, pointing to a heap of Rhine wine bottles. "But not the Americans who took the place," remarked Jack. "The bottles are empty."

All around us were artillery placements and machine-gun nests. "Here," said the commissioner, "you may grasp, better perhaps than anywhere else in France, an idea of American fighting efficiency. This place was taken by assault. You see no trenches here. Our boys simply charged through the woods in the face of the machine-gun fire. God knows what the capture cost us in lives—but"—he added the note of victory as if in compensation for the lives—"we won."

Hearn had been so long overseas that he had gotten the spirit of the fight, and even peace had not taken it from him. "But we won!" How many voices have sent that melancholy bit of consolation down the centuries! "But we won!" Every history book has kept repeating the ominous words till they have become a universal challenge. If we are to avoid future wars we may need to forget even victories.

The first American grave we saw was in a ditch by the side of the road. When I noticed the little flag on it I insisted on stopping to say a prayer. The soldier's name was on the cross over it, and it was a German name. Here was tragedy indeed; a German-American soldier with the Fatherland's machine-gun bullets in his riddled body.

There were not nearly as many trenches as we had seen on the upper road, showing that much of the fighting in the American sector had been done by advances in the open. It marked the last push to victory. How we must have paid for it! The proof of the payment was seen in the well-kept American cemeteries with their long rows of white cross markers.

It was on the 14th that we arrived in Verdun and saw another cathedral in ruins. I thought how significant were these heaps of stone which once had housed the Prince of Peace—and how appropriate too, for He was gone out of them. It was as if He had fled away rather than witness the folly of men who had lost the good will which alone merits His blessing. The message of the ruined cathedrals was written plainly on what was left of them: "He is not here. Behold the place where they laid Him."

We found bodies in the trenches before Verdun. I picked up a

military boot and shook bones out of it. We still had Chateau
Thierry and Belleau Woods to see, but the spring had covered up
most of their horrors. We stopped to walk in the green grass and
stumbled on belts and helmets. There were trees covered with
leaves, but most of them had been cut short by artillery fire, and
the branches had been broken off. We had enough, and started via
Meaux for Paris.

The car, full of war relics that we had picked up on both roads,
rolled into the city. All I clung to of the relics was my volume of
Lacordaire's sermons. I never again saw the shells empty of powder
and the helmets empty of heads. I never wanted to see them again.

⇜§ 24 §⇝

THE CONFERENCE

PARIS welcomed us back. Everybody was welcome there for the visitor business was booming. Some of the hotels had been taken over by national delegations to the Conference. The Americans were in the Crillon, but President Wilson had a house to himself. The Italians had the Edouard VII. The Japanese held the Bristol. The English were quite alone up near the Arch of Triumph in the Majestic. People who came to pick up news for the press, or to lobby, or just to hang around, were mostly quartered in the centrally located hotels which faced the Gardens of the Tuileries or the Place Vendome. It was an adventure to take dinner at the Ritz. The tables were so closely packed that there was always danger of an elbow pushed a few inches too far back knocking food off the fork of someone behind. The situation was wonderful for eavesdroppers, of which tribe there was then a great plenty in Paris. Parties called together both to eat and talk business usually took their food downstairs over chats about the weather and went upstairs to a private suite for the real business. But downstairs was interesting if only to see the near great. The real great were not much in evidence. They had to eat somewhere but somewhere was rarely where others might hear as well as see. Upstairs was still more interesting when one was a guest at a large private party with a few celebrities in it. When the door closed the talk was on, for talks were the attractions of most international social gatherings in the Paris of the Peace Conference. There was in them the piquant charm of sportsmanship because it was quite well understood, but never confessed, that what was said might be retailed to higher-ups before the next morning. People talked very slowly and there was as much reticence as there was conversation when someone carelessly, as it seemed, threw out what obviously was a feeler. Not the least humorous incidents in such gatherings were the opportunities to note the way diplomats had of calling each other liars by seeming to accept what was told them as the gospel truth. Thus if I told the simple truth about my reason for being in Paris everybody apparently accepted it, and at once proceeded to discuss it with zest, but I knew that few believed me. I garnered the credit of being a very astute person by not trying to be anything of the kind. The truth in these hectic days of history-making was always under suspicion.

One evening was particularly interesting. The host was an American businessman, his distinguished guest a great authority on Russia and the Near East, one whose anteroom at the hotel was, during receiving hours, like that of a popular society physician with an exclusive office practice. I had heard a lot about the man. He had been a student for the priesthood but had dropped his clerical garb, after one of the best universities of Europe had given him all it had, to enter journalism. His philosophical and theological training turned to good account in Czarist Russia where he became all things to a major statesman. The fact that the Russian politics of the time had ecclesiastical branchings made one of his great opportunities. He could talk theology with any Patriarch. But talk and faith were different things. Traditionally he was a Catholic. Politically he had to have a standing—the Russians pray standing—acquaintance with the Orthodox Church. He had, too, the cosmopolitan advantage of being Irish, and therefore, at the time, of no recognized or interesting political color. He could be trusted not to favor any side but the one that employed him. I was of the opinion that he could not be trusted at all. It was at a lunch a few days before the great dinner that I had gotten this impression. All the guests at the lunch were either Catholics or American Protestants except this gentleman's wife and himself. The hostess asked me to say grace. I kept an eye on the ex-seminarian. When he heard the, to him, unusual request of the hostess he threw a cautious and, I thought, half-frightened glance around. Most of the company made the sign of the cross as if God really had an interest left in postwar Paris. He muffed it, though it was obvious that he had tried hard to remember how to do it. Having thus established confidence he went to eating and talking as one of the family of the Faith. He got away with it too and even secured a new job from the host when the Peace Conference broke up its sessions—and the world's furniture.

To that party upstairs came later a former American Ambassador known to be in the confidence of the President. It was the very day the news had been given out that Geneva was to be the seat of the League of Nations. Few seemed to like the selection, since the war record of Belgium was thought glorious enough to give Brussels a fair claim. One of the guests mentioned the matter and threw out a feeler. No one ventured to guess who had influenced the selection but there were several assurances as to who had not. I listened to the noise of the scamper away from responsibility and remembered, while thus silent, that the word Covenant had been used and certain references to Covenanters had recently been made by our Presbyterian President. Thinking only to inject a bit of humor into the gathering I remarked that perhaps I could make a fairly accurate guess in answer to the general inquiry. At once there was a demand for the guess. "Who do you think was responsible, Monseigneur?"

"I think," I said, "that it might have been John Calvin."

"John Calvin? John Calvin?" snapped the former Ambassador, "I have not seen him around here."

"He's not here," his wife uttered an alarmed warning. "Monseigneur means the reformer—Geneva, you know."

All the husband could do was to mutter, "I thought Monseigneur was referring to someone in Paris."

There was a double reason for the laugh that went around. When it was over, the Russo-Irishman said quietly, "Monseigneur may be more than half right." The gentleman must have had a mental flash back to his seminary days.

There was one place in Paris that knew well how to keep its counsel. It was the "Irish Embassy" quartered at the Grand Hotel with Sean O'Ceallaigh at its head. I used to envy Mr. O'Ceallaigh the spelling of his name, which really was my own, for O'Ceallaigh is the Irish for Kelley; or better, the son of Kelley. Why had we permitted the Sassenach to Anglicize such a fine old Gaelic name? I envied Sean who spelled his name correctly. No one ever knew what Sean O'Ceallaigh was doing unless he could read his title clear to Sinn Fein confidences. Lunch with Sean and his staff was a joy, often an intellectual one. There would be talks on history, diplomacy, religion, cooking, or Tierra del Fuego—if you know what I mean—but never a word—should I say "divil a word"?—about Sean O'Ceallaigh's business that the whole world did not already know. Three Irish-American delegates came over to be of service, one of them my old friend Governor Dunne of Illinois. All the intimate details of the "Embassy's" business they got—at least so I figured—could be put into the shell of a hazelnut. The Irish-American delegates were lacking in the gift of caution. Perhaps I could better express my thought about them by saying that all the diplomacy they had was the downright shillalah kind. They knew what they wanted and how to go after it in Donnybrook style. Ireland, not Paris, was the place for them. So, by the gracious permission of Lloyd George—granted at the urgent request of Colonel House—they went to Ireland. When Lloyd George read in the English papers what they had said there it was reported that the Colonel had some explaining to do. He must have done it well, for, when I chatted with him in New York after the show was over, the Colonel was getting much humor out of his memory of the affair. "The Irish," he said, "wanted everything and wanted it quick. I thought they would have been wiser to advance by slower stages, sticking a peg in the ground gained to mark their advance, resting there and then starting afresh. But who knows? They did get on, and I admire them for their sticking qualities."

I was quite sure that my Irish namesake—perhaps relative many lustrums between—was one of those who wondered what I was doing in Paris. If so he was another man deceived by the truth.

In post-bellum Paris one of the most precious possessions a stranger could have was a card of some kind attesting membership in—anything, if it were printed in another language than French and carried a seal and a photograph. The French police could not read the foreign language and a fine large seal was a sacred thing to them. The photograph was, of course, a convincing proof that the owner of the card was important. Jack worked even his Press Club card for entrance to many places where his only business was an insatiable curiosity and a wish to make the most of an hour not likely to be equaled again in his lifetime. I never blamed him. His only handicap was the fact that he was master of but a single tongue, but he did acquire a marvelous command over signs and shrugs. He never failed to get what he wanted as he wanted it and when he wanted it. Life in Paris for Jack was one thrill after another with many laughs between. Every night he went over with me the story of his day and it was always worth hearing. Monsignor Aceves had a literary editor whose name was Muñoz, a Spaniard. It was an experience to hear Jack and Signor Muñoz holding long conversations in English and Spanish, neither one knowing what the other was saying, but sign and shrug making the conversation seemingly quite clear to both.

There is a grave misunderstanding amongst Americans as to the smartness of their diplomats, because of the fact—alas, too plain—that so many were retired politicians. Whatever the weakness on the top, I did not find it reflected in the experienced and trained secretaries, and I met many of them. Usually the secretary type in diplomacy was clean-cut and its impression good. But some of them did love to play the game of cleverness that they knew so well. One experience will illustrate.

Mister—let us say Q—was giving me audience for his Chief on the liberty of conscience article before the Commission on the Covenant. I waxed as eloquent as I could in pointing out that if no other nation wanted it in the Covenant, the United States of America did, or should. My discourse was interrupted frequently by calls for the secretary on the telephone. No one could have handled them better. The man was a most polite watchdog at his Chief's gate. At last he had to say something to me. On the principle of the thing he knew I had him, but that did not mean much in practice. He began to talk about Japan. He talked a lot about Japan before I caught the import. He was allowing me to put my own interpretation on his words; to think that Japan would object to a liberty of conscience article. He succeeded splendidly.

As I was walking away from the Crillon after the interview I heard my name called and turned around to face a smiling Japanese gentleman whom I recognized at once as Captain Yamamoto of the Imperial Japanese Navy; already mentioned as one I had met at the home of a mutual friend in Rome when the captain was Naval Attaché to the Japanese Embassy there. The captain told me that he was serving as Naval Adviser to the Japanese Delegation and living at the Bristol. He begged me to come to his apartment for a chat. I went with him, told him what I had heard at the Crillon and asked what he thought about it.

"What I think about it, Monseigneur, does not matter in the least so far as your mission is concerned," he replied. "Naturally, as a Japanese Catholic, I see with you the propriety of such an article as you advocate for the Covenant. But I am a naval officer, not a statesman. There is only one man here who can answer your question. May I leave you and put it to Baron Makino, the chief of our Delegation?"

Naturally I was glad to wait as long as necessary. He went out. In twenty minutes he returned all smiles. "Baron Makino authorizes me to say, and you to quote him, that Japan has not objected to the proposed liberty of conscience article. Japan favors it."

I could not get back fast enough to Mr. Secretary to tell him what Baron Makino had said. But Mr. Secretary was not a bit nonplussed. "You did not grasp my meaning," he assured me, "Japan has made no protest against the article on liberty of conscience, but the Baron has proposed a race equality addition to it. You know how that would be taken in California and British Columbia. If we insist on the liberty of conscience article Japan will insist on a race equality addition. To avoid that the whole matter may have to be dropped."

I returned at once to see my Japanese friend. Once more he went to Baron Makino and returned with a new statement: "Japan has all along asked for recognition of race equality. She will continue to do so whether the liberty of conscience article is adopted or not. Even if Japan does not succeed in securing what she asks for she will nevertheless support the article in favor of liberty of conscience."

Again a trip to Mr. Secretary. He only laughed and invited me to dinner. It was a good dinner in excellent company. Mr. Secretary had lost nothing of his charm when later I met him at the American Embassy in Rome. He had gone up higher and is likely to go higher still—good luck to him.

The liberty of conscience article as it first went before the Commission on the Covenant was Number XIX. Later it was XXI. Proposed by the British it read as follows:

"Recognizing religious persecution as a fertile source of war the High Contracting Parties solemnly undertake to extirpate such evils from their territories, and they authorize the Executive Council, wherever it is of opinion that the peace of the world is threatened by the existence in any State of evils of this nature, to make such representations or take such other steps as it may consider that the case requires."

This wording of the article did not find favor and someone re-drafted it for President Wilson:

"The High Contracting Parties agreed that they will make no law prohibiting or interfering with the free exercise of religion, and they resolve that they will not permit the practice of any particular creed, religion, or belief, whose practices are not inconsistent with public order or with public morals, to interfere with the life, liberty or pursuit of happiness of their people."

Pretty terrible as English.

There were objections but it was sent to the Drafting Committee which saw difficulties and proposed to eliminate it altogether. It came up for discussion with that suggestion attached, in the tenth meeting of the Commission on the Covenant, Colonel House presiding and President Wilson absent. The chairman notified the Commission that the President wished to keep the article in the Covenant. Opposed were Lord Robert Cecil of Great Britain, Mr. Larnaude of France, Mr. Vesnitch of Serbia and Mr. Venizelos of Greece, the latter leading the attack. Their report was as follows:

"The Committee feels that, in view of the complications of this question, it would be preferable to omit this article altogether. If, however, there is a strong feeling in the Commission that some such provision should be inserted, they suggest the following drafting: The High Contracting Parties agree that they will not prohibit or interfere with the free exercise of any creed, religion or belief whose practices are not inconsistent with public order or public morals, and that no person within their respective jurisdictions shall be molested in life, liberty or the pursuit of happiness by reason of his adherence to any such creed, religion or belief."

Venizelos insisted that there was a connection between Japan's proposals on race equality and Article XIX. He based his opposition to the latter on that alleged fact. After the meeting President Wilson withdrew his support from the article and at his word it was dropped.

But it appeared again indirectly in Article XXII which required nations governing mandated peoples to give them "freedom of conscience and religion." On the logic that no one could give what he did not possess, this could be interpreted as the liberty of conscience article in another form. But it would take a decision of the World Court to establish the fact. The World Court has never been asked to pass upon it.

It was held by some that the liberty of conscience article would have been fatal to the League. The exact contrary is true; it might have saved the League. The first blow given the League was the refusal of the United States to enter it. One of the arguments in support of that action was based on the fact that the Covenant did not safeguard liberty of conscience. Catholics would have been for the League if that right had been properly recognized. As it was they were against it. The whole Catholic press could have been rallied to support the League but it had nothing to rally around. President Wilson was right, and it is to be regretted that, weakening at the last moment, he thus lost the cause. I say "thus lost the cause" because it was plain that the Commission would not have opposed him on the point. The minutes of the meeting are quite clear on that.

Why the opposition of Venizelos? He himself stated that it was because of the race equality addition of Japan. But Japan did not make its support of the liberty of conscience article a condition for the adoption of its race equality proposal. Japan would have supported Article XIX even if its own proposal were rejected. Venizelos tried to explain away his opposition on the ground that he might have supported Article XIX had he known that the race equality suggestion would not be insisted upon. He "reminded the Commission that he had been largely responsible for the disappearance of the religious liberty clause from the Covenant. He had thought that if this clause were cut out the difficulty relative to the racial question would likewise be eliminated. Today, however, the question had appeared in a different light and Japan had taken her stand upon another ground; they were talking not of the equality of races, but of the equality of nations themselves and of just treatment of their nationals."

What is most to be remembered is the fact that the Commission did reject a proposal that liberalism proclaimed to be vital in its system. Yet the Commission was made up mainly of liberals. It was these liberals who rejected it. The Conference of Peace and the Commission on the Covenant forged chains on the world by such acts as its ungenerous and unjust treatment of Germany, the partition of Austria, the isolation of Italy, and the abandonment of its own accepted principles as shown by the rejection of Article XIX. Liberalism has since become a meaningless slogan or a mask for something more deadly.

The rejection of Article XIX turned out to be a disaster for Jews and Christians. It is true that the former had ample justification for devoting themselves chiefly to the rights of racial and religious minorities, since they nowhere form by themselves a majority in any state. I said that Poland seemed to fill the eye of their Paris meeting, but I thought then, as I think now, that Article XIX would have, in the long run, done more for them than did the treaty called "Little Versailles" which Poland was forced by the Conference to accept. It was resented not only by the Polish delegates but by the Polish people. The Poles felt, and with fair historical right, that of all nations with Jewish minorities, they had treated their Jewish fellow-citizens with the greatest generosity. The treaty was a mistake that should have been foreseen for what it plainly was, an invitation to trouble. President Wilson himself would never have tolerated the suggestion of signing such a treaty if its provisions were to be universally applied. He could not have accepted it for his own country. Truth is that "Little Versailles" was an insult. If its terms were good why should they not be applied universally? But Wilson knew, and Cecil knew, and Clemenceau knew, that none of their nations could accept what they were forcing on others. "Little Versailles" did not live long for that very reason; and because it made a League of Nations case out of the most trivial of possible local disturbances. But "Little Versailles" had its good point. It did pretend to safeguard racial and religious minorities in the states forced to accept it, by giving them what they certainly have not in greater nations. Listen to this provision in its Article IX:

"In towns and districts where there is a considerable proportion of Polish nationals belonging to racial, religious or linguistic minorities, these minorities shall be assured an equitable share in the enjoyment and application of the sums which may be provided out of public funds under the State, municipal or other budget, for educational, religious or charitable purposes."

Add this from Article XII:

"Poland agrees that the stipulations in the foregoing Articles, so far as they affect persons belonging to racial, religious or linguistic minorities, constitute obligations of international concern and shall be placed under the guarantee of the League of Nations. They shall not be modified without the assent of a majority of the Council of the League of Nations. The United States, the British Empire, France, Italy and Japan hereby agree not to withhold their assent from any modification in these Articles which is in due form assented to by a majority of the Council of the League of Nations."

"Little Versailles" was destined to die, not for what it gave the Jews but for the resentment it was sure to stir up. But Article XIX in the Covenant that was to be the charter of the League could have been accepted by all states without fear of trouble. It did not threaten any member-state in the League but simply set down a fair and just test for membership which, at the time, no state could well refuse to accept. It was liberalism's chance but the liberals muffed it. The persecuted Jews of Germany are paying the bill today. Both Protestants and Catholics there and elsewhere will be paying it tomorrow. It has given its death sentence to the League because, by failing to stand against religious persecution, it cut the ground from under the inalienable things. In the scales of modern statesmanship, as against wealth and power, they were seen to be as light as a feather.

Before I left Paris Captain Yamamoto came around to see me and to voice a request, "Would Monseigneur do him the honor of accepting an invitation to meet some of his friends, all Japanese, at a dinner at Henri's?" Monseigneur would and did, though quite certain that the captain's friends were likely to be more interesting to him than he to them.

The Conference

"And would Monseigneur be so kind and gracious as to permit these Japanese gentlemen to ask him questions of a religious nature?" The captain explained that he felt it only right to say that they were most anxious to hear Monseigneur's answers, since they were highly educated men and one in particular had been a professor in a Japanese university.

The dinner was delightful, a men's affair from caviar to conversation. Japanese politeness is a bit overwhelming to matter-of-fact Americans but we enjoy it nevertheless. The spokesman of the party was the ex-professor who admitted that he had once been lightly dipped in Presbyterianism but had dried off. His suspicion seemed to be that somewhere in Christianity—he did not know where—the light of ages would yet be found. The captain smiled. I knew that he was thinking that he, at least, already had found it. The ex-professor kept diving deep. There is one great satisfaction in talking to men of his type: they are free from the prejudices that obstruct the clear thinking of so many professed Protestants. I did not have to tell the Japanese gentlemen, for example, that the infallibility of the Pope did not mean his impeccability; nor that the books of a private doctor who happened to be a Pope were not included in the scope of the infallibility. They only wanted me to indicate the exact boundaries. Inside these, they quite understood that for the Catholic position the infallibility was a logical necessity and for thinkers outside an attraction worth considering. It was with the nature of Truth they chiefly seemed to be concerned. They wasted no words. They went off on no side lines. There were no red herrings dragged across the track. They knew what they wanted to know and asked for it. I wished that I too had been a professor. But somehow I seemed to be getting by. Before I could come around to the Bristol next morning to thank Captain Yamamoto for his hospitality his card was handed to me. The moment he entered the room he thanked me for what he seemed still to consider an honor conferred on him and his guests. They had expressed themselves, he said, as having been both entertained and enlightened. I admitted that I too had been entertained and not a little enlightened by the Japanese way of getting down to fundamentals. Many events of seemingly greater importance than a dinner with Japanese at Henri's have happened in my lifetime but, somehow, they have passed into the subconscious record. This one has not.

Definitely I knew from conversations at different delegations that the proposed article on liberty of conscience had been dropped for other reasons than the one alleged. Perhaps old Tiger Clemenceau had supported Venizelos. Such an article as XIX would have been an implied censure on his own political past. The Combes memory was still alive. The Tiger was a good hater and a loud denouncer. I was impressed with the idea that there was a wealth of personal power behind him but, in truth, also a not inconsiderable amount of bluff. Lloyd George was a fine promiser—though he promised me nothing, for I never spoke to him—but he could change with a shake of his white mane and a grin. Flattery could be used with considerable success on him. Everybody knew Wilson's one objective. Everything on the road to it was trivial and debatable. He was not dishonest. He was not weak. He only wanted something of doubtful value altogether too much. Orlando, as subsequent happenings showed, had been maneuvered out of the influence he had a right to enjoy. The consequences were interesting.

❦ 25 ❧

HIGH SPOT

THE subject discussed by Cardinal Mercier with me during
our private conversation in his palace was the Roman question. The substance of that discussion was made public property
through the publishing, ten years later, of two reports: one that of
Monsignor Bonaventure Cerretti, the other my own, in the review
Vita e Pensiero of the University of the Sacred Heart, Milan. At the
time his report was made Monsignor Cerretti was Under-Secretary
for Extraordinary Affairs in the Department of State of the Vatican.
Later he was Nuncio to Paris. He died a cardinal. What I am jotting
down here is nothing more than was contained in the published
reports with a background and a few details.

Since the Roman question in its acute form dated from 1870 it
suffered from the gradual obscuring process that the years bring to
every historical event. But between 1870 and 1919 it was always a
recurring question, especially through protests issued by succeeding
Popes. Perhaps it was always best understood in Germany where
for both political and religious reasons it was kept constantly before
the public by resolutions passed in annual Catholic congresses. It
was never well understood by the Catholic laity in America or in
England. Protestants, of course, have always thought of it as an agitation by a usurping Pope against a liberal and united Italy. The
French government used it to suit the political convenience of the
times. It is safe to say that outside ecclesiastical circles few studied
the question from the standpoints of justice or principle.

What was the Roman question? To state the case simply, and
show the trend of Italian liberalism at the same time, an extract
from the speech of Count Cavour on March 24, 1861, will serve
the double purpose: "We must go to Rome, but on two conditions:

261

we must go there in agreement with France; and in such a way that the uniting of this City with the kingdom of Italy may not be interpreted by the great mass of Catholics in Italy and outside Italy as a sign of the enslaving of the Church. We must go to Rome, but without bringing about any diminution of the independence of the Pope. We must go to Rome, but without allowing the civil authority to extend its power to the spiritual order. If we succeed in realizing the second of the above-mentioned conditions, the first will not present many difficulties; if we succeed in uniting Rome to Italy without arousing grave fears in the Catholic body; if we, I say, succeed in persuading the great mass of Catholics that the union of Rome with Italy can be made without the Church ceasing to be independent, I think the problem will be solved."

The reader will kindly note the words "without the Church ceasing to be independent." Though the Roman question came out of the seizure of the Papal States by the Kingdom of Italy, and for some years remained a protest against that seizure, nevertheless, up to 1929 it really lived because the Church protested that Italy had failed to insure the Pope's independence. To guard that independence the Pope became a voluntary prisoner in the Vatican.

The Roman question was always a weakness in Italy's relations to other states. These states could and sometimes did resurrect it in political controversies with Italy. It is doubtful if any of them wanted to settle it, since they did not feel like giving up opportunities to use it for their own ends. Even Great Britain's statesmen had said enough about the rights of the Pope to independence to justify their keeping the question alive. As long as Italy went along with the rest of the powers—better say "was dragged along"—the Roman question seemingly was forgotten, but Italy always knew that it had merely been laid on the table and might be taken up in her hour of need. Thus Lords Palmerston, Brougham, Lansdowne, and Ellenborough, each in his own day of power, had made clear their attitude, if not their convictions, on the rights of the Holy See. The most succinct statement from many of them was a dispatch from Lord Palmerston to Lord Normanby as follows: "It is without doubt to be desired that a person (the Pope), who in his spiritual character exercises a vast influence in the internal affairs of the greater part of the nations of Europe should be so independent as not to become, in the hands of any European power whatsoever, a means of embarrassing others." Lansdowne stated in Parliament that he "was not prepared to say that we (Great Britain) as a Protestant State, had not, to a certain extent, a similar interest (to that of Catholic States): that there was not a country with Catholic subjects, and Catholic possessions, which had not a deep interest in the Pope being so placed as to be able to exercise his authority unfettered and unshackled by any temporal influence which might affect his spiritual authority." These and other expressions of statesmen over all Europe clearly made the Roman question international. Italy was practically alone in insisting that it was exclusively Italian.

One has to go back to the idea of the Two Swords, which statesmen had not entirely rejected in principle, to get at the root of the trouble as they saw it. In spite of heresies the Pope was the recognized leader of the forces of Christianity and the embodiment in himself of the spiritual power. Thus that power was in a general way a unity. It could be dealt with as a responsible unity. It would stay put because it worked entirely upon well-proclaimed, well-understood and very simple principles. On the other hand the secular power was divided by nations into many parts. Unlooked-for trouble might come from any one of these parts. Indeed they could scarcely be called parts at all. One could easily upset the calculations of all the others. A treaty between them was likely to prove a scrap of paper. The spiritual power dealt with them separately and was bound to be in contention with some of them. A Pope subject to any one of these was a potential danger to all the rest. The statesmen saw, and saw very clearly, that, for the sake of all, the spiritual power represented by the Pope must be independent. But they faced facts: the Kingdom of Italy had seized the Papal States by force; the Holy See had protested and had kept on protesting against the seizure; the Popes claimed that the position of the Holy See was intolerable. Undoubted fraud by Italy had been added to force. Here was an international question. Various attempts had been made between 1870 and 1919 to settle it. The chief difficulty lay in the claim by Italy that it was an Italian question which the Italian State could settle by itself and on its own authority, and the insistence of the Pope, backed by the consensus of the opinions of statesmen outside Italy, of its international character. I have already more than hinted that there were European statesmen who would hold to that opinion for no other purpose than to keep the question alive but unanswered.

What Cardinal Mercier discussed with me was an idea that the two major parties could, in the League of Nations, find a method of reconciling the difference in their positions. Italy would certainly take it as an unfriendly act if any other European nation took up the question; and feared some of them would. As a matter of fact when Italy went into the Great War, Sonnino, her Foreign Minister, forced a clause into the London Pact stating that Italy went into the war on the side of the allies on the condition that they, all of them, should oppose any participation of the Vatican in peace negotiations. It was not enmity to the Vatican that caused Italy to take that step, but fear that the Roman question would be brought up to strengthen other Powers against her. The Cardinal's thought was that Italy might be persuaded to take the first step, not by making but by recognizing a Vatican State existing by right within her own borders; then notifying the League of her recognition of it and asking that an invitation be extended to enter the League. It was a clever way out which, the Cardinal thought, could not fail to satisfy both the Holy See and Italy. The immediate question was what Power would suggest this solution to Italy. He thought it might be America. The only reason he had for putting the matter up to me was the friendly role that the Cardinal thought America could play in bringing the matter to the attention of the Conference at Versailles. The United States was officially an outsider in European affairs. Our country would not even accept the title "ally," but insisted on being called an associate in the war. The Roman question affected the United States less than any European country. To American Catholics the Pope, bound or free, was always the Pope. Indeed there was no place in the world where the Pope was more the Pope than in the United States. American Catholics loved the Pope as the Vicar of Christ and the Successor of St. Peter. To them it would be a tremendous gratification if through their representatives a solution to the Roman question were worked out. The Cardinal knew that, for he had been in America and understood the attitude of our people. What he did not understand were our politicians. He knew nothing about the fear that would be on them if they saw such a question approaching their desks. I told His Eminence very frankly that in my judgment, while he might find the American Delegation sympathetic, he would not find it ready to act. I went into a long explanation of the reasons for my conviction and the Cardinal agreed. Nevertheless, I promised that I would take the matter up on my return to Paris and notify him promptly about what interviews I could secure. Before I left the room he said, "I do not want to go to Paris. It would be very inconvenient at this time and might attract unwanted attention. But if President Wilson, Colonel House and Mr. Lansing agree to receive and talk over the matter with us I shall be quite willing to go."

Colonel House was no more like my then somewhat benighted conception of a Texan than I, now an Oklahoman, am like what my Eastern friends think about the appearance of an Oklahoman. With the Texan and the Oklahoman, to the Eastern and Northern mind at least, goes the suggestion of ten-gallon hats, guns, chaps, and an appetite for life in the raw. The Oklahoman in particular should show a trace or more of Indian blood. With the Texan a bit of devil-may-care stubbornness might serve for identification. What fourteen years of life in Oklahoma has done to change me let others tell, but for the mental picture I had made of Colonel Edward M. House the Texan before I met him, I here and now apologize most humbly. My one excuse is that when it was made I was living in Chicago, and all the Texans I saw there—barring bishops—were mostly those who came with loads of cattle for the stockyards.

I was introduced to Colonel House by Admiral Benson who had been in command of the American Navy during the war; a gentleman, a scholar, and one whom God must have loved very much for his sincerity, his loyalty, his humble and unaffected piety, as well as his charity unfeigned. I might go into details as a tribute to his memory were I writing at length about him, but could I really say more?

All my first interview with Colonel House had been about the Mexican persecution and the proposal for a liberty of conscience article in the Covenant. He had mentioned the President's objection to anything that might seem like intervention. I wanted to put him straight on that point, so before I left Paris I sent a letter

to him dated May 6th, 1919, assuring him that the authorities of
the Church in Mexico were, like myself, opposed to intervention.

On my return to Paris the Mexican question came up again with
Colonel House. He left me under the impression that it would have
to drift along until the Conference was over and done with. I felt
that he did not see eye to eye with the President on it. Then I told
him of my interview with Cardinal Mercier. He at once said that
the President certainly would see His Eminence, but doubted if he
would discuss the Roman question. He thought that the President
would not wish to have it brought up. It was, after all, somewhat
out of the line of American interests, and there were our religious
divisions at home to consider. He thought I should write that to
the Cardinal but, at the same time, assure him that the President
would be glad to receive a friendly visit from him. After all they
were not strangers to one another and the Cardinal was a great
veteran of the war, even if he had fought only with moral and not
physical weapons.

I left the Colonel to go back to the Continental where I was
then staying, having given up the apartment on Boulevard St.
Germain to be nearer the center of interest; but I lengthened my
way for exercise' sake and approached the Hotel down the Rue de
la Paix. It was a fateful detour.

It was Saturday afternoon. The interview with Colonel House
had taken place at five o'clock. The stores on the street were closed.
As I walked rapidly along I saw a man approaching who evidently
intended to accost me. I remembered that I had met him before
I left Paris for the tour of the battlefields, at Hotel Edouard VII,
and that he was a member of the Italian Delegation. He shook
hands and reminded me that he was Brambilla, Counselor to the
Delegation. In spite of his smile of recognition I saw that he was
very much excited and in a high state of indignation. Without preliminary small talk he burst out, "Did you hear what happened
today at the Council?"

I said that I had been away from Paris. He looked toward the
doorway of the nearest shop, which happened to be an alcove, and
drew me into it out of the crowd. Once there he gave free vent to
his indignation. I must set down his talk as best my memory will
allow. "Italy has been isolated," he burst out. "We are not to have

Fiume, and that by the decision of your President. He in whom the Italian people had all confidence has betrayed us. And the other two are with him, for their own reasons of political interest. It is damnable—damnable."

He was speaking English and speaking it well. I remembered that he had an American wife and had been attached to the Italian Embassy in Washington. "Why do you want Fiume?" I asked. "A port without adjacent territory to feed it would be a liability."

"It is the Italian people who want it," he answered, "and Orlando is their servant. In fact if he does not get it his government will fall from power. Wilson is bringing that about—and at such a time!"

"The President knows that?"

"I don't think he realizes it. He is so confident of his popularity with the Italian people that he is sure they will accept his decision without question. Imagine!"

Though Marquis Brambilla's gloom was overpowering I had to smile over that. My smile got no response. His indignation was crossing the Atlantic at that moment. "The Italians in America will show their resentment against Wilson when he comes up for re-election," he said. "Don't you think so?"

"Don't bank on that," I answered. "No class of immigrants to the United States assimilates as quickly as the Italian. They set out to learn English at once. They become property owners and citizens very quickly. Some of the first arrivals do go back, but rarely the children. For them Italy is only a tradition and Italia a pretty name. The assimilation process for Italians is, if anything, too rapid for their own good."

He was astonished but too polite to question my statement. "What would you do if you had the responsibility for such a situation?" he asked.

It must be admitted that the question was a flattering one. Who did this gentleman think I was? I felt an inclination to make a pleasantry, and was about to give it utterance, when the conversation with Colonel House, not a half-hour past, flashed a fuse in my head and the joke went out.

"My dear Marquis," I parried, "I am in no position to advise in such a crisis. I am neither a statesman nor a diplomat. I have been following the rumors of the Council's doings only out of curiosity

The Bishop Jots It Down

and for amusement, since I have but one special interest in them. You know why I am here. I told you two weeks ago and discussed my business with you."

This time he actually did laugh. "Yes," he said, "you discussed a question about a proposed article for the Covenant with me. But you are here for more than that."

"Which means?"

"You are here for the Vatican, and all Catholic interests are the Vatican's interests."

I saw that he meant every word he uttered. "Look here!" I protested. "Do you think that the Holy See would send a stranger to diplomacy and an American to do what its own trained Roman diplomats could do far better? It does not make sense."

"Oh! yes it does make sense, and in many ways."

I did not know what to say before his evident but mistaken conviction, but I did what I thought best and tried to be impressive at it. "I give you my word of honor that I am not what you and probably others think me to be. There is no Vatican representative known to me here. The Holy See knows its own business and is not likely to ask for my opinion. I have no mission here but to advocate the insertion of a liberty of conscience article in the Covenant of the League. Do you not believe me?"

He dodged the question. "Does the Holy Father know that you are here?" he asked.

"He does."

"Does he know you?"

"Yes."

"Then please tell me what you would advise."

There it was again. Nothing could uproot his annoying conviction that I was more than I claimed to be. "All right," I gave up. "If it is my personal advice you want you shall have it: *settle the Roman question.*"

He looked puzzled. What had the Roman question to do with Fiume and territory for Italian expansion? He voiced his bewilderment, so I had to explain: "Italy has since 1870 and before been playing in with the enemies of the Church, but Italy's true interests have never been there and every good Italian knows it. You have gone so deep into an alliance with the anti-clerical camp that they

268

think you'll stay no matter what happens. It is not Wilson who is against you but those who are influencing him. He knows little about European problems. Don't therefore blame Wilson overmuch. What your old allies do not expect is a move that would end in Italy becoming a chief instead of a follower. The first and most necessary advance toward that end is peace with the Church, and that calls for the settlement of the Roman question."

"But the Holy Father will want all his States back. They are now the very heart of Italy."

"Why jump to that conclusion? An Archbishop of Udine was not rebuked for saying that the question was one of independence rather than territory, and even suggesting a way out of the problem which did not call for a return of the old Papal States."

The counselor's eyes were shining with interest. He had grasped possibilities at which I had only hinted. He caught my arm excitedly and said, "You must talk with Orlando."

That frightened me. I shook my head. "I told you that I had no authority. I offered only a personal opinion. If I call on Orlando others will make the same mistake that you have made. The reporters will fly to guessing and I shall be put down as a meddler. No, I should not even have said as much as I did."

"There need be no reporters," he urged. "I can arrange the meeting so as to throw off all suspicion. May not one Catholic gentleman talk over a public question with another Catholic gentleman in all propriety?"

"Yes. If the interview is on that basis, and so understood by Signor Orlando, I shall be glad to meet him."

Before I went to bed that night I had an invitation from the Marquis to a tea at the Ritz the next afternoon. I understood. Brambilla was a quick worker. But I went to bed worried. Suppose the reporters did get suspicious? Suppose some of their guesses and conjectures got to Rome? But I was going to see it out whatever happened.

Next afternoon there was a crowd at the tea, nearly all Italians. How it had been gathered in on such short notice I never knew. The Brambilla method of securing privacy was to make the setting semipublic. I was placed near a window alcove. There was a flutter of polite excitement when a distinguished-looking gentleman with a great crop of gray, almost white hair came in and began to pass around the room, bowing and shaking hands as he progressed toward the place where evidently he knew I was. He stopped there. I was introduced. He looked at a little table nearby and remarked, "Why should I not take my tea here—with Monsignore?" Why not indeed? So it had been arranged. We conversed in French— about nothing at all. People came to be presented and went away. I was always a "Monsignore from America, the great and wonderful country of the Marchioness Brambilla." I might have been visiting them in Paris as an old family friend. The crowd consumed the tea and cakes and began to thin out. In a short time there were none left but the host and the hostess, the Premier of Italy and a nervous "Monsignore from America." The hostess quickly developed a diplomatic headache. Her husband excused himself to take her away. He said he would return in a few minutes but he did not return for an hour.

The Prime Minister's account of that meeting was printed in the *Saturday Evening Post* ten years later; to be exact under the date of May 4th, 1929. He offered the article in the "hope that the great American public will be interested in this hitherto unpublished story, not only for its universal importance but also for the influence which was exercised by American citizens, directly or indirectly, in a favorable or hostile manner, at a decisive moment." He then proceeds to give the historical background of the Roman question, because "an agreement can only be arrived at through a disagreement, and that this disagreement, with its various phases, gives us the necessary foundation of the agreement." "When the Law of Guarantees was passed by the Italian parliament," he said, "a Deputy asked what would happen to it in case Italy became involved in a war, and Ruggero Bonghi replied: 'We have struggled so much to create an arrangement which may serve in time of peace; for heaven's sake, let us avoid foreseeing what would happen in time of war. God will provide for us!'" But let Mr. Orlando tell in his own words what did happen in that case when war did come. I make no apology for the long quotation:

"This unheard-of thing happened: The attempt was made to use as a weapon against victorious Italy that Roman Question which the enemies of Italy and of the Entente had intended to raise against a vanquished Italy. Someone tried to speculate on the wrath of Wilson, which at that time was as terrible as that which Homer attributes to Jupiter, and to punish that rebellious Italy which persevered obstinately in the protection of its rights by wounding her in her most delicate and vital interest. Similar intentions were not only expressed in Catholic countries, as Spain and Belgium, but also in the Catholic circles of states in which the majority is non-Catholic, as in England and perhaps also in the United States. Naturally, the extreme solution planned by the Germans was not proposed; the purpose aimed at was more modest. It would perhaps have been sufficient to effect the admission of the Pope into the League of Nations. Nothing in such a plan appeared to me intolerable; what I considered intolerable was that an event, even if innocent in itself, should be carried through against the will of Italy, so as to imply for her the deepest humiliation.

"I must frankly declare that similar tendencies did not find any encouragement in the two parties to which they addressed themselves. They were not favored by Wilson and the Allied nations because, great as was the irritation against Italy, the spirit of the representatives of those countries did not sympathize with the vindication of the Holy See: Wilson and Lloyd-George were non-Catholics. Clemenceau was an anticlerical. As to the Holy See, I am bound to acknowledge that its spirit maintained itself such as had been revealed by the recorded declaration of Cardinal Gasparri. The Pope did not wish to achieve a success which might provoke irreparable hostility toward Italy. The concurrence of these causes prevented the imminence and even the gravity of that danger; but I was, all the same, obliged to take it into consideration and to do my best to protect Italy against it.

"At this point, during the second half of May, an American prelate of Chicago, Monsignor K., came to Paris and had some interviews with Marquis Brambilla, an Italian diplomat, whose wife was the daughter of Mr. George von Lengerke Meyer, former ambassador of the United States to Italy and ex-Secretary of the Navy. The purpose of those interviews was to arrive at a direct agreement between Italy and the Holy See. Marquis Brambilla informed me of this, and I realized that it was advisable that I should deal with those negotiations myself. Friendly interviews took place between Marquis Brambilla, Monsignor K. and me. Monsignor K. immediately left for Rome and met Cardinal Gasparri, who, in his turn, informed His Holiness of the matter."

My departure for Rome was on the Tuesday following the meeting with Orlando. I must admit that I had misgivings. I wanted to report the incident to the Secretariat of State in writing, but Brambilla would not hear of it and I knew he was talking for the Premier. I suggested calling Cardinal Mercier in to take the matter off my hands. Brambilla told me plainly that no one would be permitted to touch it till the American who started it with him had handed it over to the Holy See. Evidently Orlando preferred an American. Even if I had acted without authority, Brambilla said, I was still a prelate of the Pope's household and a priest pledged to the interests of the Church. He came to see me three times to impress that on me, brought another diplomat with him on one visit, and left this note when he found me absent:

"I have been thinking of the conversation you had with Signor Orlando, and the more I think of it, the more I convince myself that it would be impossible to convey a complete impression of such a conversation in writing.

"The questions that were dwelt upon and the problems they involve are of such momentous and far-reaching importance, the prospects of success seem, indeed, so hopeful, that nothing should be left to chance and I venture to suggest that you report what has been said in person.

"As far as I am aware and although the meeting was purely 'social,' it is the first time that one of our Ministers has met a Representative of the Church when it was known beforehand that the Roman question would be discussed, and the words that were spoken were such that I feel sure you will find it worth the while to postpone your sailing for America and take the way of Rome instead."

Surely, there was nothing for me to do but go to Rome.

On the train I prepared a précis of my conversation with Signor Orlando, chiefly of the arguments I had used to show why it would be to Italy's advantage, apart from the supreme question of justice, to bring the Roman question to a right ending. Some are so very American that I now see good reasons for the smile with which the Prime Minister received them. Here they are, translated from sign language and paraphrased from my notebook. They were published with my letter:

"1. Preface about Cardinal Mercier's request and his opinion that the settlement could be made without large territorial concessions.—Recalled Udine pastoral— What I wrote to the Cardinal and the unwillingness of Orlando to bring anyone else into the affair.

"2. How a just settlement would benefit Italy: (a) Benefit to Italians out of Italy, but also out of touch with their co-religionists because of Italy's treatment of the Pope. (b) Bad effect of present situation politically and commercially on Italy and Italians. (c) Bad effect on the political stability of Italy itself. (d) The Holy See a commercial asset to Italy which, in a business nation like the United States or England, would be appreciated and protected. (e) Evident break between Italy and her allies and advantage to be drawn from it. (f) Interest in the coming centralization of Catholic missionary activities in Rome. (g) Loss of Austria as the first Catholic power leaves her place *sede vacante*. (h) Importance to Italy of a world-wide unification of Catholic missionary activities under a free Pope.

"3. The territorial concession suggested: (a) A square mile for the Vatican beginning at the street below the Castle of St. Angelo and with two bridges as gates at the Tiber. (b) Access to the sea. (c) Italy to agree on limits, recognize the new State, and so inform the League of Nations; thus taking the lead— Notification to the League of the recognition of the international character of the settlement."

It was on Thursday afternoon that I went to the Vatican and called on my friend Monsignor Cerretti, then Secretary of Extraordinary Affairs. He brought me at once to Cardinal Gasparri who wanted me to go with Cerretti and himself to Benedict XV. I begged off on the excuse of not being properly dressed for an audience. Cerretti saved me. The two went to see the Holy Father together while I waited in Cardinal Gasparri's apartment. It was a long wait. When they returned we again sat down to talk. The Cardinal asked me what I would advise under the circumstances. Presuming that the terms I had suggested might have to be changed or adjusted, I at once replied that all my advice consisted of a request to take it off my hands and send a Vatican diplomat to Paris.

"But who?" persisted His Eminence.

"As near an approach to Archbishop Cerretti as Your Eminence can find," I answered, "that is, if he himself cannot be spared from his duties in Rome."

"Very well," agreed the Cardinal, "it will be Cerretti himself; and you are to return with him; but you will go on another mission which he will explain to you on the way. In Paris it will, however, be your duty to put Cerretti in touch with Orlando and Brambilla. Then you may have your wish to rid yourself of the responsibility and work at the other mission as long as Cerretti needs your assistance. Do not go back to America until he needs you no longer. What was it you said to Orlando about Austria?"

"That the place of the first Catholic nation was now *sede vacante*, Your Eminence."

"*Sede vacante*, eh? Bene! Bene! It was an idea, that!" And His portly Eminence had a hearty laugh over what he considered "a good one."

Signor Orlando's narrative tells the rest of the story:

"Monsignor Cerretti arrived in Paris toward the end of May and met Marquis Brambilla. The historical interview I had on the first of June with Monsignor Cerretti at the Hotel Ritz was thus arranged. He handed me a scheme containing the chief lines of an agreement between Italy and the Holy See. The fact of its being written and signed by Cardinal Gasparri gave it the highest authority. Its purport corresponded to that of the agreement now concluded—in February, 1929—that is, to confer the character of state, with international independence and sovereignty, on the inclosure of the Vatican, with a certain inclination, however, to include some other confining boundaries.

"I have to add that no allusion was made in the document or in the interview to any financial contribution from Italy, nor to any amendment to its legal system capable of exerting an influence on the common law. There was only a general hint of a convention which should successively regulate the relations of ecclesiastical law. I declared that I accepted that scheme in principle—that is, as a base of discussion—and that I limited my immediate reservations as to its contents to pointing out the inconvenience of asking for further extensions of the territory actually occupied by the Vatican. I remarked that the addition of a few thousand square yards would not in any way change things, though it could give rise to difficulties. I remember that I availed myself of a simile which Monsignor Cerretti acknowledged to be impressive. I said that the important question was whether the state should or should not exist and that its larger or smaller dimension was of little importance—as in the field of biology, a microbe was as much entitled to the name of a living organism as an elephant. . . .

"On the tenth of June I left Paris, never to go back again. On the nineteenth of that month I presented myself at the Chamber of Deputies, where I myself on that very day provoked the vote which, placing my cabinet in the minority, determined my resignation of office and the end of my government. . . .

"From a point of view of historical curiosity, my remark at the beginning of this article proves to be true. I said that America influenced in two ways this attempt of Agreement: Positively and negatively. Positively, because the suggestion which brought about the interview came from an American prelate. Negatively, because, without my tragic dissension with President Wilson, my prestige as head of the government which had won the war and concluded the peace would have remained untouched, and the Italian people would have been peaceful and contented. The two conditions whose absence prevented the conclusion of the agreement would then have been fulfilled."

Ten years later the Roman question was settled by a treaty signed by Cardinal Gasparri for the Holy See and Prime Minister Mussolini for the Kingdom of Italy. The *Saturday Evening Post* article of the former Premier marked a situation which must have been recognized by both Powers, namely: that behind the Treaty of 1929 was an Italy united in approval. The Liberals represented the only possible opposition to the 1929 settlement, and their leader had agreed to a Treaty of the same kind ten years before. That made the Lateran Treaty unanimous.

In 1929, after the signing of the Lateran Treaty, I made an official visit to Rome as a bishop, and called on Cardinal Gasparri according to a long-established custom for visiting bishops. He was still Secretary of State. I intended to offer congratulations on the signing of the Treaty. While I waited in the antechamber of the Cardinal I thought of a longer wait ten years before and of his hearty laugh over the *sede vacante* suggestion. He passed me with a bow as he came from a Papal audience and went into his receiving room. Alas! the Cardinal had grown much older and the spring was out of his step. A minute later I was called for and entered. He was standing near the door. He asked me who I was.

"*Sic transit gloria mundi.*"

❧ 26 ❧

THE FOURTH LONDON

THERE was a fourth London for me. The first I saw was the pre-war city—rich, confident, politely arrogant; not a mere world capital but the capital of the world; a city that would make any American less than a millionaire or an ambassador—often the same thing—mad at it. My second London was the war city; uniformed, distressed, hungry for the fleshpots of the old day, cheerless, dark, plucky, and brave—very. My third London was a dazed, shaky-on-its-feet, uncertain, back-to-civies, muddled-through—what? kind of place. But London Four was only London One chastened by a near-licking, yet standing straight on its pins and beginning to put on airs again. Certainly there were four Londons. Count them.

Man made the four Londons but nature made only one, for London town is a fortress built by man in a permanent war between himself and a nasty climate. The chills combine against the city in an effort to drive man out of it, but they fight against an incurable imperial sentimentalist who, though he may live elsewhere, has made London the center of his adoration. The Londoner himself has dug in and stays. One of his fogs would discourage anybody else on earth, two distress him, three banish him. Not so with the Londoner. To him the fog is a not unwelcome change from the little he has of sunshine. But how could he know anything about sunshine? And he is wrong about the fog. He is wrong about the rain. They can't be explained away. But London is a sentiment, a monumented past which saves it from being again the swamp it was in the days of the Angles. Traditions do not mind the climate. Who cares about last year's storms? Who bothers about last week's fog? Not the Tower, not the Bridge, not Big Ben, not Piccadilly, not

Cheapside, not anything in London that was there before the Londoner's great great grandfather was born. The elements will not give up their fight—ever; but they never will conquer London.

Whitehall is the heart of the British Empire. It is very English, if only in the fact that it is not a hall and not white. Whitehall is a group of dark office buildings—really one building—surrounding a paved courtyard. The heart mentioned is right in the center of that courtyard. One may step on it or stand on it and nobody will mind. Nothing will stop and nobody will even look. The buildings themselves are the most London-like possible; which means that the atmosphere is about the same within and without. They feel so foggy and damp that the visitor from lands of sunshine is moved to keep his umbrella up when he enters. The only shock is to find elevators—pardon me, *lifts*—but they seem to have been there before any Londoner's great great grandfather was born. They were originally made so strong that they will never wear out, so they remain as one of the Great Sustaining Influences. Because they still work they may not be discarded.

The offices in Whitehall are not really offices. Each one is a combination office, drawing and bedroom, somewhat run down and dusty. When the Cabinet Minister, or the Chief Under-Secretary—who in most matters is the Cabinet Minister's tutor—is at his desk, the room is an office; when he leaves it becomes the drawing room of a clerk—*clark*, thank you! When the day's darkness thickens into night the clerk makes a bed for himself out of the sofa. I did not see these things done, but my informant did not appear to be fooling me—I mean, of course, did not appear to be spoofing me.

In the business of letting the Empire govern Whitehall one sees immediately the influence of the climatic war. Government officials carry silence as they do umbrellas. Not that there are so many secrets, but that silence is considered the best answer when there is no answer. It takes long training to produce the silence— Eton, Oxford, a bit of foreign service and "a lot of that sort of rot, you know!" Once learned it is invaluable and, best of all, it works. Things come out quite right in the end. Really it's no bother at all. There are few secrets in a statesmen's daily duties, but for practice in secrecy everything must be considered secret—quite.

It was all very strange but I took kindly to it. I liked it—rather!

I knew that everybody knew that someone had blundered in the business that brought me back to London in 1920, but I knew better than to expect an admission that anyone at Whitehall ever did or ever could do anything so very un-English. I expected to be snubbed as an amateur who had not been to any equivalent of Eton and Oxford somewhere, though of course there could not possibly be an equivalent to either anywhere. I expected—but nothing happened at all. No one snubbed me. Everyone listened politely to me. Some took me to lunch at clubs as old as Whitehall, and just as English because they did not look like clubs but were. They fed me fish, joint, cabbage, and peas. Some only gave me tea and cake. Of course I tried to talk business in the American way on such occasions and of course had no success. There was no business except myself for the moment—if you see what I mean. I was under gentlemanly observation. When it was over and done with I could be sure—quite—that I was a "decent sort" and need not bother about the fog. So the Day of Judgment no longer impresses me as once it did. I've been through an imitation and a forerunner of it.

An unofficial invitation tendered by heads of the British Foreign Office, to come over and discuss the problem of the future of missions conducted and supported by Germans and Austrians before the war, and threatened with destruction after, brought me back to London. It was a problem made more difficult by the fact that there had been unpleasant reactions in America; some made by editorial pens, and mine one of them. The question was not wholly a Catholic one. In fact German Protestant missions were even more involved than were those of the Catholic religious orders. There had been heavy firing on the Allied policy of expulsion, from German Protestant press and pulpit, but it had accomplished nothing. Such blasts were considered merely the harmless continuation of wartime propaganda. Catholic protests were more serious, for they were likely to be world-wide and based, not upon irritation over a defeat, but on fundamental principles. The German Protestant protests did find some sympathetic hearers in England, but the English had not yet forgotten the war atrocity inventions. The Holy See had taken up the question through her usual diplomatic channels and thus had had a hearing. But there was more delay and further consideration of possible evil consequences to the colonies. Manifestation of American interest in the question slowed up still more the policy of expelling missionaries from fields they had developed. But the great damage had been done. Two years after the war the question was, for the most part, how to arrest it. America loomed large there, since the missions were looking to America for men and money as well as sympathy.

In truth the determination of the Allied governments to expel German and Austrian Christian missionaries was what the Holy See called it: a blow at the right of the Church to preach the Gospel of Christ to all men. It was an attack on what one editor well called "the supernationality of the Gospel of Christ." Though made on the excuse of military necessity, in effect it was a war horror which struck at a vital underlying Christian principle. But those responsible had not thought of that while the fighting was on nor immediately after. It was chiefly the Holy See defending a principle that made people outside Germany and Austria think of it at all.

Almost unknown then to the people of Great Britain and the United States, the movement begun in a very small way during the war had developed at its close into a policy and a stunning surprise. Only a few old and infirm missionaries were spared. Decrees called for expulsion, confiscation, imprisonment, closing of mission stations, and abandonment of schools and colleges. In India it struck with terrific force. The whole staff of the Jesuit College at Bombay was affected, and the missionary work in Assam, entirely conducted by German Salvatorians, was crippled.

The effect on mission schools for both Europeans and natives was disastrous. Many German missionaries, especially Jesuits, had come out of their novitiate in India as native to the country as the English residents themselves, though their chief support had always been from Germany. Some of these missionaries had even received decorations from the Indian Government. At the consecration of a new church in Schillong in 1913 the Chief Commissioner and officials gave a complimentary dinner to the Prefect Apostolic who had built it, eulogizing his service and those of his clergy to the province. Before the building was quite finished Prefect and clergy had to leave it. On the little schools fell the hardest blow.

Working for them was an order of teaching nuns with a remarkable history, the Sisters of Loreto. They had been founded centuries before by an English lady, Mary Ward, but their development had largely been on the Continent, especially in Germany where the Sisters became known popularly as the English Ladies. They had many schools in India. Authorities were a little slower in reaching out for the nuns than they had been for the priests and brothers, but in the end one hundred and fifty "English Ladies" were interned at Ahmadnagar as a preliminary to expulsion. In November, 1915, and in March, 1916, about one hundred and thirty-five missionaries were driven out of India. Toward the end of 1915 the Allies called upon China to do the same. Expulsion followed from Egypt and other points in Africa. The whole missionary organization of German East Africa was destroyed. And all this was done contrary to the Congo Act which imposed the duty of protecting missions in the interest of Christian civilization. Groups were sent out of the Sudan and the South Sea Islands. France, though having only a small number of German missionaries, did her share thoroughly. Portugal followed. Japan expelled some missionaries from the South Sea Islands but none from the homeland or Korea. The United States interned a few in the Philippines. All this was done before the world knew what was going on, for at the time censorship had not ceased to operate.

In 1919 China decided to follow the example of the other Allies. It happened, however, that China could not do all that was expected of her. The United States, being involved as an Associated Power in the war, had to take note of the fact that American missionaries there were mixed with the Germans. One of the largest institutions for preparing missionaries for China was in the archdiocese of Chicago. Archbishop Mundelein made representations to the American Government in favor of these missions on the ground that they were dependent upon American support and therefore practically American, indeed Chicagoan. His protest awakened our government to the folly of the policy as well as to its danger. The missions of the Fathers of the Divine Word in China were saved by the Archbishop's prompt action, much to the satisfaction of Chinese Christians as well as the Chinese government. But before the awakening hundreds of missionaries had been expelled.

The Treaty of Peace took for granted the expulsion of German missionaries, since its terms arranged for boards of management to hold their properties. This meant the taking of the properties from those who had built, supported, or endowed them. Benedict XV protested through his special envoy Archbishop Cerretti, who succeeded in securing the concession that Catholic missions were to be recognized as belonging to the Holy See. Protestant missions could and did take advantage of that concession to save their rights · to what they had built up and sustained. But it was evident that behind the whole movement was the desire on the part of some persons for state control.

The protests of American Catholics, especially that of Archbishop Mundelein, and the consequent withdrawal of the United States from the agreement of expulsion, brought the matter to the direct attention of the more responsible leaders of American and British public opinion. Almost without exception British colonial powers had favored Christian missions, not only because of their religious influence on the native populations but also because of the educational and philanthropic benefits they brought with them. At the height of the anti-clerical movement in France, even when religious orders were being suppressed, foreign missions had been treated with consideration. France had always an army of missionaries with posts in every part of the world. The French missionary had more than once paved the way for French colonial expansion, and the French language was for a long time almost the only language of many Catholic missions.

The Catholic missionary movement in Germany had almost leaped into importance. Not only were Germans working in their own colonies but they had active and successful foundations in Africa, China, India, and Australia. They brought much order and system into missionary work, and in some cases made their missions self-supporting by trade development. The British especially were quick to see the importance of fostering such practical efforts for both the evangelization and the education of the native population. Though the chief support of these missions came from Germany, in British territory the German language was not taught. Nor were the Germans at all too German. The college at Schillong, already mentioned, though built and supported by the German Prefect

Apostolic, nevertheless was on his invitation directed and staffed by Irish Christian Brothers. The first European girls' school in the Province of Assam was founded by Father Becker of the German Salvatorians. He also started the first high school for boys in the same province. The British chief commissioner at the time, Sir Archdale Earle, fostered these foundations in accord with approved governmental policy. Even during the war, English schools for mixed populations were established in India by Germans. The Assam mission had about thirty elementary schools for natives. There were also orphanages and other charitable institutions similarly managed and directed.

How it happened that an invitation was extended to me to go to England and there discuss the matter unofficially I do not know, but I believe that my name was suggested by Mr. Robert Wilberforce, then at the British Embassy in Washington. About that time a little pamphlet, for which I had written the preface, appeared on the question. The following extract from that preface will show quite clearly that the Foreign Office had not selected me as a friend:

"In this little book we face the story of a new attack on the supernationality of the Gospel; a new effort to make the Church of Christ subservient to the ambitions of states and rulers; a new effort to render to Caesar not only what is Caesar's but also what is God's; a blind uncomprehension of the rights of Christian states, perhaps, rather than a deliberate attempt to deny the rights of God, but none the less dangerous. It is the same error as to the prerogatives of the Teaching Church that has been an enemy of Christ from the beginning; the error that crucified Him, and has been crucifying Him ever since."

I left for London on the "Celtic" in the summer of 1920. All the British Foreign Office wanted was an unofficial discussion of the situation for its own information, but the importance it attached to the matter was indicated by the fact that Mr. Wilberforce was directed to accompany me to London and make the formal introductions. I could not have had a more delightful companion. He had entered the service of the Foreign Office from Oxford, married an American, and had had his longest assignment in our country. Besides, being a Catholic himself, and by no means a lax one, he understood how grave the affair might turn out to be; especially since the case involved also the Protestant missions. In London he knew everyone I had to meet and saw to it that I met them under the most favorable circumstances.

It was arranged that my host in London would be Cardinal Bourne, then the Archbishop of Westminster. I am afraid that he had read what I had written on the mission question and had already put me down as a person worth watching. Nor did I blame His Eminence. I had written strongly. When the Foreign Office asked the Cardinal to entertain me in his house during my stay in London—I learned this only on a return visit—he had not failed to utter a warning. But whether he liked me or not at the start, when the affair was over and done with we were friends. To the day of his lamented death his house in Westminster was, by his invitation and even command, a London home for me.

Strange as it may seem, my Canadian birth and youthful upbring-ing had done nothing to make me like England. No part of the British overseas Empire is more loyal to the Throne than Canada, but as a rule Canadians do not like Englishmen any too well. Seem-ingly there is no logic in the situation. Yet there is. The Canadian takes the Empire on a strictly business basis. It suits his purposes to buy what it has to offer, which is protection. There is, however, no special protection for the individual Englishman in Canada. For one thing he may be and often is Scotch. The Canadian wants to make the money himself. What profits a man if he wants the world and has to deal with a Scot? In industry the Canadian is no small rival of the Englishman. Then the Canadian has little use for titles. He is an unaffected person and believes that the Englishman is not. The Canadian puts on few airs and thinks the Englishman puts on too many. An Englishman finds himself much more comfort-able in the United States than in Canada. But the Canadian never fails to respond to a call for cheers for King and Empire. They both belong to him. Then in my case there was the Irish question. I had decided views about Ireland. I could never forget my early reading. I never wanted to. I hoped for Ireland all the freedom she could safely lay her hands upon. It will be seen that I was not at all in love with the English when I went to England.

In London I soon reversed the order I had learned in Canada

and began to like the Englishman and to think that the Empire
was not good enough for him. The poor fellow was oppressed. He
was not permitted to govern himself. He needed the independence
the Irish were pummeling him to get for themselves. The Scots,
the Welsh, and the Jews were running him. The colonies were
picking his pockets. Englishmen were a minority even in their own
Cabinet. Later one of them put it to me in this unforgettable form,
"My word! If the Irish would only stay with us; what? It would
be a blasted sight more agreeable to have them govern us, since
it seems we're too blasted busy to govern ourselves. There's not
even a smile left in the House of Commons since the Irish left.
We never knew till they were gone how much we really liked having them. What?"

The poor chap was sincere. Sympathy is the gate of love. I got to
the point of throwing off my prejudice and extending a lot of
sympathy to the poor oppressed English. Perhaps it was the kind
of Englishmen I met who changed me. I visited and preached in
the poorest parish in London, down in Commercial Road where
Canon Ring was in command. There I learned something of the
sterling patience of the Englishman in adversity—even in poverty.
And there I saw honest devotion and genuine love for the poor
shown by the Irish Canon and his English curates. No week went by
in that parish without constant visitation of homes and flock. In
Hyde Park I saw the faith of the laity in splendid action. G. K.
Chesterton—God rest him—was in himself alone a magnet which
attracted me to the people who produced him. One of the pleas-
antest afternoons of my life was passed with Hilaire Belloc sharing
with me the comfort of an open fireplace on a typical chilly and
rainy London day. The Cardinal, once the ice was broken, sat many
an evening in the same place. I found two bishops before my fire one
afternoon after a trying visit to Whitehall. One was Casartelli,
who, in spite of his Italian name, was typically an English gentleman of the old school, even to the whiskers. The other was Burton
of Clifton, a man with a heart overflowing with goodness and a
head overflowing with brains. I had lunch with Sydney Dark of
the *Church Times* and found myself praying for his conversion—
the greatest compliment I could give to any man alive. Ernest Old-
meadow—novelist, editor, and connoisseur of wines—himself cooked

the lunch to which he invited me, and served it with his own hands hot off the stove. What a lunch! The very memory of it makes me long once more to climb that old stairs to the top of his musty building—which should have had a vintage label on it—and present him with a forged rain-check. At the office of the *Universe* there was always the shy welcome of the editor, Dean, who looked as if he knew everybody's ancestors—and did. I had a typical English secretary, now with Dean on the *Universe*, George Barnard. A Western cowboy would give him his highest and best by swearing that his stability was like unto that of a hitching post; though the cowboy would not go at making the compliment in such a labored way. One morning when I was vested for Mass in the cathedral, a gentleman asked "the privilege of serving." I found out later that my white-haired altar boy had been Under-Secretary of State for the Colonies. Prince René of Bourbon-Parma once served my Mass, claiming it as a privilege of his family, but my English commoner did it quite as well as the French prince. In both cases "it was the Mass that mattered."

At the Foreign Office three gentlemen were awaiting me: Sir William Tyrrell, Mr. Christopher Phillips, and Mr. P. A. Koppel. It was with these three I had to deal. Later, the first became Baron Tyrrell and British Ambassador to France. The second went to the Department of Education from which his talents had been borrowed by the Foreign Office. The third is dead—God rest him. Sir William was at the time Permanent Under-Secretary of State for Foreign Affairs, a manager and director of diplomats. It was a testimony to the importance of the missions question that he was taking personal charge; since Sir William, to quote Shane Leslie, was "the power at the Foreign Office, one of the ablest and subtlest diplomats that England ever had." A cousin of poor Father Tyrrell, Sir William was Irish and a Catholic. He had lost all his sons in the war. In these three Englishmen there was nothing of the affectation my early Canadian training had led me to expect. They were very fine and very human. They even made me like tea, which, by the way, was made for them at the correct hour each afternoon by a confidential secretary—Miss Best, from, of all places, that Boston which was famous for having thrown tea overboard.

Of the facts about the German missions I soon found that I

knew all too little, and suggested that discussions be postponed until I could learn more by a visit to Germany where many expelled missionaries were living. Time out was granted. But how to get into Germany? Officially America and Germany were still at war. A German consular agent had, however, been accredited to London and the good offices of Mr. Phillips secured a very unofficial pass for Father Shannon, who had come over with me on editorial instinct, and myself. We left to show our passes at the Holland frontier and, by stopping at the mission house of the Fathers of the Divine Word at Steyl, to secure introductions across the border. There we met a priest who told us that the expelled Jesuit Fathers of Bombay were located at Bonn. He himself was Superior of the mission house of his own Order at Hanglar near the University city.

We did our last steady and satisfactory eating in Holland. If I were asked to give a special name to the frontier post at which we entered Germany I should call it Hunger. Its official name was Kalden Kirken. A line of German women had crossed the border into the strip of neutral ground where some Dutch merchants had set up huts for selling food. A definite and small amount only was admitted free of duty for each person. It was soon evident why only women were buying. Their skirts were good hiding places, and such food as hams could be attached to concealed belts. The only way to detect the smuggling would have been to weigh each woman both entering and returning. But the frontier guards understood. They looked into baskets and bags but did not trouble about a very apparent gain in female avoirdupois in the space of ten or fifteen minutes.

At the little railway station a lot of battered passenger coaches were being attached to an equally decrepit engine. Third class was crowded with women carrying food. We were alone in the one first-class compartment. A young aristocrat—he had a cane and spats—was strolling along the station platform, his well-worn clothes carefully pressed and his fedora tilted at the proper angle. A piece of bread was lying on the ground near the platform, evidently fallen from one of the bags and now soiled by the cinders. The young man walked toward it, gave a quick look around, leaned over, picked it up and put it in his pocket. We ourselves ate a lunch we had taken over from Steyl. Our German professor finished his share first. Then he carefully gathered the crumbs left in the paper bag into the palm of his hand and used them for dessert. No food was being wasted in Germany. At Cologne people were bringing their own eggs into the hotel dining room. All the hotel served was *ersatz* coffee and war-bread. Families were dining luxuriously on that and the hard-boiled eggs they had carried in with them. We were ready for the worst at Bonn—and got it.

Two young professors from the college in Bombay, speaking perfect English, were at the Jesuit house. It was near the lunch hour. In a shamefaced way they told us that they could not invite us to lunch—"It is so very scanty and poor in these days, you know." We asked if there was a hotel or restaurant to which we could invite them. They cheered up visibly and led us to a hotel overlooking the Rhine where we had the choice of a small dish of stewed meat or nothing. We ordered the stew. When it came Father Shannon pressed my foot under the table and signaled me to look at our guests. Their eyes were devouring the meat. Father Shannon barely touched his serving and I followed suit, thankful to his kind heart for giving me the hint. There was not a scrap of meat or gravy on any of the plates when the professors had finished. These were hard times indeed for German appetites. We sat there overlooking the Rhine for hours as the young priests told their story. There was no bitterness in it. They were of India, not Germany, since it was India they were longing for. India was pulling on the cords of their hearts, and how they did want to go back!

We went to Hanglar next day, the young Indian-Germans with us, where an afternoon conference was to be held; but the conference was broken into by a sad tragedy. In front of a farm home we had passed on our way to the mission house children had been playing, an older boy watching from an open window. Some soldiers in occupation came down the road in an army wagon. Seeing the children they stopped and one of them threw a hand grenade at the boy, shattering his face. It was the awful wailing of his grandmother, who came to find a priest, that broke into our conference. Father Shannon left to hear the proceedings in the magistrate's court. We were told later that the affair had been hushed up.

Nothing could be done about it. We went back to London with sadness in our hearts, having learned more than we expected or wanted to learn. Nazism was being born in Germany, and its parents were Hunger and Shame.

War drags men back to savagery. I remembered an incident in Florida at the close of the Spanish War when a group of volunteers got out of hand. They invaded a cemetery, broke into tombs and dragged the dead bodies out of them. In the cemetery was a chapel over the grave of the Cuban patriot Felix Varila. Only the weight of the stone slab over it saved his body from desecration. Everything breakable in the chapel was left in splinters. These men were Americans filled with drink and bigotry. Men are alike everywhere when the bars of decency are down. Is civilization only a veneer? Perhaps not, but many a mark left by war on the souls of nations is a mark of the Cloven Foot.

When I returned to London with my notebook well filled, the conversations began, still unofficial. They seemed, however, to drag out interminably and I had work to do at home. It took a month before I knew what concessions could be had. Then I went to Rome and there the story ends so far as this narrative is concerned, for when I left to return to London my status had changed and my mission was official. What writing is done about official missions is all in the form of reports and these do not belong to the writer once they are filed. But there are always interesting things to be seen and enjoyed "on the side" and, in this case, it was the wish of both parties that the newspapers be given information on the subject once it was settled.

An amusing incident occurred at the end of the conversations in London, the telling of which will not be an indiscretion. It was over a fight I had been making from the unofficial beginning to save the Loreto nuns from expulsion. It was also my test case. If I lost it I lost everything, so, naturally, all the persuasion and eloquence I had was put into it. I had succeeded in obtaining a respite of four months, but when the time was up the original order for expulsion would come back into force. The Indian government was worried about the nuns, especially about the danger of sending them from the heart of India back to Munich with winter coming on. The officials actually saw to it that warm clothing was issued to them. There was no lack of sympathy in the face of what was thought to be hard necessity. The postponement of the expulsion was secured on the ground that I was obliged to return to America while the whole question was still under consideration. I suggested that expulsion of the nuns at that time would be nothing less than a premature adverse decision on the whole question. The contention was accepted and the expulsion delayed, but the nuns were kept interned at Ahmadnagar.

When I returned to London a few days before the New Year of 1921, I found that a change of mind for the better had taken place at Whitehall. The matter had come to be a question, not of the justice or injustice of the decrees of expulsion but of how far exceptions might be made in the enforcement of them. As I felt from the beginning, the pivotal point was India. A hint from Cardinal Bourne gave me the advance information that Lord Redding would be named Viceroy of India. I went to Lord Redding's London house to talk the situation over with him. Next day the news of his appointment was out and I finished giving him my side of the case at the India Office. From then on things moved swiftly. Cardinal Bourne was a most encouraging person. He gave me lift after lift and suggestion after suggestion, but always left me free. It was when the decision that the nuns might stay in India was communicated to me that the amusing incident occurred.

I had been making my diplomacy the foundation of many a pleasantry against myself. Now I insisted that I was no longer a joke but a simon-pure diplomat. As such I could not, of course, trust anyone, for I had to live the part. Lacking the gold-embroidered uniform, plumed hat, and sword, I felt it a duty to my dignity to see personally that there could be no slip. I requested the privilege of writing the dispatch to India which canceled the expulsion order. It was granted so I sat down at a battered old desk of the Dickens period—Mr. Micawber might well have used one like it before it was seized for debt—and wrote that order. At Whitehall interdepartmental communications go from office to office in little iron boxes covered—or once covered—with red morocco leather. I wanted to put the dispatch into the box with my own hands, address the slip, turn the key, and give the box over to the messenger.

I was asked ironically if I did not want also to click it off on the telegraph instruments, but declined in the fear that I had forgotten the Morse code which, I admitted, I had once known. But I did find a glorious satisfaction in writing that dispatch and thinking of the joy it would bring to one hundred and fifty teachers longing to go back to their Indian pupils. That night when the Cardinal came to my room after dinner for a chat before the open fire, I gave him little opportunity to do any of the talking. The end of my job and home were in sight.

It did not take long after that to reach an agreement. All the harm that had been done could not be undone, but a plan was adopted to permit German missionaries to enter British territory, with the exception of East Africa where there had been hard fighting during the war. Cardinal Bourne was given the right to "visa" all applications for Catholic missionaries of German and Austrian nationality with the understanding that his powers were wide and that he should use them generously. A somewhat similar arrangement was adopted by the India and Colonial offices for Protestant missionaries. These two plans were, I heard later, sent to Australia and New Zealand where they were accepted in an even more liberal spirit by their governments.

The German mission question had one surprising reawakening soon after. It had been decided that the Jesuit College in Bombay should be taken over by the Fathers of the New York Province. The German Fathers had all been expelled before the question had come up for discussion in London, and even a government hates to seem to reverse itself; perhaps hates to confess by so doing that it had been wrong. Bombay would have preferred the former teachers to any substitutes, but if they could not come back Americans would be the most welcome. The English Jesuit Province had not enough Fathers to man the college. A first contingent of American volunteers for India was selected and ready to leave when suddenly the British Embassy in Washington refused to grant visas. A report followed that the refusal was based on the fact that some of the Fathers had Irish names. The affair caused no small embarrassment in London when I brought it to the attention of the India and Foreign Offices after getting the news by cable. The Irish trouble was at that very time headed for peaceful conference, and the word of the government had been passed on the missions. How had the new contretemps happened?

Government bureaus in the Old World are most secretive and slow. The news about a preliminary understanding had evidently not reached Washington, and there was someone in the embassy very suspicious of the Irish—how strange! London acted quickly. When I left, a few days after the news from America reached me, I carried with me an official grant of the visas direct from the India Office, and an assurance that there would be no trouble about those to be asked for later. But all was not well in New York. Thinking that the visas would not be granted, the General of the Jesuits had changed the assignment of the American Fathers and had ordered them to go to the Philippine Islands instead of to Bombay. The latter charge he confided to a Spanish Province which still has it. The task must have seemed hard to the Spaniards, faced with the necessity of learning a new language.

There are, I believe, few at present of the postwar restrictions on Christian missions in any part of the British Empire. Germans are still working in the South Seas, even in Australia. One of the great objections to the activities of German missionaries on the part of Great Britain came out of trade, and was aimed especially at a Lutheran missionary society with headquarters in Switzerland. This German society had separate religious and trade divisions, the latter supporting the former. The society paid its own way and was thought to be doing a bit more. It was thought too that it had arrived at a point where the trade had become of greater importance than the missions. There was also a Catholic mission in the South Seas paying its own way through copra plantations, but no charge of promoting German trade in British possessions had been made against it. These missions are still at work, but I suppose that the business side of them has come in for some regulation with an eye to Great Britain's getting the trade.

A few months after my return I read an article clipped from a newspaper in India and published in London under the caption, "A Diplomatic Settlement." It detailed the plan adopted in London for the admission of missionaries of non-British nationality into India. All the credit was assigned to the Cardinal Archbishop of Westminster. At the end appeared this comment: "(It) should encourage those of us who 'hope all things' where the Catholic conscience is served by a sane intermediary and the Catholic Church possessed of a statesmanlike representative."

I rubbed my eyes. The Cardinal would not like it any more than I did. But when I put it away as the last contribution to my notes, I thought a lot about that strange thing called human nature. The nice old gentleman who had written that article had not lifted a finger to help at any stage of the negotiations, and in practice actually had assumed the attitude that "the Germans got what they deserved." But then his nation had been the first invaded and was the greatest sufferer from the war. The German Ambassador to the Holy See invited me to a sort of thanksgiving dinner at the embassy in Rome. It was an excellent dinner. I could not have eaten an Iron Cross.

Non-Catholics often ask the reason why the Holy See maintains diplomatic relations with the nations of the world and why so many of these nations are so anxious to be represented at the Vatican. Lord Clonmore, in his interesting book *Pope Pius XI and World Peace*, has a paragraph giving the viewpoint of a large number of people with a knowledge of international conditions: "One can only think that a closer connection between the United States and the Vatican would be to the advantage of both parties, and that the States in their decision to send no ambassador have made a mistake. In view of the large proportion of Catholics in the States, there would almost certainly be plenty of business which could be profitably transacted, and we shall see, when we examine conditions in Mexico, that there are ways in which he might be of the greatest use to other inhabitants of the American continent, for he would hear a point of view which he is not likely to hear so clearly expressed anywhere else, and which voices a wider scope of opinion than anything to be heard at Geneva."

Diplomats would offer another answer without denying the force of Lord Clonmore's. I heard one of them state his view and that of others: "The Vatican is the only all-time diplomatic neutral ground in the world. Because it is that, the diplomatic corps has made it the whispering gallery of diplomacy. To this advantage is added another which is most valuable for the training of diplomats: The Vatican sees the world's troubles from a vantage ground above them. It is the principle that must be kept to the fore in dealing with the Vatican. It is a good training to be exposed to that somewhat unusual light ray."

My own answer would not call the force of the other answers into question. I should only offer the German and Austrian missions question as a pertinent example. It was admitted that the question affected Protestant as well as Catholic missions. The former could only utter individual protests which beat vainly upon locked chancery doors. Individuals could and did differ with missionary bodies representing their own denominations. War prejudice played a nasty part as usual. Protestant missionary societies had no unity, no one authorized voice to speak for all, and no recognized way of approaching governments. It was different with the Vatican which represented as a final authority all Catholic missionary bodies in the world. To this was added a recognized diplomatic standing which gave it a right to speak its mind. It had no guarantee that its views would prevail, but it had the guarantee of a way to present them.

It happened to be a fortunate thing even for the Protestant missions that the Vatican had both diplomatic standing and authority. The Vatican did not present the case of any missions other than its own. The result, however, was the vindication of a principle that could be and was taken advantage of by missions that were not Catholic.

The Holy See seeks to preserve the peace of the world. Expediency counts far less at the Vatican than in any other court. The Church deals in principles to such an extent that any diplomat with long experience at the Vatican can pretty well tell in advance what its attitude will be on any question. I was given an illustration of that latter fact in a matter outside diplomacy by the late Anglican Bishop Anderson of Chicago. I had met him with two other Anglican bishops, Vincent of Cincinnati and Webber of Fond du Lac, on the Paris-Rome Express before the War. The three were over there to sound out the Pope and the Patriarchs of Eastern churches on their attitude to a proposed Conference on Faith and Order to be called at Lausanne. Their interview with Benedict XV had already been arranged. Meeting Bishop Anderson in Chicago later on, he gave me an outline of what had occurred at that interview. To me the most interesting thing about it was what happened immediately before and immediately after. I shall allow the Bishop to tell it in his own way: "Before we left the hotel to drive to the Vatican, I wrote down something on a sheet of paper, sealed it in an envelope, and handed it to Bishop Vincent, saying, 'When we return here open this and you will read the Pope's answer.' When the envelope was opened what I had written was found to be in substance what the Holy Father said."

But I have a conviction of my own on the subject that perhaps the diplomats would not think of voicing. Since the days of the "Reformers" Christianity has been subjected by their followers to a chipping-off process which has brought it more and more into the servitude of the State. The Reformation, proclaimed as a declaration of independence, won its success through princes at the cost of liberty. One Christian dogma after another has been discarded or obscured. Even the Divinity of Christ is no longer fully accepted by the larger non-Catholic denominations. It remains only in old professions of faith. With nothing definite to preserve or fight for, expediency allows the State more and more to cross the dividing line and encroach on ground not her own.

But it is not alone non-Catholic bodies and individuals who have shown a willingness thus to yield ground to the State. Modernism within the Church was a doctrinal movement inevitably leading to that end. Its condemnation and failure did not do away with its evil objective. Postwar troubles and social disturbances became appeals for radical political changes which, for the greater part, were directed to the rise of totalitarian states claiming jurisdiction in both the spiritual and temporal order. Often it was hunger that made men barter their fundamental freedom for these.

The Church of Christ is universal in more than a territorial meaning. Its mission is not only to every part of the world but to all the peoples and nations of the world. Its universality is as much a part of its heritage in courts as it is in peoples. Its teachings and the liberties born of them are as much at home by right in college and university as in temple and hamlet. No nation is above them or exempt from the moral law that comes out of them. Christ then has a place amongst the nations as much as He had a place amongst the shepherds. That place becomes a citadel for the defense of the rights of men; one spot at least on earth where eternal principles rule and where expediency has no power to supplant them. What the Holy See did for "the supernationality of the Gospel of Christ" was done in its own name and by its own strength. It was the eternal principle that was at stake. Out of that defense of principles others profited. The Vatican as a court to which ambassadors come and out of which ambassadors are sent is the confession of faith of the nations of our civilization in the saving power of Christian principles. The Church could exist without it but wise statesmen have learned by experience that its existence is a safeguard of inestimable value.

I expect to be pardoned the preachment. No bishop could miss such an opening.

GHOSTS

ROBERT HUGH BENSON'S personal friends knew that he dearly loved ghosts, and readers of his books more than suspected it. The wide-awake prelate would go far to find a haunted house. His last novel, *Oddsfish*, introduced a lady who became a ghost in the days of Charles II. It offered a detailed description of the house she honored with her mysterious presence and told of her moaning midnight walks up and down its stairs.

England has so many ancient, ruined abbeys, priories, and monastic halls—now belonging to descendants of, or purchasers from, the spoilers—that it would be small wonder indeed if these had not their spiritual guardians: gray-friars, brown-friars, black-friars, gloomy abbots and melancholy abbesses. English novels have not missed them. Their stories had inspired in me a great curiosity, though I was quite sure it would never lead me as far as Benson was always willing to go. I wanted only to hear about them. But I was destined not only to hear about that lady in *Oddsfish* but to hear her. I visited the house, slept in it, and—but let's not get ahead of the story.

There was one bothersome thing about my being in England on the business of trying to save what was left of the German missions in British territory. It can be put into two words: Sinn Fein. The words were ominous. I knew my Irish. The little drop of Scotch blood in me had long ago been assimilated by the more exciting Irish flow, which, ordinarily peaceful enough, always stirred into life both irresistible and dangerous when the heart started driving it beyond the speed limit. Cucuhlain and Finn and Brian—even the latter's lieutenant on the left wing at Clontarf, my presumed ancestor, the O'Ceallaigh of Hy-Maine—had come to life

297

in me early, and neither Dane nor Saxon could put them to sleep again. Nineteen-twenty certainly was no time for an O'Ceallaigh to be visiting with friendly countenance the heart of the Sassenach Empire on any business not fully understood by the leaders of the new Erin. But my friend Monsignor Cerretti was an understanding man. He told me to make no secret of the object of my mission, for even a small misunderstanding could make difficulties. It was a relief then to know that I might explain myself. It is a greater relief now.

Before leaving Chicago I was a guest at a luncheon given to Eamon de Valera. When the crowd had broken up I had an opportunity of speaking with him in private. I told him when and why I was going to London. He promised to see that no misunderstandings would arise. I told him frankly how I felt about Sinn Fein, which feeling carried one doubt about its ultimate success. There was a twinkle in De Valera's eye as he gave me a clever as well as enlightening answer, "Your difficulty, Monsignor, is like that of a man driving in an automobile along a hilly road to a certain destination. He cannot always see what is on the other side of a hill nor what is down in a valley. All he knows for a certainty is that he is on the right road. Does that express it?"

"It does," I answered, "it expresses it perfectly."

"Then don't worry a bit, Monsignor," he said, "I am on the same road. I cannot see over the hill or down into the valley, but I know that I am on the right road."

I left for London very much reassured; but when half-settled there I suspected that De Valera had not succeeded in getting word over ahead of me. I felt that I was being watched. In fact I became rather well acquainted with an Irish gentleman who appeared to be taking special interest in me. He became a regular visitor; a tall fine looking man expounding an idea about church finances and doing it remarkably well. But I noticed that never once in his visits did he fail to steer the conversation to the Irish question. Nevertheless, his visits were always welcome. He had lived long in London, knew many people, and was most informative. After a few visits he knew what I had come for and had a correct idea of my personal sentiments about the Irish question, which, I suspected, was his immediate interest. I was sorry when his visits became fewer, though they did not entirely cease.

Sinn Fein had the best, in the sense of being the most effective, secret service in Europe; no small accomplishment for a movement with such small financial resources. Its intelligence officers seemed to be covering every point of importance and their information in the main was remarkably accurate. The leaders knew well that their cause had friends not Irish, even friends at court. The war had worked a change in English public opinion and the people were taking the propaganda of yesterday less seriously. One day, when I called for a fitting, I found my tailor buried in a newspaper spread out on his cutting board. "What interests you so greatly?" I asked.

"The report of the Thomas Commission on conditions in Ireland," he replied.

"Pretty bad?"

"Sir," he said, with his jaw set, "if I believed that Englishmen could do what Thomas says those damn Black and Tans are doing in Ireland I'd be a Sinn Feiner myself."

"You don't believe it?"

"I can't see why Thomas should be lying about it, but it's hard to think that even exceptional Englishmen could be such rotters."

That man, representing a large class of intelligent workers, was more than half on the sympathy side of Sinn Fein.

Everybody I met wanted to talk about the Irish situation, but I found in their talk less of the old-time bitterness. A group of officials were present one day at the India Office when I was to submit the case for my missionary clients. The leading official broke in on my appeal. "I cannot quite understand, Monsignor," he said, "why you, an American Catholic, want to discuss the preservation of the German Catholic missions in India when your own people seem bent on driving all Christianity out of India by your sympathy with Indian revolutionists. Surely you know that if they succeed India must fall back into pagan or Moslem hands. What then would happen to your missions?"

I saw where that question would lead me and played for time. "American Catholics," I said, "certainly have no thought of making India pagan or Moslem." It was a weak reply and I knew it.

The questioner came back at me in a flash and gave day and date for a "march past" of Indian revolutionaries in a St. Patrick's Day parade, adding some high lights to a picture that astonished and disconcerted me. While I knew nothing about the parade, I did know that what he said about it was by no means improbable. He added a touch about people applauding as the Indian revolutionaries passed the reviewing stand.

I explained about processions in America, telling the gentleman, Sir Frederick Duke, how accustomed we were to salute and applaud any striking or colorful division of marchers. But my dilemma by this time had made me resentful and, seeing that my lame explanation was only amusing the company, I drove on thoughtlessly, "Why bother about it at all? It has nothing to do with this case and it drags in an Irish question which I have no mission at all to discuss or even any right to speak about." Then I threw caution to the winds and added, "Besides, I am a Sinn Feiner myself."

I could have bitten off the end of my tongue when the words were out. A pretty sort of counsel I was to antagonize these officials with one thoughtless sentence which might well have been left unsaid. There was dead silence in the room, but no one seemed a bit angry or even surprised. The silence was broken by a burly Scot with the tan of his native moors on his honest face. "What do you mean by a Sinn Feiner, Monsignor?" he asked.

I was again in a tight place. I knew little about Sinn Fein beyond what had been implied in De Valera's clever answer to me in Chicago. "Sinn Fein," I stammered, "means For Ourselves. I think that any intelligent people can make a better job of governing themselves and managing their own affairs than strangers."

"Go on with the presentation of your case, Monsignor." The man who had started the trouble ended it with a good natured laugh. "We are all Sinn Feiners with proper qualifications."

But I felt that I had weakened my case and something had to be done about that. In America we hold to the conviction that an Englishman is slow to grasp a joke. Nevertheless, I now badly needed a joke. If I could make these men laugh they might forget the slip I had made by proclaiming attachment to rebellion. When my pleading called for witnesses to the good conduct and usefulness of the German missionaries I had dozens of quotations to present. I selected one from a former Viceroy of India. When I looked at his name in my notebook I took courage. The joke was in sight. "I should like," I said, "to read what Lord ———." There I hesitated. "The name is spelled S-y-n-d-e-n-h-a-m but I really do not know how it is pronounced in England. In America we would say Syndenham but here—perhaps I should call him Jones."

The laugh came as the chance shot hit. Actually the name was pronounced Sin-den.

As I was leaving the building I met the hearty Scot. "I am very glad to meet you again, Monsignor," he said cordially. "Do you by any chance know any of the Seton family in America?"

"I know a retired archbishop of that name."

"He is my relative."

"You are then connected by blood with the American Setons?"

"The same stock," he replied. "One family."

"I do not know Archbishop Seton very well," I said. "He was active in America before my day, but for a long time has lived in Rome. He is not, however, the great American Seton. Elizabeth has that distinction. As foundress of the American Sisters of Charity she put the Setons into our Church history."

"We are not Catholics here, you know," said Sir Malcolm, "but we are very proud of our Catholic relatives in America. I hope you will be successful in your mission, Monsignor. It will be a great pleasure for me to do what I can to help you should another occasion arise. I think that we are all on your side."

So I thought myself, and later events proved that we both were right.

Just as soon as any nation in Europe gets into a mess with another the Pope is certain to receive much gratuitous advice. Every such fight resolves itself into a "strictly moral issue" in which the English especially always agree that they are on the side of morality. They ask pointedly why the Pope does not fulminate against their adversaries. Even over the late Italian expedition into Ethiopia England rang with demands that the Pope should condemn Italy. During the Great War both Germany and England had complained bitterly against the Holy See. Cardinal Merry del Val was the Papal Secretary of State who had to bear the brunt of the assault on the neutrality of Peter during the first months of the war. The Irish in him saw humor in the situation; at least there was some in the explanation he made to me. "Both sides," he said, "ask the Holy Father to pass on the issues of the war but are careful not to make the appeal official. They do not see, while demanding that the Holy Father speak, that they really ask him to be judge and arbitrator. Did not courtesy forbid we might ask them when they took an abrupt about-face on the question of the Holy Father's right to open a world court to decide political issues. Do they thus admit his authority? They will not say they do. But even if they did, how could any just judge decide a case without hearing it? Or would the nations at war cease to fight if the Pope called on them to lay down their arms and submit the issues to him? Where is his court for such a purpose? And what folly it is to ask for a decision which, accepted only by the side it favors, would settle nothing! War makes the peoples involved very unreasonable."

It was that way with the Irish troubles. Over and over again I was asked by individuals why the Pope did not "tell the Irish to behave themselves." Had the Holy Father followed their wishes they could have charged him later on with interfering in political matters. "Did I not always say that he claimed political power over all nations?" they would ask.

In view of that situation I was well aware of the fact that the Irish question was not for me to touch. But wherever I went, to whomsoever I talked, it was sure to be brought into the conversations, requiring me to duck under with the same regularity as it ducked up.

When my work was over and done with, however, Ireland came up once more and that time I did not duck. My tall visitor with the financial idea to expound—I had not seen him for weeks—came back one day after my passage home had already been booked. I could afford to listen and learn since soon I would be out of the way of temptation. But I had not reckoned on the persuasive power the man could bring to bear on me. He lost no time about doing that, "If I ask a question that might embarrass you to answer, Monsignor, please tell me frankly that it is none of my business." I assured him that I would do just that.

"Then, since I may ask without offense, can you tell me what are the true sentiments of His Eminence Cardinal Bourne on the Irish question?"

"His Eminence has never made a secret of them to me," I answered, "nor has he required me to keep them a secret from others. In fact it always appeared to me as if he would be glad to have the whole world know them if the whole world would only listen."

"What are they?"

"The Cardinal," I said, "does not favor Ireland's complete withdrawal from the Empire; holding that such a step might have the effect on one side of cutting Ireland away from her best customer, and on the other of weakening the defenses of the Empire itself. He wants what he thinks would be freedom for Ireland with prosperity, and safety for the Empire with friendship. I think that covers the ground."

"But he never said so much to the public."

"How could he? You took it for granted that he was against you and made it annoying for him more than once. After all, you must remember that he is the unofficial representative of the Holy See in England and bound to remember that fact in all his public utterances."

"But he did reissue a pastoral of Manning on ——."

"On secret societies."

"We'll pass that. It's the present that matters. What I am anxious about is what the Cardinal thinks now."

"But do you want him to say what he thinks? If he does not go all the way you do not want his company at all."

"You're wrong there, Monsignor. Let me explain. Ireland needs just a little push at this moment."

"I see. Perhaps you are thinking of the proposed conference?"

"Yes."

"What can the Cardinal do if he feels he is not wanted and if he can't go all the way?"

"Monsignor," my visitor said impressively, "the British government has always thought that English Catholics had no sympathy for Ireland. The old aristocratic lay leaders, like the Duke of Norfolk, impressed that conviction on every government. It was never true of the majority. But it was the minority that had wealth—respectability if you will—and the voice that was heard. Norfolk is dead—God rest him and all the souls of the faithful departed! There is now only one voice that will be heard, the Cardinal's. He has sympathy for Ireland—small wonder, for he had an Irish mother. Let him speak out that sympathy even if he can't go as far as the rest of us, and I think—I feel sure—that good results will follow. I know whereof I speak, Monsignor. Ireland's cause now needs that little push."

"I see. You want me to solicit the little push from His Eminence?"

"Exactly."

"I am booked to sail in a few days and have a lecture to give at St. Bede's College in Manchester on Sunday. The Cardinal is not in London."

"I know that he is at his country house, but you could go there."

"Yes, and disappoint St. Bede's."

"Now, Monsignor, all the grandfathers and grandmothers you had were Irish. Could you do more for their memory than help now? Why bother about a lecture you can give any time you come over? Sure, you'll do it for the auld sod, won't you?"

"I'll try, but I am afraid it will not be easy. The Cardinal resents the treatment he has had from ——."

"People who didn't understand, Monsignor. We know that he likes you. I tell you, Monsignor, he'll do it if you ask him."

"All right. I'll send a telegram to Manchester and ask His Eminence by telephone if I may go out to see him."

Incidentally, the Cardinal had already invited me to spend the week end with him in the country. When he was informed by telephone that I was not going to Manchester he repeated the invitation and directed Monsignor Coote, one of his secretaries, to drive me some sixty miles to the Hare Street House.

Enter the Ghost.

Hare Street, like Whitehall, was very English in that it was not a street but a village. The house itself had been the home of Monsignor Benson, who bequeathed it as a summer residence to the archbishops of Westminster. A defect in the will rendered the bequest invalid, but the Bensons—the widow of the late Anglican Archbishop of Canterbury and her sons—saw to it that the wish of Hugh was carried out. It was thus the family of an Anglican archbishop of Canterbury who made the gift of a country home to the Catholic archbishops of Westminster. Monsignor Benson was buried in the garden of Hare Street House, and a beautiful chapel, used by the Cardinal for his daily Mass while there, covered the grave of one of the most devoted, eloquent, and talented converts of the generation.

We met the Cardinal in intimate converse with a road-mender a few miles from Hare Street. He came back with us in the car. "Now, Monsignor," he said to me on arrival, "you must first have a welcome from every room as well as the garden of the famous Hare Street House."

"Not yet, if you please, Your Eminence. I want first to talk with you on a matter of importance. Let me get it off my mind and on yours."

The Cardinal threw open the door of his study at once, pulled up a chair for me and sat down himself. "Now!" he said. "You can talk in comfort."

Frankly and fully I told him the story and—waited. I made no request. His Eminence looked out the window for a few moments before he spoke. "I do not see how I can do that, Monsignor. I should like to do it, but would it not seem, considering all the misunderstandings to which you referred, as if—well, as if the Sinn Fein people had rather forced me out? I have to remember my position and the dignity it calls on me to maintain. These people have not hesitated to say bitter things that hurt me. But I am not thinking of that as much as the impression the public might get if I now break a long silence. Do you see the difficulty?"

"I do, Your Eminence, and I think I also see a way out of it. You have heard of American reporters. Why could not one of them break in on your privacy out here and get an interview? Everybody would understand that you couldn't well push him out once he got in."

"But where, my dear Monsignor, are we to find that convenient American reporter?"

"Am I not an editor? To catch a Cardinal should not the boss himself go fishing?"

"Are not Cardinals supposed to be birds, not fish?"

"Then we'll make it hunting, Your Eminence. May I draw my gun?"

"You may. But try mine. There are pencils and paper over on the table."

"With Your Eminence's permission I shall take them to another room. Why trouble you with questions when I know your opinions so well from our fireside conversations in London? Let me go back where Benson did his writing and prepare the interview. This evening it will be in your hands and you may use the blue pencil on it. Tomorrow I'll return with it to London and give it to an American correspondent who will take care of the English papers also."

"Very good," the Cardinal said, "do it your way. I'll send in your tea and the bell will announce dinner."

When the bell did its duty I was ready and the Cardinal had the interview in his hands. He did not even glance at it before saying "good night" and taking it upstairs to his room. I remained up with Monsignor Coote for an hour longer before I went to my own room.

"This room," remarked the secretary as he ushered me in, "is the one Monsignor Benson himself occupied."

It was a strange-looking place. The walls were paneled in oak so old that it had turned black. The bed was a cot with deep purple hangings and the blankets were of the same somber color. Even the cloth over a bed table was dark purple. On it was a combination ash tray and match box. Benson smoked while he was awake.

"It is just as it was when Monsignor Benson left it for the last time," the secretary assured me before leaving.

Again I looked around the room though there were few details that I had not already noticed. One, however, there was, a skull looking out at the bed from a niche in the paneling. Then I remembered. Hare Street House was the ghost house of *Oddsfish*. The priest-novelist who loved ghosts would naturally have selected the room nearest to the haunted stairs. Sure enough, this room of mine was right at the head of the stairs on which the lady of the days of Charles II wandered up and down at midnight with her moanings.

I said my prayers that night with a marked increase of fervor and got into bed with a trifle more alacrity than was usual with me, but sleep would not come. I tried a cigarette, remembering as I took a match from the stand on the bed table that I was using the same box the dead Monsignor who loved ghosts had used the night before he left home to die. For more than an hour I tossed and tumbled. Then I turned on the light and looked at my watch. Did I hear a noise? I did. It was after midnight. There was a sound from the stairs outside my door. Did that skull in the wall actually grin when I glanced its way?

The noise on the stairs increased. It sounded like footsteps going up, then down; going up, then down; going up, then—I heard the moans. And, strange as it may seem, before they stopped I had fallen asleep. I must have awakened five or six times that night. The sounds of the footsteps had ceased but not the moaning. It stopped only with daybreak.

When I finished my Mass in the chapel over Benson's tomb in the morning I met the Cardinal walking in the garden. Evidently he had not been disturbed, for he greeted me with a hearty, "Good morning! I hope you had a fine night's rest, Monsignor."

"I believe in telling the exact truth, Your Eminence," I answered. "I made a very poor night of it."

"I am sorry indeed. It is so peaceful and quiet out here away from London that I was sure you would fall asleep at once. Did you stay up reading?"

"No, Your Eminence, I stayed up ghosting. If you kept your household ghosts in better order I am sure I should have slept."

Was that a smile I detected on his grave face? "Come with me, Monsignor." He started off, leading me to a spot in the garden from which I could see the windows of my room. "It is altogether too bad," he said, "to take away from you what could not but prove your most vivid memory of the England that is supposed to have ghosts in every old house, but in the interest of truth I must do it. These are your windows, are they not?" I answered that I was quite sure they were. "First," he went on, "as to the sound of footsteps: the stairs are very old, and the oak boards out of which the steps were made are not fastened by nails but by wooden plugs. During the day constant passing over them sets the steps down tight. At night, after a few hours of relief from the weight and perhaps because it is colder, the plugs loosen a little and the steps come back. The sound made resembles that of footsteps."

"But how do you know all that, Your Eminence?" I asked.

"Because I went out with an electric hand torch one night to investigate—and found the ghost."

"But the moans?"

"They were my reason for bringing you over here. See what is above your windows. In there is a colony of English owls, not ghosts, and it is at night one hears them. Now you are disappointed. What is a visit to an old English house for an American without ghosts?"

Next day I accompanied the Cardinal back to London, and as soon as possible after arrival went to see John Steele of the *Chicago Tribune*. He had been very kind and helpful to me and I wanted to show my appreciation. He read the interview through before speaking. "Where did this come from, Monsignor?" he asked.

"Direct from the Cardinal."

"Given to what reporter?"

"To me."

"You are, of course, going to let the Associated Press have it?"

"I am going to put a release date on it and give it to the *Tribune*."

"You mean that? Why, the whole world has wanted to get something of this kind from the Cardinal. It is mighty good of you to give it to us."

The door of the office opened and Colonel McCormick, editor of the *Tribune* at home, came in—a surprise visit.

After introductions the interview was shown him. "What are you going to do with it, John?" he asked.

"Give a copy to the *Sunday Times* with a release date and send it on to Chicago by mail."

"Why not by cable?"

"Think of the cost—fifteen hundred words at least."

"Never mind the cost," replied the Colonel, "get it on the wire now and remember the *Freeman's Journal* in Dublin as well as the *Times*."

The copy reached home before I did.

The Cardinal had laid one ghost for me at Hare Street House. If he did not lay an older one it was not his fault. No more could anyone do than his best. The conference soon was called and the aurora of peace filled the troubled air with promise. I heard nothing from London as to the effect of the interview, except through one little note from my tall friend—a line of thanks. Whether he did the thing for Sinn Fein or on his own I never knew, but I had my suspicions.

Years later I told the story at a dinner in Louvain, Belgium. Cardinal Bourne and Cardinal O'Donnell of Armagh were both present. It stirred up a small sensation.

~§ 28 §~

IMPERIAL SUNSET

AUSTRIA will always be a center of world interest. She is that as I write, though Nazi Germany has taken possession of what Versailles left. As I look back over what I saw and felt about Austria in 1920 I am convinced that the thing was inevitable. But at that time I did not see how it could be, for the Allied Powers were determined that Germany should never expand beyond the frontiers they had fixed for her. The alliances of conquerors tend to soften, slip, and come apart. Versailles gave the Austrians too hard a task to do. It was too big even for genius. Yet Austria is needed in Europe. Her people are German in blood and language, but her culture seems to visitors more Latin than German. Can it be made over on a Nazi nod? It is difficult to uproot great traditions, and most of Austria's are not of the kind that will live in loving companionship with Northern ones. The history of the making of the Hohenzollern Empire shows that. It would be a miracle if Austria remained long content as a mere province of a nation in which Prussia has the leading influence. The old Austrian Empire had many troubles, but it best could keep Europe out of trouble. It might have stood the loss of an arm, but it could not stand the loss of both arms and both legs. So Austria has passed into history. But I cannot help thinking that if Europe, crushed by armaments or wars, ever becomes sane enough to form a union for her own salvation, the capital of the United States of Europe will be Vienna.

I wanted to give a whole chapter to Austria and therefore made no reference to it in its proper place. I had gone to Vienna from Germany, after meeting the missionaries at Bonn and Hanglar, to give financial aid to hungry clergy and religious. Father Shannon had been good enough to volunteer his help which I was glad to have. We stayed long enough to do some relief work ourselves and make arrangements for its continuation. We went from Vienna to Rome, and from there back to London. Father Shannon had to return to his editorial duties in Chicago while I remained in England. While the missions question was being discussed I found time to direct the relief work in Vienna at long distance.

The question "Who won the war?" has never been answered to anyone's satisfaction. But if the question were reversed into "Who lost the war?" it could be answered at least in part very promptly. Austria did. Any postwar visitor to Vienna would know that, for he could not fail to see that the city, before the war the pride of Europe, was dying. I had seen Vienna in her glory. When I registered at its famed Bristol Hotel in the summer of 1920 I was given the suite in which I had once been entertained by Colonel Kerens, then Ambassador of the United States to the Austrian Empire. It consisted of vestibule, parlor, two bedrooms and two baths. It cost me about three dollars a day. Times had changed. The Ambassador must have paid ten times that much. He had given me a royal time and sight of my first emperor. There was no emperor and no court in 1920. We actually opened our relief office in one of his royal palaces.

An American writer who had visited Vienna for a few days before we came, Mr. Kaufman, published impressions gathered up in a few days of superficial looking about. I answered him: "Austria is now only nominally a nation. Every province is actually independent. The rule of the Republic extends only to the province in which Vienna is located. The other provinces have practically shut Vienna and its poor republic in upon itself. Self-preservation still remains the first law of nature. Austria outside Vienna does not propose to starve with Vienna. The Treaty of Versailles has been the cause of all this. As far as Austria is concerned the Treaty is a monstrous injustice, the work of men blind to facts, the juggling of children with the blocks of other people's destinies. Austria is the standing condemnation of and reproach to Versailles. Not only did the Allied Commissioners dismember and ruin, but they condemned a whole nation to starvation and extinction; and, worse still, imposed an indemnity after taking from the people not only the power to pay it, but even the means of living. Austria cannot pay, for Austria has nothing with which to pay. Her investments were in Bohemia, near the coal lands. These Bohemia has taken. Her money is so low that an enterprising wine merchant used the notes as labels on his bottles. They were cheaper and prettier than any labels he could have printed; besides being useful for advertising purposes. Austria is judged and condemned to death. That is the plain truth. . . . 'Austria can work out her worst problems?' How? With what? Granted that she is 'clever, imaginative, adept, a creator, a designer, a fabricator,' etc., how can she create without materials? What good is a design on paper? Will imagination stand for a meal? . . . The sad condition of Austria today, and the hopelessness of her situation unless she is permitted to make some sort of alliance with neighbors who can supply her with raw materials for the skilled hands of her intelligent workers, is defeating the very end for which our President assured us that we entered the war—to 'make the world safe for democracy.' In Austria the people ask what democracy has done for them, while sadly stating that they feel keenly what democracy has done to them."

The picture was not attractive but there were soft lights in it nevertheless—lights of charity. Other relief agencies were at work in Vienna. America and England were both aiding their former foes generously. Mr. Hoover's name was as well known as that of the dead Franz Josef himself—and more honored. In other centers than Vienna the name spelled bread and bacon and sounded like a grace before meals.

Passing through London Father Shannon had met a Jewish friend from Chicago who, learning the object of the mission to Austria, asked him to spend five hundred dollars for him. Shannon had no trouble at all getting rid of this very special donation and got much joy out of the distribution of the money. He did it in a most original way. When we learned that every religious house, rectory, and institution in Vienna was in need, when we knew that there were convents where nuns had to take turns wearing the few habits left fit for use, when we heard the pathetic prayer for "Fats, Fats, please!" it was decided that I should spend the money I had for clothing and Hoover food packages, while Shannon was free to go out alone and dispose of his five hundred dollars in his own way. In the evenings he told me how he did it. "Today," he would say,

"I saw an old monk going along with an empty basket on his arm, evidently begging. He stopped before a store displaying some food. It was pitiful to see how his eyes devoured the contents of that window display. I stepped up behind him, took up one of his hands, filled it with kronen, and walked on before he recovered. From the crowd I looked back. The wonderment on his face was worth the money. He went into the shop. There will be something to eat in the monastery tonight." Another of Shannon's charitable tricks was to ring a convent doorbell and, when a nun opened it, to press a roll of money into her hand and go away without saying a word or letting her say one.

"When the history of this famine is written," I commented, "there will be stories told of an angel disguised in American clericals sent from heaven in answer to prayers. Or if ever some of those nuns get a snapshot picture of their unknown benefactor you may yet see yourself as a saint in plaster before you die."

While any of that five hundred good American dollars, a fortune in kronen, remained, Shannon did yeoman work for his charitable Jewish friend of Chicago. How much he added out of his own pocket only God and himself can tell.

That it would be hard to buy the food needed, we knew when we tried to get breakfast for ourselves the morning after our arrival. There was coffee of a kind but no milk. There was bread of a kind but no butter. On the side, the waiters could supply a bit of bacon, strictly against the law, since the State was rationing everybody. But on Vienna had descended swarms of food bootleggers from Galicia who dealt with waiters when they could not deal with managers. For ourselves we had to find a knowing guide who could tell us what restaurants to patronize and when. He was glad to come with us, for he, too, was hungry. He turned out to be a Bohemian well acquainted with all the religious houses in Vienna, and therefore invaluable for us. But he could not tell us where to get milk. I found that out for myself. At the Hoover offices I was told that the British specialty was feeding children. That meant milk. I called at once on the British. The official in charge was an army officer left over from the war. When he read my name on the card I gave him he smiled broadly, "It's hard to keep the Irish out of anything that makes a pull on the heartstrings, eh Father?" He shot out his hand. "My name's Dugan, late captain of the ———." Of course I forgot what regiment.

I was more than pleased. If I could not get what I needed out of a Dugan the drop of Scotch in me had taken over all the Irish. "I am glad indeed that it is a Dugan I have to deal with," I said, "I came to beg. My dear Captain, be a good fellow and let me have some condensed milk."

"Of course," he answered at once and called a clerk. "Here, wrap up two tins of milk for the Father. You didn't get a drop for your coffee this morning, I'll warrant. Now did you?"

Two tins? What could I do with two tins? Shannon and I could get along without milk in our coffee. It was milk by the thousands of tins I wanted. But I took the two he offered. "Now attend and be reasonable, my dear Captain," I said. "That's no way to treat a Kelley, putting him off with milk for his own coffee. Do you know what has brought me over here?"

"I do. The Americans told me that you came to help the sisters."

"And clergy."

"Well, of course. But the clergy are men and can go to the bread lines. With the old clothes they are wearing no one knows them. But I don't want to see the sisters do that. I'm glad you came. Our agency is for the children. The Americans are giving food packages to families. There's no one to help the nuns."

"Oh, yes there is. You are going to help them, Captain. I want milk, a lot of milk, as a start hundreds of cases."

"Man alive," the astonished captain said, "I haven't hundreds of cases of milk in Vienna."

"I know that," I countered. "But you have plenty in Trieste and you have Austrian ex-army officers guarding it there and on the trains as you bring it in. And you know, my dear Captain, that a telegram to London will hurry a shipment to you any time. Now be a good chap and let me buy a thousand cases to begin with."

"Father dear," he said, "I can't sell anything. I can give milk away if it's for children but ——."

"Did you ever know any people more childlike than innocent nuns? And don't they feed children with what they can get and never bother you?"

"They do. But rules are rules."

"That's so, and heads are heads, made to interpret rules. But I see your difficulty. Is this a way out? If you give me the milk I'll promise—word of an Irish gentleman—that when I go to London, as I must on my way home, I'll call at the headquarters of your agency there and make a free donation to the work of—let us say one thousand pounds sterling."

I think the captain suggested making it guineas instead of pounds. There must have been a Scotch drop in that fellow too.

The milk came, cases and cases and cases of it. The Caritashaus distributed it gladly for me when the favor was asked of its kind and efficient officials. For the immediate relief of the clergy I asked the favor of buying food packages from the Hoover agency, and sent them a list of priests supplied by the diocesan chancery. One of the recipients was Monsignor Seipel, then only a chaplain, but later the Chancellor of Austria.

Visits to two of the large Mother Houses of teaching sisters and to a hospital run by brothers—I think the latter were called the Brothers of St. John of God—decided me to purchase cloth on my return to London. I had to have a representative in Vienna, and again the captain came to my aid. He told me of a lady, Mrs. Charlotte Baynes, who had been doing relief work, was well connected in Vienna and knew the city and the institutions. I was informed that she would be delighted to donate her services, especially in view of the fact that the sad condition of the religious communities was so well known to her. The arrangement was made and we were free to leave after visiting a few more institutions.

The first of the Mother Houses we visited was also a beautiful boarding school conducted by Dominican Sisters. When the Superior came to the parlor to see us I noticed that, while the once white habits she and her assistants wore were immaculately clean, they were nevertheless more yellow than white and patched to the point of near-extinction. The Superior was very reticent about speaking to us of the condition of the Sisters; but she was the one who first broke out with a cry for fats. It was when I asked her what she needed most that her hands were lifted as if she were praying and she exclaimed, "Oh! Herr Prelat, Fats! Fats! Fats! We need them so badly. And we have no soap. We must wash our habits as best we can. We need fats in any shape. All of my Sisters are wearing out from undernourishment. I cannot give them the proper food to sustain them."

I strongly suspect that this particular convent received a generous part of Shannon's own money, and I suspect, moreover, that it was not forgotten when he returned to Chicago.

It was in the second Mother House that I learned most about the need of clothing. I had seen priests in patched trousers with vari-colored old coats on the streets. But I had not known that a community of three hundred and fifty nuns was forced to keep the majority in bed so that the few habits left could be used in turn. It was here, too, that I saw what looked like a flower garden with vegetables of all kinds growing between its well laid out walks. But even in turning their flower garden into a kitchen garden the nuns had an eye for the beautiful. In spite of the potatoes and cabbages in the beds it still looked very much like a flower garden. Here the demand was for cloth.

The visit to the hospital was the most distressing. It was conducted by men for men, and was one of the largest in Vienna. The Brother Superior showed us around the wards. There were no sheets on the beds, and what they had of blankets were evidently relics of the war repaired by the Brothers and heavily patched with pieces taken from others too worn for use. The patients were all emaciated, for the Brothers simply could not find proper nourishment for them. Most were charges on the charity of the community. I remarked to the Brother Superior that here at least it did not appear as if clothes were needed by the religious. He smiled rather sadly and pulled his habit up to his knees. He had neither socks nor trousers. The habit, slippers, and a rubber collar were all he had on. "Some of us," he said, "have not even that. "But," he added, "it will be all right for some months while the weather is warm. What we fear is the coming winter." I told him that he need not worry about winter. He could bank on friends in America who would see that he had cloth. I could buy that from the mills in England at wholesale prices. We left for Rome while Mrs. Baynes was making the rounds of the convents to find out what kind of cloth and how much was needed by each community.

How to get to Italy? We were told that an Italian military train went through to Rome via Trieste and Udine, but no one was sure how often. Our Bohemian guide got the information for us, and the Italian officials permitted us to go along. I have many recollections of hard trips. An old lecturer could not help accumulating them. But that trip from Vienna to Rome will stand out till the day of my death as the very worst. The coaches were veritable war relics. We had a little compartment with a hard bench and barely enough room for the knees when we sat down. Sleep was impossible, and there was no time schedule. We knew when we were going to start from Vienna but not when we would arrive anywhere. One thing was certain, we were likely to be at least two nights and two days on the road to Rome.

One evening during the trip, when the train pulled into Udine and we had a chance to get something to eat, we both felt so dirty that we risked missing the food to go where there was a pipe with running water in the station yard. No water was ever more welcome, though the best we could do was to let it flow over hands and heads. Happily there was a longer delay than we expected and the restaurant at Udine had good, if far from fancy, food. We were curiosities to the people at the tables. One old fellow came up and sat with us, bent on finding out who we were. He could speak neither French nor English. Father Shannon, who knew more Italian than I, was too tired to bother with him but soon saw that he could get a lot of amusement listening to my attempts to converse with our visitor in a language I did not know. When the announcement was made that the train was about to move out, the old man got up and insisted on solemnly shaking hands while assuring me—a good-natured and gentlemanly liar he was—that I spoke Italian perfectly. When we got back to our little cubbyhole on the train Father Shannon added that, while the old fellow had stretched his conscience a bit in paying the compliment, nevertheless he himself had been vastly edified over the use I made of the ten words I then knew of Italian.

We did not remain long in Rome, but long enough to be received by the Holy Father and carry away his blessing.

In London, Monsignor Jackman, the Cardinal's secretary, was invaluable. He knew Mrs. Baynes and congratulated me on securing her services. He also knew a former army officer in London who would be delighted to help in the purchase of the cloth. It happened that this officer had, for me at least, gotten into the right kind of business after the war and knew all the manufacturers. I called at the headquarters of Captain Dugan's agency with a check for five thousand dollars, which was the donation I had promised and which covered the cost of the milk. I am afraid I gave heart failure to the astonished honorable treasurer. I was sure that the captain had believed me and had expressed his faith to his superiors in London, but without making a deep impression upon them. When I left the London office I knew that they had been converted to faith in American promises. Nor did I fail to express my thanks and advise them that an Irishman who uses his head for interpreting rules is a valuable man.

It was after I left that the office in one of the old royal palaces of Vienna was opened and the name of The Catholic Church Extension Society placed on its door. It was a busy office when the shipments of cloth arrived, but when all was ready for delivery it was the turn of Mrs. Baynes to get a surprise. The Sisters especially insisted on paying, but the instructions I had left were that everything should be given free. Many were unwilling to accept the cloth under that condition and the case had to be referred to me. I telegraphed Mrs. Baynes to let them have the cloth on their own terms, which meant that they could pay whatever they thought they could afford, a krone a yard or five hundred kronen a yard. The krone had dropped down to nearly nothing. There was no safe in the office, so Mrs. Baynes stuffed the money, as it was paid, into a barrel. When the job was done she told me that the barrel was full and wanted to know what to do with it. I told her to give it to the poor and that is what she did. I hope the barrel was rolled up the steps of the Caritashaus and left there. It would have been an experience indeed for any charity house actually to receive a barrel of money. If the Caritashaus got it that way and spent it promptly it would have fed and clothed many. But if they held it for long it could be used only for wallpaper, since very soon the Austrian krone was tumbling down in emulation of the antics of the German mark.

The memory of that Austrian adventure is a sad one. Palaces could be had for business purposes in Vienna, and magnificent residences rented or purchased for almost nothing. Several members of the Hoover agency had clubbed together to rent a house. It was more a mansion than a home, yet for it the young men paid thirty-five dollars a month. The country could not produce enough coal to do more than run its railroads, not even enough for that. The Austrian Republic had practically no raw materials for manufacturing except what wood could be taken from the forests. To find enough to eat, outside of war-bread, recourse had to be had to the food bootleggers who really were of some use, though they charged outrageous prices and enriched themselves until the fall of the krone wiped out their profits. People once wealthy were forced to accept donations of castoff clothing which came from everywhere in Europe. The world sympathized greatly with Austria in her sad plight, for everyone who knew Austrians loved them. They were always a refined, soft-spoken, gentle, and well-educated part of the Teutonic race. Hearts and purses, in spite of war bitterness, opened up to help, and it was consoling to know that the people were trying to make the best of a bad situation. Even the castoff clothes the Austrian could wear with a certain distinction, and politeness was never forgotten. In days that tried souls the Austrian remained a gentleman.

The reports we sent to the Archbishop of Chicago increased his sympathy. He wrote a personal appeal, based on these documents, and extended it to include Germany. Later he ordered a general collection in his diocese for the relief of both peoples and interested other members of the hierarchy. He chartered a ship and loaded it with flour. What funds the society received were turned over to a new work carried on by the Archbishop's representatives, principally in Germany. A note I wrote on the way through Germany will show how badly the help was needed there, "All day long we have been going through green pastures that have no cattle in them. Today we saw only four cows. They were all working in harness. There is no fresh milk. We hear that America is going to send over one hundred thousand cows. They will be surprised cows when they come to Germany. The life of leisure to which an American cow is accustomed does not await them on this side. Cows work here. We do not envy the pampered cows of America their trip to Europe."

CHANGE

ORDINARILY there is little perceptible change in the passing of one generation into another, but there was a perceptible, even shocking, change as the world before the Great War became the world that chafes the bent back of humanity today. We in America scarcely felt the sores in 1922, but we were afraid nevertheless as cries of pain flew toward us from across the Atlantic. In 1929 our time came and we realized that we had to face a turning point in history. A momentous change was our inheritance, and not a change for the better.

A New Zealand poet, Eileen Duggan, writing she said only for New Zealand children about their beautiful country's native birds, created one thought pregnant of meaning for those who feel deeply and lament the change. Her verse was about the Moa, a bird that once could fly over sea and land but came to love the fertile feeding grounds of the latter so much that it deserted the sea. I quote only the verses needed to clothe the thought:

> "Said God to the Moa: now for many springs
> I have watched you walking, I will take your wings.
>
> Said the foolish Moa: Take them, I'll not cry.
> With the land to tread on who would need the sky?
>
> But their bones grew feeble, rotted in the sun,
> By the swamps and rivers died they one by one.
>
> Came canoes in plenty, breaking the still sea.
> Staring cried the Moa: What may these things be?
>
> Ah! Escape ye Moas, fly, oh fly, oh fly!
> But their wings had vanished. They had lost the sky."

On the fields of battle, in the hates of war, around the barter table of Versailles, our world too had lost its sky. Better off than the Moa, however, we keep the power to regain it. Paul Claudel, another poet, struck a hopeful note: "We never reach the rich core of our nature unless some overwhelming humiliation has driven us there, and until tears have welled from our hearts." We are near that rich core, perhaps, for the greatest of humiliations is upon us. We who thought that at last the peoples could govern themselves have discovered that for many of them the conviction was nothing but a brilliant bubble blown by a dream pipe. How few the peoples today who still pretend to govern themselves! How swiftly have they all come back under the stroke of ill-fortune to the destructive cry for bread and circuses! The sky is ours no more. We think only of the feeding grounds. A small and weak political heresy has grown into a monster. Patriotism has become racialism, and from it, as a witch-mother, ugly things have been born: the subversive movements of the day that already in the name of justice have murdered more than the war killed. Few realize the truth that in no century of the world's history has there been more blood shed in religious persecution than in this one generation. Nor is the end yet, for the thinker has almost disappeared. Professors now laugh at logic; philosophers at syllogisms. The man who shouts the loudest and dares the greatest wins the crowd. Blind obedience is then his decree while he makes states over and tears their constitutions to tatters.

Seemingly there is no salvation in sight. The cost of armaments and their destructive efficiency makes an end to any hope for the return of "embattled farmers," or of future Tells, Winkelreids, Reveres, or Emmetts. What force could pitchforks and pikes in the hands of patriots have before the machine guns, tanks, and bombers of organized tyranny? What force can the thoughtful few have before an avalanche of the votes of the deceived? Perhaps never again will a people who love liberty be able to win it by their own willing sacrifices. Liberty sickened when the inventor placed in one man's hand the power to shower death over a thousand.

Education, upon which we relied so much, has changed by becoming more shallow and utilitarian. Colleges, except in science, are not turning out scholars but job hunters who, because there are not enough of what they seek to go around, only add to the mass problem. But there is no stopping the overflow, since universities, with a few honorable exceptions, test their success only by the size of their enrollment. All sorts of easy ways to knowledge are planned. But what enters the head by an easy swinging door soon knows that the door swings as easily out as in. On the primary plane of education, at least, results should long ago have shown. They do, but the showing is far from what was expected. Statesmen? They are hidden by the memories of the giants of other days; giants who had no easy road to learning, yet became the more learned for the obstacles they had to overcome. The back of the world of today is bent double with debt and it limps under taxation, for a sound principle of government has been set aside. No longer is "the best government the one that governs the least."

After 1921 I began to realize that what was happening to the world was, in a minor but yet distressing way, happening to me—but in reverse. I had not lost my sky but I had lost my earth. I came back from Europe to find that others had done more than merely keep the ship sailing. They had taken over almost all my duties and were performing them well. I was still "The Boss," but a boss who could be spared. A few hours daily at the office, a few reports to be looked over, a few editorials and appeals to write, a few drops of oil here and there in the machinery, and my room was better than my company. I should have known the signs but I failed to read them. They heralded for me a change that I had already begun to feel in my soul. Others knew before the thought of the impending change came to me. A friend said one day, "You will soon be a bishop."

"Why," I asked, "should I become a bishop? With all due respect to the office, I think that I have more and greater opportunities for doing good where I am than I could possibly have as the ruler of a diocese."

"Quite true," he answered, "You have. But it is a great honor for anyone to be called to the episcopate, especially in America. We have more than twenty-five thousand priests in the United States and only a few over a hundred bishops. To be the ruler of the very smallest and poorest diocese is to be one out of a hundred. Each

Apostle himself was only one out of twelve. Is there a greater honor than being selected to be a successor of the Twelve?"

I remember telling him a story about an old seminary rector which had been related to me by one of his favorite students. The appointment of a new bishop had been announced that very morning and the student suspected that his rector had had a hand in the making of him. "Why don't you become a bishop yourself, Father?" he asked, "You are always putting others up for the episcopate. Don't you want to be a bishop?"

"Son," said the old man, "I should be glad to have the plenitude of the priesthood that I love so dearly and for which I have prepared so many, and I know what a great honor indeed it is to be a successor of the Apostles. But the conditions are too onerous for me. It is hard enough to direct and administer a seminary. To be a bishop who has a charge ten or twenty times heavier would be taking on too much labor and responsibility at my age. No, under such circumstances, it would not be good for me to be a bishop."

"But for you," commented my friend, "it would be different. The burden would be lighter than the one you carried for twenty years. Anyhow you might as well get ready. There's nothing to do with you but make you a bishop. You need a change too before you grow too old. And it *is* an honor."

I was human and liked to win honors. I also liked to see fireworks; especially the kind that scatter the darkness of the sky with multicolored stars leaving it darker than before. But a change? I began to think that I should welcome it. Ledvina, my right hand, was already Bishop of Corpus Christi. Roe, poor fellow, was dead before his time. The army had claimed Landry. But O'Brien, the first comer, was stepping out and showing speed. McGuinness, of Philadelphia, now Bishop of Raleigh, was splendidly efficient, and there was Griffin of Indianapolis to watch the pennies take care of the dollars. Baldus, a layman who took on the magazine task, had settled down firmly at his littered desk and evidently intended to stay to the end. The society itself was well founded and had assumed its permanent form. Its growing pains were over. No one was criticising any more. No one was bothering whether we sat on mahogany chairs or kitchen chairs. Most former critics favored the mahogany as good business. The society's income was mounting. The magazine was paying.

The—but why draw it out? The truth was that I could leave at any time and no one would long miss me. Was not the society too much a "one man" affair? Would it be for its good to depend over much on its founder? Do not founders grow old and become set in their ways? Perhaps—I hated to think of that—they also become a bit cranky. Yes, the barometer that was myself was set at "Change," though for a long time I had not even glanced at it. Once before, change had been in the air for me and I did not want it. It had been avoided. I should have welcomed it then, but the hint about it came so suddenly and so mysteriously that in the shock I merely tightened my grip on what I felt was mine by right of creation. It was a foolish thing to do, but change at that time looked too much like a leap into the outer darkness.

The change came. It was heralded one bright June morning in 1924. A registered special delivery letter was lying unopened and forgotten in my pocket as I was driving to the city. An attempt had been made the evening before to deliver it at my house but I had not returned home for dinner, and only a personal signature on the receipt would be accepted. The post office had closed for the night when I arrived. Next morning I called and took the letter with me on my way to the city where I had an engagement. I opened it in the car. I had been appointed Bishop of Oklahoma.

What does it mean to be a bishop of the Church Catholic? I am told that there are those who think a bishop must be a mysterious person because he has a mysterious office. But there is nothing mysterious about office or man.

Catholic bishops are human. They are not only successors of the Apostles but individuals of the race Christ came to save by His teaching and example. Left without His grace they would do as humans always do—make a mess of things. In fact there were always some in history who did make a mess of what things they could affect by their blindness. Christ did not guarantee that bishops would be like angels; nor could He endow them with Divine prerogatives. What He could do was to give them a grace of state— which He did—so that, no matter what happened in the man, the Church which was Himself on earth would, in spite of the failure, remain the one safe refuge of His Truth. Safety for Truth was placed in the communion of all bishops with the See of Peter and it would live till the end of time. Where Peter was, there the Church had to be. All bishops take their mission from it. Peter's successor alone can call and make his brethren; alone can depose them. Thus they are in a bond of brotherhood with the Vicar of Christ. Thus they keep the unity which is a mark and sign of Truth. This is the bond that explains the marvelous continuity and universality of the teaching Church as well as her preservation, and her power in the end to overcome all man-made difficulties; the cord that binds together all the Catholic bishops of the world.

Christian civilization owes its all to bishops. Theirs was the labor that kept the world together when the tie of Empire was broken. They had to become the leaders to Christianize and civilize the hordes that cut it. Bishops, working often through monasticism, preserved what was left of Greek and Roman culture throughout the Dark Ages. Bishops lighted the dim candles and then the brilliant lamps which dispelled the darkness before the sun began again to break through the clouds of feudalism. Bishops were at Runnymede, and their names are on the Great Charter. Bishops were in the Crusades which enlarged the bounds of Western civilization. Bishops founded the universities, and their pictured faces still look down from the walls of the greatest schools on earth. A bishop gave America, North and South, its first college and its first university. Versatile men they were in the onward march of civilization. Ambrose of Milan was a statesman, an orator, a doctor. Augustine of Hippo was philosopher, rhetorician, and theologian. Nicholas of Cusa was an early light in the world of science.

The problems facing the world today will inevitably be brought for solution to bishops when the modern theorist has left them all twisted, tangled, and seemingly hopeless. It is for bishops to find the lost sky. So has it been for two thousand years. When men break away from the liberty of Christ they may still do wonderful things, because doing them is part of man's earthly destiny. They will still invent, still sing, still plan. They will soar into the clouds. They will produce literature. But, doing these things unaided by the grace of Christ they will also, and inevitably, try head and hand at destruction; for they will attempt to be gods themselves and invade the province of the spiritual. New social theories, untried and untested, they may offer, and the world will be forced into dangerous ways. Man will play with the liberties of his fellows. He will as a consequence bring on confusion of thought, fears, wars, and misery. When the inevitable disaster follows, bishops who saw the tragedy from the beginning will become the first sufferers from it. But history once more will repeat itself, and confused humanity will turn to Christ with its red-stained hands outstretched, because bishops will call them. Humanity must meet its Saviour as did Theodosius—at the door of the cathedral; there to be told by the bishop how their stains may be washed away.

All these things are symbolized in the life of even the lowliest of bishops. His ordinary day is passed doing what to the world are quite ordinary things. He mounts a pulpit to teach a handful of the faithful. He goes out to lay hands on the heads of a few children and give them the Sacrament of strength. He sits down with poor people who have prepared the best they had to welcome him, but meets the great also in their mansions. Oftener he walks in narrow paths alone, glad to be unnoticed. The hour comes, however, when he is not just a bishop. He puts on the great cape, takes into his hand the golden crozier, and sits on a throne while the centuries-old pageant of the Pontifical Mass circles around him. Over him breaks the inspired music of long-dead masters in sobbing kyries, joyful glorias, brave credos, inspiring offertories. On that throne he is the Bishop who does not die, because the Church does not die, because Christ does not die in the world He saved. Twenty years before, the face on the throne might have been a different one. Ten years forward, and again there may come a change. Tragedies follow. Peace again comes out of tragedies. The vaulted cathedral roof may fall and a new one may or may not rise to take its place. The city itself may know riches or poverty, growth or extinction. The nation may pass to the Valhalla of states. New times may bring new triumphs of human ingenuity or destroy the old. Genius may mount Parnassus or descend into Hades. There may be no throne any longer where once there was one, or there may be ten; but the Bishop will always be somewhere near. Whether it be in the glory of Chartres, the poverty of Alaska, the uncertainties of China, or the martyrdom of Barcelona, it will remain as it always was since Bethlehem, and ever will be, by the mercy of God, good for the world to have bishops and good for one to have the opportunity to become a bishop.

That then was what I was to be—a bishop. I could have refused. I hesitated a few hours to recall what I had seen of the offered field of labor. Twenty-two years before I had been in Oklahoma, two territories then being made into one state, and I had carried away no attractive picture of it. I now saw myself again standing on the platform of the old railway junction at El Reno. The roofs of the town were in sight over a stretch of flat prairie. The grass between had been burned yellow, since for a long time there had been no rain. Dust was in the air. It hung over the prairie like a haze and shut off the glare of the sun. How badly then I wanted to finish the work that had brought me down where the South begins and return to a sight of forests, hills, and lakes! Now I was to go back and stay, but I was not sorry. The prairie would be no more depressing than memories of great cities full of fears, juggling statesmen, desolate fields on which War had stamped his cloven foot, hungry children and ruined villages, cathedrals battered down, a young aristocrat picking a piece of bread out of the cinders, longing eyes devouring the sight of meat, and even one broken and lonesome old king in the Garden of the Tuileries trying to tempt a few little tots to play with him. There were those who wondered how one who had seen so much of the crowded places, who had become so accustomed to the rush of their pulsating life, who had been immersed in the flood of events, could be cheerful about turning his back on them all, as well as on everything he had built up so carefully and painfully. They need not have wondered. I knew that there must be a new and a greater Oklahoma waiting after these twenty-two years, and—I had to find my lost bit of earth.

Perhaps—but that may be another story.

INDEX

Index

Index

Hearn, Edward L., 241-242, 243, 245
Hennessey, George, 155-156
Hennessy, John, 67, 115, 129-130, 136
Hill, James J., 89
Hinchey, Jim, 99-100
History of the Church, 70
History of the French in Canada, 146-147
Hodgson, Governor, 29-30
Hodnett, Pope, 67
Hogan, Abbé, 80
Hoover, Herbert, 312
House, Edward M., 252, 255, 265-266
Howlan, Governor, 144
Hughes, Dr., 109
Human Problem, 79-82
Humboldt, 187
Huneker, James Gibbons, 227-228
Huxley, 80, 81

If Christ Came to Chicago, 125
Influence of automobile on church-going, 156
Insurrection versus Resurrection, 80
Ireland, John, 89-91, 93, 118, 132, 138
Irish College at Rome, 59
Irish Land League, 70, 71
Irish question, 298-306

Jewish international conferences, 239
Jones, Sam, 109
Joyce, Chaplain, 188

Keane, John J., 132, 133, 139
Kelley, "Father Ed," 133
Kennedy, Thomas, 163, 167, 171, 172
Kerens, Richard, 140, 311
Kilroy, William, 69
Kipling, 87
Knowles, Major, 100
Knox, Ronald, 225
Kuntz, Peter, 154

Lacordaire, 77, 245, 248
La Follette, Bob, 108
Lamartine, 237
Language differences causing misunderstanding, 144-145
Lateran Treaty, 275
Laurenti, Cardinal, 183
Laval University, 24, 37, 55, 57, 148
Lazarus, 132, 134
League of Nations, 226, 251, 256, 257-258, 264, 271

Lee, General, 102, 104
Leo XIII, 61
Lepage, John, 15
Leslie, Shane, 232-233, 234, 286
Letters to Jack, 161
Lewis, James Hamilton, 88
Liberty, 105
  of conscience, 194, 206, 226, 236-237, 239, 253-256, 265
"Little Shanty Story," 115-117, 118
"Little Versailles," 257-258
London, impressions of, 228-229, 277-279
Longfellow, 6
Loughnane, Emma, 84
Loughran, Peter, 69
Luckey, Arthur, 115-117
Luçon, Cardinal, 245
Lunn, Arnold, 225
Lyceum lectures, 106-112
Lynch, Archbishop, 91

McAuley, Alexander, 20-23
MacDonald, Charles, 22
MacDonald, John A., 22, 23-24
McEvay, Fergus Patrick, 148, 150-152
McGolrick, Bishop, 93
McGuigan, Archbishop, 148
McGurrin, Colonel, 98-99, 101, 120-121
McIntyre, Peter, 30
McIntyre, Robert, 109
McKernon, Father, 154
McKinley Bill, 33
McKinley, William, 86, 87, 96
McKinnon, William, 68-69
McNeill, Archbishop, 147-148
McQuaid, Bernard, 91-94
Mack, Julian, 239
Madero, President, 184, 225
Magnien, Abbé, 71, 114
Maines, Charles, 106
Makino, Baron, 254
Mann, Horace, 27
Mannix, Archbishop, 233-234
Marini, Cardinal, 183
Maybury, William C., 64-65
"Memories" of Benjamin Bremner, 16
Mendel, Abbot, 9
Mercier, Cardinal, 73, 243-244, 261, 264-265
Merrett, General, 68
Merry del Val, Raphael, 167-169, 170-171, 172-173, 181, 183, 301-302

Index

Index